T0332478

UNDERSTANDING EDITORIAL TEXT:
A Computer Model of Argument Comprehension

THE KLUWER INTERNATIONAL SERIES IN ENGINEERING AND COMPUTER SCIENCE

NATURAL LANGUAGE PROCESSING AND MACHINE TRANSLATION

Consulting Editor

Jaime Carbonell

Other books in the series:

EFFICIENT PARSING FOR NATURAL LANGUAGE: A FAST ALGORITHM FOR PRACTICAL SYSTEMS, M. Tomita
ISBN 0-89838-202-5

A NATURAL LANGUAGE INTERFACE FOR COMPUTER AIDED DESIGN, T. Samad
ISBN 0-89838-222-X

INTEGRATED NATURAL LANGUAGE DIALOGUE: A COMPUTATIONAL MODEL, R.E. Frederking
ISBN 0-89838-255-6

NAIVE SEMANTICS FOR NATURAL LANGUAGE UNDERSTANDING, K. Dahlgren
ISBN 0-89838-287-4

UNDERSTANDING EDITORIAL TEXT:
A Computer Model of Argument Comprehension

by

Sergio J. Alvarado

University of California, Davis

KLUWER ACADEMIC PUBLISHERS
Boston/Dordrecht/London

Distributors for North America:
Kluwer Academic Publishers
101 Philip Drive
Assinippi Park
Norwell, Massachusetts 02061 USA

Distributors for all others countries:
Kluwer Academic Publishers Group
Distribution Centre
Post Office Box 322
3300 AH Dordrecht, THE NETHERLANDS

Library of Congress Cataloging-in-Publication Data

Alvarado, Sergio Jose, 1957–
    Understanding editorial text : a computer model of argument
comprehension / by Sergio J. Alvarado.
        p.   cm.   — (Kluwer international series in engineering and
computer science)
    Originally presented as the author's thesis (Ph. D.)—University
of California, Los Angeles.
    Includes bibliographical references and index.
    ISBN 0–7923–9123–3
    1. Editorials—Data processing.   2. Natural language processing
(Computer science)   3. Text processing (Computer science)
I. Title.   II. Series.
PN4784.E28A48   1990
006.3—dc20   90–4813
                                                            CIP

Copyright © 1990 by Kluwer Academic Publishers

All rights reserved. No part of this publication may be reproduced, stored in a retrieval
system or transmitted in any form or by any means, mechanical, photo-copying, recording,
or otherwise, without the prior written permission of the publisher, Kluwer Academic
Publishers, 101 Philip Drive, Assinippi Park, Norwell, Massachusetts 02061.

Printed in the United States of America

To Ingrid

Table of Contents

List of Figures

List of Tables

Foreword

by

Michael G. Dyer

Natural language processing (NLP) is an area of research within Artificial Intelligence (AI) concerned with the comprehension and generation of natural language text. Comprehension involves the dynamic construction of conceptual representations, linked by causal relationships and organized/indexed for subsequent retrieval. Once these conceptual representations have been created, comprehension can be tested by means of such tasks as paraphrasing, question answering, and summarization. Higher-level cognitive tasks are also modeled within the NLP paradigm and include: translation, acquisition of word meanings and concepts through reading, analysis of goals and plans in multi-agent environments (e.g., coalition and counterplanning behavior by narrative characters), invention of novel stories, recognition of abstract themes (such as irony and hypocrisy), extraction of the moral or point of a story, and justification/refutation of beliefs through argumentation.

The robustness of conceptually-based text comprehension systems is directly related to the nature and scope of the knowledge constructs applied during conceptual analysis of the text. Until recently, conceptually-based natural language systems were developed for, and applied to, the task of narrative comprehension (Dyer, 1983a; Schank and Abelson, 1977; Wilensky, 1983). These systems worked by recognizing the goals and plans of narrative characters, and using this knowledge to build a conceptual representation of the narrative, including actions and intentions which must be inferred to complete the representation.

A large portion of text appearing in newspapers and magazines, however, is editorial in nature. The ability to understand such non-narrative text remains outside the theoretical limits of current narrative comprehension programs, due to the fact that editorial comprehension relies upon an additional set of knowledge and processing constructs. Editorial text comprehension requires construction of a network of beliefs which are supported by methods of reasoning and strategies of argumentation.

In this book, Dr. Sergio Alvarado presents a highly knowledge-based approach to editorial text comprehension. The theory of argument comprehension discussed here has been implemented in a prototype computer program, called OpEd, currently capable of reading editorial segments in the domain of politico-economics, and answering questions about their argument content. The process of editorial comprehension is viewed as one of managing many different knowledge sources, including: scripts, social acts, affects, causal chains of reasoning, economic entities, goals, plans, actions, characters, beliefs, and belief relationships.

Alvarado postulates the existence of *Argument Units (AUs)* as central, organizing constructs of argument knowledge, which consist of configurations of belief attack and support relationships, where the content of each belief refers to abstract goal/plan situations. AUs encode knowledge of argumentation which is highly abstract and independent of any particular domain. As a result, knowledge of argument units allows a comprehension system to recognize and interpret arguments in disparate domains, as long as the system has sufficient planning skill and domain knowledge to build up instances of the particular goals, plans and beliefs occurring within that domain.

Traditionally, reasoning and argumentation have been characterized as a process of logic. This is not surprising since some of the first people to address reasoning were logicians. Also, a common tactic in arguments and editorials is to accuse one's opponent of being "illogical." However, protocols indicate that people do not reason by syllogisms, nor do they employ carefully constructed proof-style chains of deductive reasoning. In this book, Alvarado does not emphasize the role of formal logic *per se*. His work is not aimed at developing programs which comprehend valid or correct reasoning in a strictly logical sense. Instead, he is interested in modeling how a refutation or accusation is recognized as such, and how this affects the process of comprehension, memory construction, and subsequent retrieval during question answering. His overall approach has been to combine (1) in-depth language comprehension techniques developed for the conceptual analysis of narrative text (Dyer, 1983a), and (2) techniques of reasoning and belief representation used in modeling argument dialogues (Flowers et al., 1982), with (3) a taxonomy of Argument Units, to create in OpEd a system for comprehending arguments which arise in editorial text.

Alvarado's work contains a number of original and substantial contributions to the field of AI. The design of OpEd, even if limited in the number and type of editorials processed, yields much computational insight in the following areas: common sense knowledge and everyday human reasoning in politico-economic arguments; representation of beliefs and arguments; strategies for reasoning about plans and goals; interactions among different sources of knowledge; memory organization, indexing, and retrieval strategies involved in argument comprehension; processing strategies for retrieving answers to belief-related questions; and conceptual analysis of natural language use in editorial text. The notion of argument units represents a significant step forward in modeling the ability to understand arguments. This theory of argument comprehension should ultimately serve as the basis for modeling the processes of generating refutations, persuading and being persuaded, learning and teaching persuasiveness and debating, and acquiring knowledge of ideological reasoning. Thus, Alvarado's work should be of much interest to researchers in artificial intelligence, natural language processing, linguistics, rhetoric, epistemology, cognitive psychology, and to researchers interested in modeling belief systems in politics and economics.

Michael G. Dyer
University of California
Los Angeles, California

Preface

The work described in this book was performed as part of the author's doctoral studies in Computer Science at the University of California at Los Angeles. The book was prepared at the University of California at Davis, where the author is currently an Assistant Professor of Computer Science. The book consists of the text of his Ph.D. dissertation.

The dissertation presents a theory of the domain knowledge, conceptual representations, and natural language processing strategies involved in understanding editorial text and answering questions about the content of editorials. The theory has been implemented in OpEd, which is a prototype editorial comprehension and question-answering system in the domain of protectionism. OpEd achieves its performance through the use of a wide variety of representational and processing constructs. To encode knowledge of the domain, OpEd contains: (a) *authority triangles and social acts,* to represent conflicts in international trade; (b) *goals and plans,* to represent political and economic actions in terms of desired economic states; (c) a *trade graph,* to represent causal relationships among the economic quantities associated with producers and consumers; and (d) *reasoning scripts,* to represent common chains of cause-effect relationships.

To encode the argument structure of an editorial, OpEd instantiates *beliefs* concerning plans and the goals they achieve or thwart. Beliefs are related to one another by *support* and/or *attack* relationships. These relationships are the basic building blocks organized by *Argument Units (AUs),* which encode language-free and domain-free knowledge about argument structure and content. With the aid of domain-specific knowledge, AUs can be instantiated to model arguments about plans in any domain. Arguments about arguments are represented as *meta-AUs,* which specify argument errors that result from: (a) inconsistencies between actions and beliefs; or (b) support strategies involving plausibilities, circularities, self-contradictions, or shifts on the burden of proof.

Associated with each knowledge construct in OpEd are one or more processing strategies. These strategies are invoked to recognize knowledge constructs that are not explicitly stated in the text, but which must be inferred to understand the argument, planning and causal structure of the text. The result of processing strategies is the construction of an *argument graph,* organized in terms of beliefs, belief relationships, and argument units. To answer belief-related questions about an editorial, OpEd analyzes each question into one of five conceptual categories and each category leads to the execution of a specific strategy of search and retrieval of the argument graph.

Acknowledgments

First, I would like to thank my advisor Professor Michael Dyer, who introduced me to the fields of cognitive modeling and natural language processing. He has been a constant source of invaluable ideas, guidance, and support through the years I have been a member of the UCLA Artificial Intelligence laboratory. Without his encouragement and enthusiasm, this dissertation would not have been possible.

I would also like to express my gratitude for the valuable comments and suggestions received from the other members of my committee: Professor Margot Flowers, Professor Michel Melkanoff, Professor Daniel Mitchell, and Professor Ronald Rogowski. The work by Professor Flowers in modeling adversary arguments provided a foundation for this dissertation.

Thanks are due also to Professor Judea Pearl and Professor Moshe Rubinstein. In my early days at UCLA, Professor Pearl introduced me to the field of artificial intelligence. Professor Rubinstein gave me the opportunity to teach problem solving at UCLA.

Special thanks go to the other members of the UCLA AI lab for their friendship and willingness to give helpful comments: Stephanie August, Charlie Dolan, Richard Feifer, Maria Fuenmayor, Michael Gasser, Anna Gibbons, Seth Goldman, Jack Hodges, Erik Mueller, Valeriy Nenov, Michael Pazzani, Alex Quillici, Walter Read, John Reeves, Eve Schooler, Ron Sumida, Scott Turner, and Uri Zernik. Anna Gibbons provided administrative lab assistance. Seth and Eve provided computing support. Erik helped me understand the GATE system. Stephanie, Charlie, and Uri offered encouragement. Stephanie also read an earlier draft of this dissertation and made valuable suggestions.

I am also grateful to my colleagues at the Division of Computer Science at the University of California at Davis. I would like to acknowledge the friendship of Professor Karl Levitt and Professor Richard Walters. Professor Walters also read an earlier draft of this dissertation and made valuable suggestions.

I would like to acknowledge the love my family has given me through the years. My wonderful parents, Luis and Maria, have taught me that one of the best things to get in life is a good education. My brothers, Jorge and Arturo, have always been willing to help me in every way they can. My parents-in-law, Francisco and Ada, my sister-in-law Betty, and my brother-in-law Jose, have all provided immeasurable moral support.

This dissertation would not have been possible without the help from my wife Ingrid Valera. She has been understanding and loving. She has provided the encouragement and inspiration needed to get through difficult and frustrating moments. Ingrid also read and corrected every draft of this dissertation, while completing her own graduate studies and working at her own job. For all these wonderful things, I will always be grateful to her.

Finally, this research was supported in part by: a fellowship from the International Joint Conference on Artificial Intelligence, a grant from the JTF Program of the DoD, an IBM Faculty Development Award, and a grant from the W. M. Keck Foundation.

Sergio J. Alvarado

UNDERSTANDING EDITORIAL TEXT:
A Computer Model of Argument Comprehension

Chapter 1

The Nature of Argument Comprehension

1.1. Introduction

The nature of research in Artificial Intelligence (AI) is highly experimental and can be viewed from two complementary perspectives: (1) understanding the basic components of intelligence; and (2) replicating intelligent behavior in computers. To achieve these goals, researchers design, implement, and experiment with computer models involving skills central to human intelligence. One such skill is the ability to understand and engage in arguments. This ability is essential to understanding newspaper editorials, TV debate programs, and defense/prosecution arguments in trials. Similarly, humans use this ability to express and defend their opinions when discussing world affairs, presenting court cases, giving expert advice, and writing newspaper editorials.

Why should computers be able to argue? As computer systems become more widely used to aid in decision making and give expert advice, they should exhibit the same cognitive skills possessed by their human-expert counterparts. That is, computers should be able not only to evaluate given situations and present their beliefs on possible courses of actions, but also to justify their beliefs, understand opposing beliefs, and argue persuasively against them. We would not accept advice from human experts who cannot explain or defend their own points of view. Similarly, we should not accept advice from computer systems that lack these abilities.

A first step towards building computer systems capable of arguing is to address the problem of computer comprehension of arguments. Designing a computer program capable of understanding people's opinions and justifications requires a theory of the knowledge structures and processes used in argument comprehension. This theory has been implemented in *OpEd (Opinions to/from the Editor)* (Alvarado et al., 1985a, 1985b, 1985c, 1986, in press), a computer program that reads short politico-economic editorial segments and answers questions about their contents. OpEd also includes a theory of memory search and retrieval developed as an extension to previous work by Lehnert (1978) and Dyer (1983a). This chapter presents an overview of OpEd's process model of argument comprehension, representation, and retrieval.

1.2. Argument Comprehension in OpEd

Editorials are similar to argument dialogues: in both, argument participants present and justify their opinions. However, editorials lack the interactive elements of argument dialogues due to the fact that editorial writers are the only active argument participants. As a result, editorials can be viewed as *one-sided arguments* where writers contrast their opinions against those of their implicit opponents (Bush, 1932; Stonecipher, 1979).

Understanding editorials remains beyond the scope of narrative understanding programs such as those developed by Cullingford (1978), DeJong (1979), Dyer (1983a), Lebowitz (1980), and Wilensky (1983). Those programs can understand stories dealing with stereotypical situations, goal and planning situations, and complex interpersonal relationships. However, understanding editorials requires applying abstract knowledge of argumentation and reasoning in addition to knowledge structures and processing strategies used in narrative comprehension. The philosophy behind OpEd's design has been to extend those previous theories of conceptual analysis of narrative text into the domain of editorial text.

In OpEd, understanding editorial text involves six major issues: (1) applying domain-specific knowledge (i.e., politico-economic knowledge); (2) recognizing beliefs and belief relationships; (3) following causal chains of reasoning about goals and plans; (4) applying abstract knowledge of argument structure; (5) mapping input text into conceptual structures which compose the internal representations of editorial arguments; and (6) indexing recognized concepts for later retrieval during question answering. Input editorial segments are in English and contain the essential wording, issues, and arguments of the original editorials. Here "essential" means that the original editorials have been edited to remove those parts which involve addressing issues that fall outside the scope of OpEd's process model, such as understanding references to historic events, completing analogies, and handling sarcastic or humorous statements.

To understand the nature and complexity of the issues addressed in OpEd, consider an actual sample of its current input/output behavior when processing ED-JOBS, a fragment of an editorial by Milton Friedman (1982). This editorial fragment presents Friedman's arguments against the Reagan administration's policies in international trade. Input text and questions to OpEd are shown in bold, lower-case letters; output is in upper case.

ED-JOBS[1]

Recent protectionist measures by the Reagan administration have disappointed us. Voluntary limits on Japanese automobiles and voluntary limits on steel by the Common Market are bad for the nation. They do not promote the long-run health of the industries affected. The problem of the automobile and steel industries is: in both industries, average wage rates are twice as high as the average. Far from saving jobs, the limitations on imports will cost jobs. If we import less, foreign countries will earn fewer dollars. They will have less to spend on American exports. The result will be fewer jobs in export industries.

Q1: What has disappointed Milton Friedman?
A1: PROTECTIONIST POLICIES BY THE REAGAN ADMINISTRATION.

Q2: Who believes that the limitations on imports will save jobs?
A2: THE REAGAN ADMINISTRATION.

Q3: What is the result of the limitations on imports?
A3: MILTON FRIEDMAN BELIEVES THAT PROTECTIONIST POLICIES BY THE REAGAN ADMINISTRATION DO NOT LEAD TO THE ACHIEVEMENT OF NORMAL PROFITS OF THE STEEL INDUSTRY AND THE AUTOMOBILE INDUSTRY.

---

[1]An example of an editorial change made in ED-JOBS is the phrase "voluntary limits." In the original text, this phrase appears as "'voluntary' limits." The single quotation marks enclosing the word "voluntary" are a sarcastic reference to the fact that the limitations on imports are not really voluntary, but rather a response by foreign countries to economic pressure by the U.S.

THE REAGAN ADMINISTRATION BELIEVES THAT PROTECTIONIST POLICIES BY THE REAGAN ADMINISTRATION LEAD TO THE ACHIEVEMENT OF NORMAL PROFITS OF THE STEEL INDUSTRY AND THE AUTOMOBILE INDUSTRY.

MILTON FRIEDMAN BELIEVES THAT PROTECTIONIST POLICIES BY THE REAGAN ADMINISTRATION WILL THWART THE PRESERVATION OF JOBS FOR U.S.

THE REAGAN ADMINISTRATION BELIEVES THAT PROTECTIONIST POLICIES BY THE REAGAN ADMINISTRATION ACHIEVE THE PRESERVATION OF JOBS FOR U.S.

Q4: What does Milton Friedman believe?

A4: MILTON FRIEDMAN BELIEVES THAT PROTECTIONIST POLICIES BY THE REAGAN ADMINISTRATION ARE BAD BECAUSE MILTON FRIEDMAN BELIEVES THAT PROTECTIONIST POLICIES BY THE REAGAN ADMINISTRATION DO NOT LEAD TO THE ACHIEVEMENT OF NORMAL PROFITS OF THE STEEL INDUSTRY AND THE AUTOMOBILE INDUSTRY. MILTON FRIEDMAN BELIEVES THAT PROTECTIONIST POLICIES BY THE REAGAN ADMINISTRATION DO NOT LEAD TO THE ACHIEVEMENT OF NORMAL PROFITS OF THE STEEL INDUSTRY AND THE AUTOMOBILE INDUSTRY BECAUSE MILTON FRIEDMAN BELIEVES THAT NORMAL SALARY IN THE STEEL INDUSTRY AND THE AUTOMOBILE INDUSTRY HIGHER THAN THE NORM THWARTS THE ACHIEVEMENT OF NORMAL PROFITS OF THE STEEL INDUSTRY AND THE AUTOMOBILE INDUSTRY. MILTON FRIEDMAN BELIEVES THAT THE REAGAN ADMINISTRATION IS WRONG BECAUSE THE REAGAN ADMINISTRATION BELIEVES THAT PROTECTIONIST POLICIES BY THE REAGAN ADMINISTRATION LEAD TO THE ACHIEVEMENT OF NORMAL PROFITS OF THE STEEL INDUSTRY AND THE AUTOMOBILE INDUSTRY.

MILTON FRIEDMAN BELIEVES THAT PROTECTIONIST POLICIES BY THE REAGAN ADMINISTRATION ARE BAD BECAUSE MILTON FRIEDMAN BELIEVES THAT PROTECTIONIST POLICIES BY THE REAGAN ADMINISTRATION WILL THWART THE PRESERVATION OF JOBS FOR U.S. MILTON FRIEDMAN BELIEVES THAT THE REAGAN ADMINISTRATION IS WRONG BECAUSE THE REAGAN ADMINISTRATION BELIEVES THAT PROTECTIONIST POLICIES BY THE REAGAN ADMINISTRATION ACHIEVE THE PRESERVATION OF JOBS FOR U.S.

Q5: Why does Milton Friedman believe that the limitations on imports will cost jobs?

A5: MILTON FRIEDMAN BELIEVES THAT PROTECTIONIST POLICIES BY THE REAGAN ADMINISTRATION WILL THWART THE PRESERVATION OF JOBS FOR U.S. BECAUSE MILTON FRIEDMAN BELIEVES THAT AS A CONSEQUENCE OF PROTECTIONIST POLICIES BY THE REAGAN ADMINISTRATION, U.S. IMPORTS FEWER PRODUCTS; AND IF U.S. IMPORTS FEWER PRODUCTS, THEN THERE IS A DECREASE IN PROFITS OF FOREIGN COUNTRIES; AND IF THERE IS A DECREASE IN PROFITS OF FOREIGN COUNTRIES, THEN FOREIGN COUNTRIES BUY FEWER AMERICAN EXPORTS; AND IF FOREIGN COUNTRIES BUY FEWER AMERICAN EXPORTS, THEN THERE IS A DECREASE IN PROFITS OF EXPORT INDUSTRIES; AND IF THERE IS A DECREASE IN PROFITS OF EXPORT

INDUSTRIES, THEN THERE IS A DECREASE IN JOBS IN EXPORT INDUSTRIES; AND A DECREASE IN JOBS IN EXPORT INDUSTRIES THWARTS THE PRESERVATION OF JOBS FOR U.S.

1.2.1. Domain-Specific Knowledge

OpEd must have a computational model of politico-economic knowledge in order to make sense of discussions about import restrictions. Consider three of the problems OpEd has to solve in order to process ED-JOBS:

(1) Concept Reference:

> **... protectionist measures by the Reagan administration ... Voluntary limits on Japanese automobiles and voluntary limits on steel by the Common Market ...**

The mention of "voluntary limits" does not constitute a sudden topic shift, but rather is a coherent continuation of Friedman's opinion concerning the Reagan administration's protectionist policies. To make such a connection possible, OpEd must understand that voluntary limits on imports are instances of protectionist policies.

(2) Concept Inference:

> **... the long-run health of the industries affected.**

What industries is Friedman referring to? Up to this point in ED-JOBS there has not been explicit reference to any industries. However, OpEd has been told that the limitations have been voluntarily imposed on exports of automobiles and steel to the U.S. Therefore, OpEd must be able to infer that Friedman is referring to the American automobile and steel industries.

(3) Causal Coherence:

> **The problem of the ... industries is ... average wage rates ...**

What do high wage rates have to do with industries? To establish the connection, OpEd must know that the profits of any industry are affected by the level of salaries it pays to its workers, i.e., the higher the salaries, the lower the profits.

OpEd's politico-economic knowledge does not have to include what an expert in politics and economics would know. Instead, OpEd's model must involve what an average, well-informed adult reader must know to understand editorials of the type of ED-JOBS. That is, OpEd's domain-specific knowledge should be a "naive" model of politics and economics. As such, this model has to have representations for each of the following classes of concepts and their instances:

- Authorities: The Reagan administration.
- Institutions: The Common Market, steel industry, and automobile industry.
- Countries: United States, Japan, and countries from the Common Market.
- Products: Imports, exports, steel, and automobiles.
- Economic Quantities: Earnings, spending, and cost.
- Occupations: Jobs in export industries.
- Goals: Saving jobs and attaining economic health of industries.
- Plans: Protectionist policies.
- Events: Importing and exporting.

OpEd's politico-economic model must also include causal relationships that exist at the level of goals, plans, and events, such as how changes in one economic quantity affect other economic quantities and which plans can be used to achieve given goals. For example, understanding ED-JOBS requires recognizing the following relationships:

- Governments can impose or negotiate import restrictions to protect jobs in domestic industries and/or to help these industries become profitable.
- An industry's rate of employment depends on the industry's volume of sales.
- The capital available for importing goods depends on the capital produced from exporting goods.

This common-sense knowledge must be represented and formalized in OpEd so that it can be accessed and applied during editorial comprehension.

1.2.2. Beliefs and Belief Relationships

Another basic problem in editorial comprehension is to recognize the writer's explicitly or implicitly stated opinions along with their justifications. For example, after reading the sentence:

... protectionist measures by the Reagan administration have disappointed us.

OpEd must infer that Friedman is against the Reagan administration's protectionist policies, although this opinion is not explicitly stated. Friedman's belief should be inferred from the affect description "disappointed," which indicates that "protectionist measures" cause goal or expectation failures. Friedman's position is later justified in the sentence:

... the limitations on imports will cost jobs.

To recognize this support relationship, OpEd has to understand that losing jobs is a goal violation. Therefore, OpEd must use knowledge of goal/planning relationships to recognize belief justifications.

In addition to recognizing the editorial writer's beliefs and their justifications, OpEd has to be able to recognize other individuals' beliefs and how they support, are supported by, or attacked by the editorial writer's beliefs. Recognizing these relationships is essential for comprehension because editorial arguments often present the writer's agreement or disagreement with respect to other individuals' beliefs. For instance, in the following sentence from ED-JOBS:

They do not promote the long-run health of the industries affected.

Friedman attacks the implicit belief by the Reagan administration that the limitations will help the automobile and steel industries recover from their economic slump.[2] To recognize this attack relationship, OpEd must access its politico-economic model to realize that voluntary import restrictions are negotiated to provide the basis for long-term economic

---

[2]The Reagan administration has always professed its belief in free international markets and never viewed the voluntary limits as restrictions on international trade to protect domestic industries. However, OpEd does not know these facts because OpEd does not support a historical memory for politico-economic events and beliefs. The model of beliefs which OpEd constructs during editorial comprehension is based *only* on those beliefs explicitly or implicitly stated in the editorial. Modeling and applying historical memories during argument comprehension fall outside the scope of OpEd.

recovery of ailing industries. Thus, recognizing opposing beliefs relies on applying domain-specific knowledge.

1.2.3. Causal Chains of Reasoning

Understanding belief justifications also requires identifying and keeping track of causal chains of reasoning. These chains are sequences of cause-effect relationships which show in greater level of detail: (a) why plans should/shouldn't be selected, implemented, or terminated; or (b) why goals should/shouldn't be pursued. To follow such chains, OpEd must recognize explicit and implicit cause-effect relationships by applying politico-economic knowledge about goals and plans. For example, consider the causal chain which supports Friedman's belief that "the limitations on imports will cost jobs":

> **If we import less, foreign countries will earn fewer dollars. They will have less to spend on American exports. The result will be fewer jobs in export industries.**

Friedman's reasoning contains the following relationships:

1) Import restrictions by the U.S. result in a decrease in imports to the U.S.

2) The decrease in imports to the U.S. causes a decrease in foreign countries' export earnings.

3) The decrease in foreign countries' earnings causes a decrease in their spending on American exports.

4) The decrease in spending on American exports results in a decrease in earnings of American export industries.

5) The decrease in earnings of American export industries causes a decrease in the number of occupations in these industries.

6) The decrease in occupations thwarts the Reagan administration's goal of saving jobs.

When processing ED-JOBS, OpEd has to be able to infer relationships (1), (4), (5), and (6) along with the implicitly stated connection between (2) and (3). Therefore, OpEd must use domain-specific knowledge to infer missing steps in incomplete chains of reasoning in editorials.

1.2.4. Abstract Knowledge of Argumentation

Editorial comprehension implies applying abstract knowledge of argumentation. This knowledge is independent of domain-specific knowledge and, thus, fundamental to understanding and generating arguments in any domain. Abstract knowledge of argumentation is organized by memory structures called *Argument Units (AUs)* (Alvarado et al., 1985a, 1986), which represent patterns of support and attack relationships among beliefs. When combined with domain-specific knowledge, AUs can be used to argue about issues involving plans, goals, and beliefs in the particular domain. As a result, argument comprehension in OpEd must be viewed as the process of recognizing, accessing, instantiating, and applying argument units.

The points of an editorial are held by AUs recognized and instantiated during editorial comprehension. For example, in ED-JOBS, Friedman uses the following argument unit:

AU-ACTUAL-CAUSE: Although opponent O believes plan P should be used to achieve goal G, SELF believes P does not achieve G because SELF believes P does not affect situation S which thwarts G. Therefore, SELF believes P should not be used.

Friedman uses AU-ACTUAL-CAUSE to argue that the Reagan administration's protectionist policies will not help the automobile and steel industries become profitable because such policies do not affect the actual cause of the industries' problems, namely, average wage rates much higher than the average. To recognize this argument unit, OpEd needs to know that: (a) import restrictions are intended to help struggling domestic industries become profitable again; (b) high workers' salaries work against industries' profits; and (c) import restrictions are not wage-control policies. Thus, OpEd must apply domain-specific knowledge to recognize argument units.

The process of recognizing argument units is also based on the capability of identifying specific linguistic constructs which signal opposition and expectation failures. For example, consider AU-OPPOSITE-EFFECT, another argument unit used in ED-JOBS:

AU-OPPOSITE-EFFECT: Although opponent O believes plan P should be used to achieve goal G, SELF believes P does not achieve G because SELF believes P thwarts G. Therefore, SELF believes P should not be used.

Friedman uses AU-OPPOSITE-EFFECT to argue that he is against import restrictions because they will not save but cost jobs. When processing ED-JOBS, OpEd must recognize AU-OPPOSITE-EFFECT after reading the sentence:

Far from saving jobs, the limitations on imports will cost jobs.

This recognition process must be triggered by the explicit relationship of opposition between expected effects of import restrictions, namely, saving jobs and costing jobs. This relationship is signaled by the construct:

"Far from" X, Y

where X and Y are opposite (mutually exclusive) effects and the phrase "far from" indicates opposition. Therefore, argument comprehension involves recognizing specific linguistic constructs, accessing the specific conceptualizations they refer to, and mapping from these conceptualizations into their appropriate argument units.

1.2.5. Conceptual Representation of Arguments

Keeping track of the contents of the editorial involves building an internal conceptual model of editorial arguments. This model, known as an *argument graph* (Flowers et al., 1982), represents explicitly relationships of support and attack among beliefs as well as causal relationships among goals, plans, events, and states. The argument graph also aids the understanding process by representing and maintaining the current context of the editorial.

OpEd must parse input words and phrases into conceptual structures and integrate these structures into the editorial's argument graph. Every new belief has to be integrated into the graph by using links that indicate whether the belief supports, attacks, or is supported by other beliefs already existing in the graph. For example, the diagram in figure 1.1 shows a simplified version of the argument graph of ED-JOBS.[3]

---

[3]For readability, the conceptual content of each belief in the argument graph is described in English.

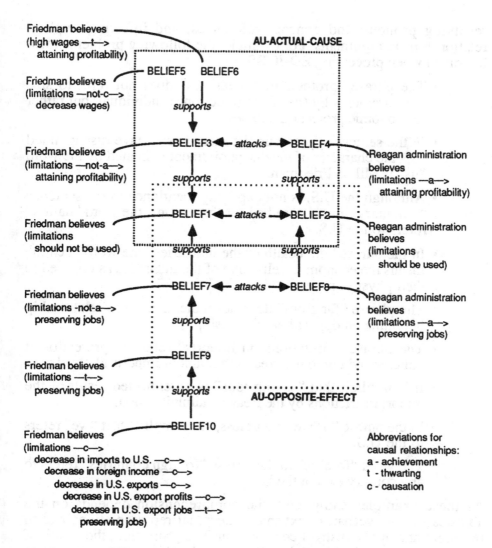

Figure 1.1. Argument Graph of ED-JOBS.

As the above diagram indicates, the bulk of the editorial representation is contained in the argument graph. The diagram also shows that patterns of support and attack relationships in the argument graph are organized by the argument units used in the editorial.

In addition to recognizing beliefs, belief relationships, and argument units, the process of mapping editorial text into conceptual representations includes other tasks such as disambiguating words, resolving pronoun and concept references, and inferring implicit relationships in arguments. For example, the following problems must be solved when processing ED-JOBS:

- The phrase "protectionist measures" does not refer to size measurements by (or of) a protectionist individual, but rather to economic protection policies.

- In the sentence "protectionist measures ... have disappointed us," the character of the disappointment indicated by the word "us" is Milton Friedman.

- Although the U.S. is not explicitly mentioned in the sentence "voluntary limits ... are bad for the nation," the word "nation" refers to the U.S.

- In the phrase "the health of the industries" the word "health" means the economic well-being of the industries as opposed to their physical state.

- The phrase "far from" does not indicate a space relationship but rather an opposition relationship.

- The phrase "limitations on imports" refers to protectionist policies and not to the greatest amount of imports allowed.

- It is implicit that "saving jobs" is an expected result of the import restrictions by the Reagan administration.

- In the phrase " If we import less," it is implicit that "we" refers to the U.S.

- The word "foreign" in the phrase "foreign countries" refers to any country except the U.S.

As these examples show, editorial comprehension depends on the abilities to map verbatim text into conceptual representations and to represent and apply abstract concepts, such as protection, the health of an organization, and saving jobs. OpEd must be able to manipulate these abstract concepts in order to construct the editorial's argument graph.

1.2.6. Memory Retrieval

The argument graph of an editorial must also include indexing structures and access links which provide initial entry to the graph. These indices and access links need to be created during editorial comprehension and later used by search and retrieval processes when answering questions about the editorial. For instance, consider one of the questions that OpEd has to be able to answer after reading ED-JOBS:

Q4:   What does Milton Friedman believe?

To answer this question, OpEd must retrieve the instantiations of the argument units used in ED-JOBS, namely AU-ACTUAL-CAUSE and AU-OPPOSITE-EFFECT. Retrieving these instantiated AUs requires: (1) indexing structures from argument participants to their professed beliefs; (2) access links between beliefs and associated argument units; and (3) a retrieval function that takes argument participants as input and retrieves argument units. Therefore, OpEd must first access its representation of Friedman's beliefs and then retrieve the instantiated AUs that contain such beliefs.

During question answering, the process of selecting appropriate retrieval strategies must depend upon parsing the question and analyzing the conceptual content into one of a number of *conceptual question categories* (Lehnert, 1978). Different question categories lead to different search and retrieval processes. These processes must select indices according to the questions' input information. Once an index is selected, these processes must traverse access and memory links in order to locate an appropriate conceptualization which will be retrieved. Answers retrieved must then be converted from memory representation into English. For example, consider OpEd's answer to question Q4:

A4:   MILTON FRIEDMAN BELIEVES THAT PROTECTIONIST POLICIES BY THE REAGAN ADMINISTRATION ARE BAD BECAUSE MILTON FRIEDMAN BELIEVES THAT PROTECTIONIST POLICIES BY THE REAGAN ADMINISTRATION DO NOT LEAD TO THE ACHIEVEMENT OF NORMAL PROFITS OF THE STEEL INDUSTRY AND THE AUTOMOBILE INDUSTRY. MILTON FRIEDMAN BELIEVES THAT PROTECTIONIST POLICIES BY THE REAGAN ADMINISTRATION DO NOT LEAD TO THE ACHIEVEMENT OF NORMAL PROFITS OF THE STEEL INDUSTRY AND THE AUTOMOBILE INDUSTRY BECAUSE MILTON FRIEDMAN BELIEVES THAT NORMAL SALARY IN THE STEEL INDUSTRY AND THE AUTOMOBILE INDUSTRY HIGHER THAN THE NORM THWARTS THE ACHIEVEMENT OF NORMAL PROFITS OF THE STEEL INDUSTRY AND THE AUTOMOBILE INDUSTRY. MILTON FRIEDMAN BELIEVES THAT THE REAGAN ADMINISTRATION IS WRONG BECAUSE THE REAGAN ADMINISTRATION BELIEVES THAT PROTECTIONIST POLICIES BY THE REAGAN ADMINISTRATION LEAD TO THE ACHIEVEMENT OF NORMAL PROFITS OF THE STEEL INDUSTRY AND THE AUTOMOBILE INDUSTRY.

MILTON FRIEDMAN BELIEVES THAT PROTECTIONIST POLICIES BY THE REAGAN ADMINISTRATION ARE BAD BECAUSE MILTON FRIEDMAN BELIEVES THAT PROTECTIONIST POLICIES BY THE REAGAN ADMINISTRATION WILL THWART THE PRESERVATION OF JOBS FOR U.S. MILTON FRIEDMAN BELIEVES THAT THE REAGAN ADMINISTRATION IS

WRONG BECAUSE THE REAGAN ADMINISTRATION BELIEVES THAT
PROTECTIONIST POLICIES BY THE REAGAN ADMINISTRATION ACHIEVE THE
PRESERVATION OF JOBS FOR U.S.

Answer A4 is a detailed account of what OpEd knows about Friedman's
opinion in ED-JOBS. The first part of the answer corresponds to the
instantiation of AU-ACTUAL-CAUSE and the second part to the
instantiation of AU-OPPOSITE-EFFECT. This detailed account of the
argument units recognized during editorial comprehension is also
verbose and contains redundant information, such as the fact that the
import restrictions were implemented by the Reagan administration.
However, linguistic style in answer generation is not a major issue
addressed in OpEd. The memory structures retrieved during question
answering are generated in English for the purpose of making them
understandable to OpEd's users.

1.3.   Scope of OpEd

The theory of argument comprehension implemented in OpEd
has been developed from the perspective of natural language
understanding. That is, argument comprehension in OpEd is not
considered as an isolated process but rather as an integral aspect of
natural language understanding. As a result, OpEd builds upon
knowledge constructs and processing strategies developed for computer
comprehension of natural language. In particular, OpEd's process
model involves the following techniques:

1) Knowledge representation constructs used in conceptual
   analysis of narratives, including events (Schank, 1975);
   social acts (Schank and Carbonell, 1979); scripts
   (Cullingford, 1978; Schank and Abelson, 1977); goals and
   plans (Carbonell, 1981; Schank and Abelson, 1977;
   Wilensky, 1983); affects (Dyer, 1983b); causal links (Dyer
   and Lehnert, 1982); and MOPs (Schank, 1982).

2) Techniques for modeling arguments, including a taxonomy
   of beliefs and argument units (Alvarado et al., 1985a, 1986),
   argument graphs (Flowers et al., 1982), and reasoning
   scripts (Dyer, Cullingford, and Alvarado, 1987; Flowers
   and Dyer, 1984).

3) Strategies for mapping natural language into conceptual
   representations (Alvarado et al., 1985b, 1985c; Dyer,
   1983a).

4) Strategies for memory search and retrieval (Alvarado et al., 1985a; Dyer 1983a; Lehnert, 1978).

These techniques are combined in OpEd to produce a system which parses editorial text into a network of beliefs by accessing and applying argument units.[4]

Editorial comprehension in OpEd does not account for the processes responsible for: (1) establishing the intention of an editorial, i.e., whether the editorial is intended to explain or persuade; (2) recognizing what it means to be persuaded by, in agreement with, or in disagreement with an argument; (3) reorganizing and updating beliefs once a persuasive argument has been recognized; and (4) recognizing whether an argument is sound or contains errors. We must first model the process of parsing editorial text into conceptual representations before we even attempt to model the processes of persuasion, agreement, belief revision, and argument-error recognition.

Currently OpEd can handle the editorial segment ED-JOBS and various conceptual question categories. To demonstrate that the theory of argument comprehension implemented in OpEd is not tailored to a particular editorial, OpEd is also able to read and answer questions about ED-RESTRICTIONS, an editorial segment taken from an editorial by Lance Morrow (1983). ED-RESTRICTIONS presents Morrow's arguments against implementing import restrictions to protect the American machine-tool industry. A sample of OpEd's input/output behavior when processing ED-RESTRICTIONS is shown below.

ED-RESTRICTIONS

The American machine-tool industry is seeking protection from foreign competition. The industry has been hurt by cheaper machine tools from Japan. The toolmakers argue that restrictions on imports must be imposed so that the industry can survive. It is a wrongheaded argument. Restrictions on imports would mean that American manufacturers would have to make do with more expensive American machine tools. Inevitably, those American manufacturers would produce more expensive products. They would

---

[4]Throughout this dissertation, it is assumed that readers have some familiarity with Conceptual Dependency theory (Schank, 1973, 1975) and techniques for narrative comprehension, representation, and retrieval. For readers lacking such a background, the following references should provide a basic introduction to those subjects: (Birnbaum and Selfridge, 1981), (Dyer and Lehnert, 1982), (Lehnert, et al., 1983), and Appendix II in (Dyer, 1983a).

**lose sales. Then those manufacturers would demand protection
against foreign competition.**

Q1: **What does the American machine-tool industry believe?**
A1: THE AMERICAN MACHINE TOOL INDUSTRY BELIEVES THAT PROTECTIONIST
POLICY BY THE AMERICAN GOVERNMENT ACHIEVES THE PRESERVATION
OF NORMAL PROFITS OF THE AMERICAN MACHINE TOOL INDUSTRY.

Q2: **What does Lance Morrow believe?**
A2: LANCE MORROW BELIEVES THAT PROTECTIONIST POLICY BY THE
AMERICAN GOVERNMENT IS BAD BECAUSE LANCE MORROW BELIEVES
THAT PROTECTIONIST POLICY BY THE AMERICAN GOVERNMENT
MOTIVATES THE PRESERVATION OF NORMAL PROFITS OF AMERICAN
INDUSTRIES. LANCE MORROW BELIEVES THAT THE AMERICAN MACHINE
TOOL INDUSTRY IS WRONG BECAUSE THE AMERICAN MACHINE TOOL
INDUSTRY BELIEVES THAT PROTECTIONIST POLICY BY THE AMERICAN
GOVERNMENT ACHIEVES THE PRESERVATION OF NORMAL PROFITS OF THE
AMERICAN MACHINE TOOL INDUSTRY.

LANCE MORROW BELIEVES THAT PROTECTIONIST POLICY BY THE
AMERICAN GOVERNMENT IS BAD BECAUSE LANCE MORROW BELIEVES
THAT PROTECTIONIST POLICY BY THE AMERICAN GOVERNMENT
MOTIVATES THE PRESERVATION OF NORMAL PROFITS OF AMERICAN
INDUSTRIES; AND THE PRESERVATION OF NORMAL PROFITS OF AMERICAN
INDUSTRIES INTENDS PERSUASION PLAN BY AMERICAN INDUSTRIES ABOUT
PROTECTIONIST POLICY BY THE AMERICAN GOVERNMENT. LANCE
MORROW BELIEVES THAT THE AMERICAN MACHINE TOOL INDUSTRY IS
WRONG BECAUSE THE AMERICAN MACHINE TOOL INDUSTRY BELIEVES
THAT PROTECTIONIST POLICY BY THE AMERICAN GOVERNMENT ACHIEVES
THE PRESERVATION OF NORMAL PROFITS OF THE AMERICAN MACHINE
TOOL INDUSTRY.

Q3: **Why does Lance Morrow believe that import restrictions would mean fewer
sales?**
A3: LANCE MORROW BELIEVES THAT PROTECTIONIST POLICY BY THE
AMERICAN GOVERNMENT MOTIVATES THE PRESERVATION OF NORMAL
PROFITS OF AMERICAN INDUSTRIES BECAUSE LANCE MORROW BELIEVES
THAT AS A CONSEQUENCE OF PROTECTIONIST POLICY BY THE AMERICAN
GOVERNMENT, AMERICAN INDUSTRY PRODUCES WITH HIGH COST
AMERICAN MACHINE TOOL; AND IF AMERICAN INDUSTRY PRODUCES WITH
HIGH COST AMERICAN MACHINE TOOL, THEN AMERICAN INDUSTRIES
PRODUCE HIGH COST PRODUCTS; AND IF AMERICAN INDUSTRIES PRODUCE
HIGH COST PRODUCTS, THEN AMERICAN INDUSTRIES SELL FEWER
PRODUCTS; AND IF AMERICAN INDUSTRIES SELL FEWER PRODUCTS, THEN
THERE IS A DECREASE IN PROFITS OF AMERICAN INDUSTRIES; AND A
DECREASE IN PROFITS OF AMERICAN INDUSTRIES MOTIVATES THE
PRESERVATION OF NORMAL PROFITS OF AMERICAN INDUSTRIES.

Although both ED-RESTRICTIONS and ED-JOBS argue
against protectionism by the U.S., Morrow's argument in ED-

RESTRICTIONS is conceptually different from that of Friedman in ED-JOBS. This difference stems from the fact that Morrow uses argument units different from those used by Friedman. The argument units used in ED-RESTRICTIONS are shown below.

> **AU-EQUIVALENCE:** Although opponent O believes plan P should be used to achieve goal G1, SELF believes P should not be used to achieve G1 because SELF believes P thwarts goal G2 which is equivalent to G1.

> **AU-SPIRAL-EFFECT:** Although opponent O believes plan P1 should be used to achieve goal G1, SELF believes P1 should not be used to achieve G1 because SELF believes P1 thwarts goal G2 and this goal failure will require using plan P2 which is equivalent to P1.

Morrow uses AU-EQUIVALENCE to argue that:

- The American machine-tool industry believes that import restrictions on Japanese machine tools should be implemented because they will achieve their goal of preserving the industry's finances.

- However, implementing these import restrictions will thwart other American manufacturers' goal of preserving their finances.

- Therefore, the import restrictions on machine tools should not be implemented.

AU-SPIRAL-EFFECT is used to argue further that these import restrictions should not be implemented because the goal violation resulting from these policies will motivate the use of more protectionist policies. That is, Morrow believes import restrictions will trigger a protectionist spiral.

To recognize the argument units in ED-RESTRICTIONS, OpEd must keep track of a causal chain of reasoning that contains the following relationships:

1) Import restrictions will result in an increase in production costs for other American manufacturers that use costly American machine tools.

2) The increase in production costs will cause an increase in the price of products made by those manufacturers.

3) The increase in the products' prices will lead to a decrease in their sales.

4) The decrease in products' sales will result in a decrease in earnings of American manufacturers.

5) The decrease in earnings thwarts those manufacturers' goal of preserving their finances.

6) Because of this goal violation, American manufacturers will petition for import restrictions.

When processing ED-RESTRICTIONS, OpEd has to be able to infer relationships (3), (4), (5), and (6) along with the implicitly stated connection between (1) and (2). In addition, mapping ED-RESTRICTIONS into conceptual representations requires solving the following problems:

- In the phrases "seeking protection from foreign competition" and "demand protection against foreign competition," it is implicit that petitions for protection are directed to the American government.

- It is also implicit that, in the phrase "import restrictions must be imposed," the American government would be the one imposing the restrictions.

- In the phrases "the industry has been hurt" and "the industry can survive," the words "hurt" and "survive" do not refer to the physical state of the industry but rather to its economic well-being.

- When referring to activities of industries, the phrase "make do with" has to be understood as "manufacture products using."

Getting OpEd to handle ED-RESTRICTIONS in addition to handling ED-JOBS did not require modifying its process model of argument comprehension, but rather: (1) augmenting its lexicon and politico-economic knowledge; (2) augmenting its knowledge of argument units to include AU-EQUIVALENCE and AU-SPIRAL-EFFECT; and (3) specifying the processing strategies needed to manipulate the conceptual structures added. In addition, OpEd's search and retrieval processes did not need any modifications to retrieve answers to questions about ED-RESTRICTIONS. For instance, to answer the question:

Q2: What does Lance Morrow believe?

OpEd must retrieve the instantiations of the above AUs by applying the same search and retrieval processes used to answer the question "What does Milton Friedman think?" within the context of ED-JOBS. Therefore, OpEd's ability to handle both ED-RESTRICTIONS and ED-JOBS demonstrates the level of generality of the theory of argument comprehension, representation, and retrieval implemented in OpEd.

1.4.   Architecture of OpEd

OpEd consists of seven major interrelated components: semantic memory, lexicon, expectation-based parser, working memory, argument graph, memory search and retrieval processes, and English generator. These components along with their interactions are shown in figure 1.2 and described below.

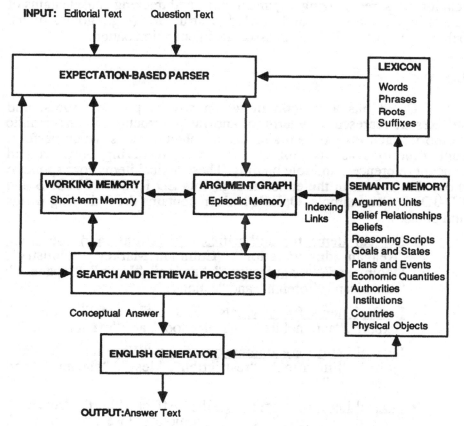

Figure 1.2. Diagram of OpEd's Components.

Semantic Memory

OpEd's semantic memory embodies a computational model of politico-economic knowledge and abstract knowledge of argumentation. OpEd's politico-economic model includes: economic protection plans and their associated goals, causal relationships among economic quantities, and reasoning scripts containing prespecified causal chains in politics and economics. OpEd's model of argumentation involves representations of argument units which organize abstract patterns of support and attack relationships among beliefs.

Each conceptual construct in semantic memory has attached processes called demons which perform knowledge application and knowledge interaction tasks, such as binding conceptualizations together, recognizing beliefs, recognizing support and attack relationships, recognizing argument units, and tracking causal chains of reasoning. Each class of knowledge structure (e.g., goals, plans, beliefs, AUs, etc.) also has an associated generation pattern.

Lexicon

OpEd has a lexicon in which words, phrases, roots, and suffixes are represented in terms of knowledge structures in its semantic memory. Each lexical item also has attached demons which perform such functions as disambiguating words, resolving pronoun and concept references, and role binding. These lexical items correspond to those that appear in the editorial segments ED-RESTRICTIONS and ED-JOBS. For example, OpEd's lexicon contains the following words and phrases:

- Lexical items for authorities, institutions, and countries: "Reagan administration", "Common Market", "industry", "toolmaker", "manufacturer", "nation", "Japan", "Japanese", "American", "foreign", and "country."

- Lexical items for products: "Product", "steel", "import", "export", "automobile", "machine tool", and "machine-tool."

- Lexical items for economic quantities: "Wage rate", "dollar", "jobs", "limitation", "restriction", "less", "cheaper", and "expensive."

- Lexical items that refer to goals: "Affect", "hurt", "survive", "be bad for", "save", "cost", "promote", "lose", "disappoint", "problem", and "competition."

- <u>Lexical items for plans and events:</u> "Protectionist", "measure", "voluntary limit", "protection", "import", "seek", "impose", "demand", "produce", "make do", "sale", "earn", and "spend."

- <u>Connectives for cause-effect relationships:</u> "So that", "inevitably", "result", "if", and "then."

- <u>Connectives for opposition relationships:</u> "Far from" and "be wrongheaded."

- <u>Lexical items for beliefs:</u> "Argue that" and "argument."

Expectation-Based Parser

Input editorial text is mapped into conceptual representations by an expectation-based (or demon-based) parser which uses the techniques for conceptual parsing implemented in BORIS (Dyer, 1983a), an in-depth understander of narrative text. Each input sentence is read from left to right on a word-by-word or phrase basis. When a lexical item is recognized, a copy of its associated conceptualization is placed into OpEd's short-term memory or working memory. Copies of the lexical item's demons and its conceptualization demons are placed into a demon agenda that contains all active demons. Then, the parser tests all active demons and executes those whose test conditions are satisfied. After demons are executed, they are removed from the agenda.

Working Memory

When demons are executed, they bind together conceptualizations in working memory and, as a result, they build the conceptual representation of the input sentence. Thus, working memory maintains the current context of the sentence being parsed. After the sentence has been read, its conceptual representation is removed from working memory and the parsing process is repeated for the next sentence in the editorial.

Argument Graph

Also resulting from demon execution, the conceptualizations created in working memory get integrated with instantiated structures currently indexed by semantic memory's structures. These instantiations compose the editorial's argument graph which represents and maintains the current context of the editorial read so far. Thus, the argument graph can be viewed as OpEd's *episodic memory* (Tulving, 1972), as opposed to OpEd's semantic memory which contains what OpEd knows before reading the editorial.

Memory Search and Retrieval Processes

During question-answering, the argument graph also maintains the current context from which questions are understood. Each input question is parsed by the expectation-based parser and the question's conceptual representation is built in working memory. Question answering demons attached to WH-words (e.g., why, what, who, etc.) are activated whenever such words are encountered at the beginning of the question. These demons determine the question's conceptual category and activate appropriate search and retrieval demons that access the argument graph and return conceptual answers.

English Generator

Once an answer is found, it is generated in English by OpEd's recursive descent generator. This generator produces English sentences in a left-to-right manner by traversing instantiated knowledge structures and using the generation patterns associated with knowledge structures in semantic memory. For example, instantiations of AU-OPPOSITE-EFFECT are generated using the pattern:

```
<BELIEF1-BY-SELF> "because" <BELIEF2-BY-SELF>.
<SELF> "believe that"
        <OPPONENT> "be wrong because" <BELIEF-BY-OPPONENT>.
```

where: (1) SELF is the instance of the arguer using AU-OPPOSITE-EFFECT; (2) OPPONENT is the instance of the arguer's opponent; (3) BELIEF1-BY-SELF is the instance the belief "P should not be used"; (4) BELIEF2-BY-SELF is the instance of the belief "P thwarts goal G"; (4) BELIEF-BY-OPPONENT is the instance of the belief "P achieves goal G"; and (5) the verbs "to believe" and "to be " are conjugated according to the contents of SELF, OPPONENT, and BELIEF-BY-OPPONENT.

1.5.   Contents of the Dissertation

This chapter has outlined the theory of argument comprehension, representation, and retrieval implemented in OpEd to understand short politico-economic editorials and answer questions about their contents. Editorial comprehension requires building an argument graph where configurations of support and attack relationships among beliefs are organized by argument units. Thus, argument comprehension in OpEd is viewed as the process of recognizing, accessing, instantiating, and applying argument units.

The remainder of this dissertation is divided into three major parts: representation (chapters 2 through 5), process model (chapters 6 and 7), and summary (chapters 8 and 9). The first section addresses issues in representation and organization of domain-specific knowledge and abstract knowledge of argumentation. Chapter 2 describes a model of knowledge in the politico-economic domain required for understanding arguments about protectionism. Chapter 3 covers a taxonomy of beliefs and relationships of support and attack among beliefs. Chapter 4 presents the theory of argument units and focuses on the use of AUs to represent arguments involving attacks on beliefs about domain-specific plans and goals. Chapter 5 examines AUs used to represent meta arguments, i.e., arguments which attack the use of entire argument strategies.

The second section deals with the process of building and retrieving argument memories. Chapter 6 describes how an editorial's argument graph is constructed through the application of techniques for recognizing beliefs, belief relationships, and argument units. Chapter 7 covers techniques for memory search and retrieval used to answer questions about editorials.

The third section is a summary of the scope of the theory of argument comprehension, representation, and retrieval. Chapter 8 discusses the implementation of OpEd and includes annotated traces of OpEd's input/output behavior during editorial comprehension and question answering. Chapter 9 discusses the relation of this work to other research in the fields of rhetoric, logic, artificial intelligence, and psychology. That chapter also sums up the claims made in this dissertation and describes current limitations of this work along with areas for future related research.

Chapter 2

Representing Politico-Economic Knowledge

2.1. Introduction

In order to understand an editorial, it is necessary to have knowledge of the domain underlying the issues addressed in that editorial. During editorial comprehension, domain-specific knowledge must be used to recognize and represent the beliefs, belief relationships, and argument units that compose the editorial's argument graph. In the case of editorials such as ED-JOBS and ED-RESTRICTIONS (chapter 1, pages 3 and 15), the comprehension process involves dealing with one-sided arguments about protectionism. To process those editorials, OpEd must have a politico-economic model that represents knowledge of protectionism from four different perspectives:

1) Social Level: The social interactions among the economic actors involved in situations of protectionism. Specifically, the events that characterize conflicts among importing and exporting countries, their governments, and their industries.

2) Economic Level: The causal relationships among the economic quantities that characterize international and domestic trade. Those economic quantities include: earnings, sales, costs, prices, spending, salaries, and employment.

3) Goal/Plan Level: The economic-protection plans that can be implemented to achieve economic goals arising from trade competition. Those goals include: (a) preserving jobs in

importing countries; and (b) preserving earnings and
attaining profitability for industries in importing countries.

4) Reasoning Level: The chains of cause-effect relationships
   involving economic quantities, economic-protection plans,
   and economic goals associated with international trade. Such
   chains show: (a) how those economic goals become active as
   a result of variations in consumer spending and product
   prices; and (b) how economic-protection plans may result in
   goal failures and/or goal achievements for industries and
   countries.

To illustrate why the above representational issues have to be
addressed in OpEd, consider the following excerpt from ED-
RESTRICTIONS:

> **The American machine-tool industry is seeking protection from
> foreign competition. The industry has been hurt by cheaper
> machine tools from Japan. The toolmakers argue that restrictions
> on imports must be imposed so that the industry can survive.**

When reading ED-RESTRICTIONS, OpEd must be able to infer the
implicit connections between the American manufacturers' act of
"seeking protection," their current state of being "hurt by cheaper
machine-tools from Japan," and their desire to "survive." Making these
connections explicit requires modeling the following relationships:

- Politico-economic conflicts: Domestic and foreign industries
  may get involved in disputes over low-priced imports sold by
  those foreign industries.

- Conflict-resolution events: To resolve trade disputes with
  foreign industries, domestic industries may petition to the
  government of their country to implement economic-protection
  plans.

- Reasoning about economic goals: Low-priced imports "hurt"
  domestic industries because: (a) low-priced imports cause a
  decrease in sales of equivalent, high-priced domestic products;
  (b) a decrease in sales produces a decrease in earnings for
  domestic manufacturers; and (c) a decrease in earnings results
  in the goal by domestic manufacturers of preserving their level
  of earnings.

- Economic-protection plans: In order to preserve the level of
  earnings of domestic industries, a government can take two
  different courses of action: (a) unilaterally impose quotas or

taxes on imports; or (b) negotiate with foreign countries in order to limit imports from those countries.

- Reasoning about economic-protection plans: Limits and taxes on imports help domestic industries to "survive" because: (a) restrictions on imports result in a decrease in domestic spending on imports; (b) a decrease in spending on imports causes an increase in spending on domestic products; and (c) an increase in spending on domestic products achieves the goal by domestic manufacturers of preserving their level of earnings.

Clearly, editorial comprehension in OpEd requires a representation of the causal relationships that exist among conflict-resolution events, economic quantities, economic goals, and protectionist plans.

OpEd's model of politico-economic knowledge is composed of four major elements: (1) authority triangles (Schank and Carbonell, 1979), which represent conflicts involving domestic and foreign industries; (2) planboxes (Schank and Abelson, 1977), which represent protectionist plans as sets of actions for resolving trade disputes; (3) a graph of economic quantities (Riesbeck, 1984), which organizes cause-effect relationships among the economic quantities associated with economic actors; and (4) reasoning scripts (Dyer, Cullingford, and Alvarado, 1987; Flowers and Dyer, 1984), which represent chains of reasoning about economic goals or about the effects of protectionist plans. This chapter describes OpEd's politico-economic constructs along with examples of their use within the framework of ED-JOBS and ED-RESTRICTIONS. The concepts described here also provide a representational foundation to be used in later chapters.

2.2.   Politico-Economic Conflicts

OpEd's representation of politico-economic conflicts is based on Schank's *basic social acts,* a representational system originally proposed by Schank (1978) and later developed and expanded by Schank and Carbonell (1979) and Carbonell (1981). In order to understand OpEd's model, it is necessary to have some exposure to the general issues addressed by those social acts. This section presents an overview of the basic social acts and describes how they are used in OpEd to encode knowledge of protectionism.

2.2.1. Basic Socials Acts and Authority Triangles

Social acts encode the basic concepts that organize knowledge in the domain of human social interactions. These constructs were conceived as a response to difficulties encountered in representing conflict-resolution events by using Conceptual Dependency primitives (Schank, 1973, 1975). Seven basic social acts have been proposed by Schank and Carbonell (1979):

1) **DISPUTE:** The initiation or escalation of a conflict between two actors.

2) **PETITION:** The request to an authority to settle a conflict.

3) **AUTHORIZE:** The issuing of a decree by an authority.

4) **ORDER:** The enforcement of a decree by an authority.

5) **INVOKE:** The initiation of a direct course of action to settle a conflict.

6) **RESOLVE:** The act of settling a conflict by means of a direct course of action.

7) **PRESSURE:** The act by a third party of applying pressure to settle a conflict.

For example, the following events in the domain of labor relationships can be represented using basic social acts: (1) a violation of a worker's civil rights by his/her boss is a DISPUTE; (2) bringing a suit to a court of law to settle the conflict is a PETITION; (3) the jury's decision is an AUTHORIZE act; (4) the enforcement of such a decision by appropriate authorities is an ORDER; (5) a call for an out-of-court settlement is an INVOKE act; (6) the resolution of the case by means of direct negotiations is a RESOLVE act; and (7) the act by the worker's peers of forcing him/her to reconsider his/her court claim is an act of PRESSURE.

Using these social acts, any conflict situation can be represented in terms of a configuration composed of two basic elements: (a) a DISPUTE between two actors; and (b) a resolution method for settling the conflict. Such a configuration is termed *authority triangle* (Carbonell, 1981). According to the resolution method used, three basic types of authority triangles can be distinguished: AUTHORIZE triangle, RESOLVE triangle, and PRESSURE triangle. These configurations are illustrated in figure 2.1.

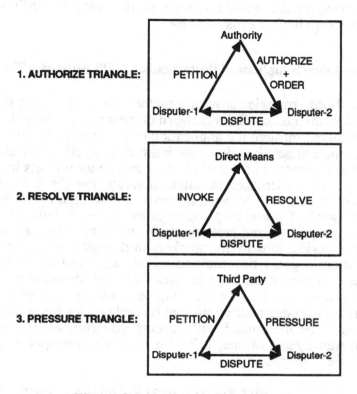

Figure 2.1. Authority Triangles.

As figure 2.1 indicates, the base of an authority triangle is a DISPUTE between two actors. The sides of the triangle represent the method used to settle of the DISPUTE. The configurations in figure 2.1 show three different methods for resolving a DISPUTE:

1) **AUTHORIZE triangle:**
   DISPUTE —> PETITION —> AUTHORIZE + ORDER

2) **RESOLVE triangle:**
   DISPUTE —> INVOKE —> RESOLVE

3) **PRESSURE triangle:**
   DISPUTE —> PETITION —> PRESSURE

For instance, in the previous example on labor relationships, the DISPUTE between a worker and his/her boss can be settled by: (1) the worker PETITIONing to a court of law so that it AUTHORIZEs in his/her favor; (2) the worker's boss INVOKing negotiations with the worker that directly RESOLVE the DISPUTE; and (3) the boss

PETITIONing to the worker's peers so that they PRESSURE that worker to accept his/her boss' position.

2.2.2. Modeling Situations of Protectionism With Authority Triangles

Authority triangles provide a method for representing situations of protectionism, i.e., conflicts between domestic and foreign industries that are resolved through the application of economic-protection plans. Those conflicts arise when domestic industries experience decreases in sales due to increases in sales of cheaper and better imports by foreign industries. Such decreases in sales motivate the three main goals underlying the conflicts between domestic and foreign industries: (1) a short-term goal of preserving earnings by domestic industries; (2) a long-term goal of attaining profitability by domestic industries; and (3) a goal of preserving jobs by the workers in domestic industries. When these economic goals become active, domestic industries ask their government to implement trade policies that either decrease the amount of low-priced imports (i.e., an import quota) or increase their price (i.e., an import tax). Those restrictions can be unilaterally imposed through legislation or be negotiated with foreign governments (Greenaway, 1983; Greenaway and Milner, 1979; Institute of Contemporary Studies, 1979; Yoffie, 1983).

How are authority triangles used in OpEd's politico-economic model? Below follows a figure that shows how situations of protectionism are modeled with authority triangles.

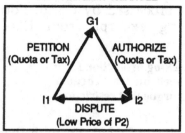

NOTATION FOR TRIANGLE ELEMENTS
G1: Government of importing country C1
G2: Government of exporting country C2
I1: Industry from C1
I2: Industry from C2
P2: Product by I2 equivalent to product P1 by I1
Quota: A decrease in amount of P2 in C1
Tax: An increase in price of P2 in C1
Negotiation: Meeting between G1 and G2 to set Quota

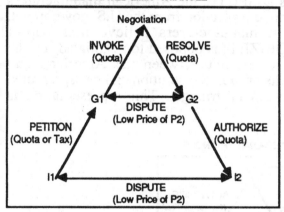

Figure 2.2. Situations of Protectionism.

As figure 2.2 illustrates, two main situations of protectionism can be distinguished:

IMPOSED-LIMIT triangle: Industry I1 from country C1 has a DISPUTE with industry I2 from country C2 over the sale price of product P2 by I2. To settle the conflict, I1 PETITIONs to government G1 of C1 for a limit (quota or tax) on P2 and G1 AUTHORIZEs such a limit.

NEGOTIATED-LIMIT triangle: Industry I1 from country C1 has a DISPUTE with industry I2 from country C2 over the sale price of product P2 by I2 in C1. To settle the conflict, I1 PETITIONs to government G1 of C1 for a limit (quota or tax) on P2. G1 RESOLVEs the conflict by INVOKing negotiations with government G2 of C2. The negotiations result in a quota that is AUTHORIZEd by G2.

These two configurations can be used to represent the situations of protectionism referred to in the editorials processed by OpEd. For example, consider again the following excerpt from ED-RESTRICTIONS:

> The American machine-tool industry is seeking protection from foreign competition. The industry has been hurt by cheaper machine tools from Japan. The toolmakers argue that restrictions on imports must be imposed ...

Here, the American machine-tool industry has a DISPUTE with the Japanese machine-tool industry over low-priced Japanese machine tools sold in the U.S. Due to this DISPUTE, the American manufacturers have PETITIONed for economic protection from the U.S. government. Furthermore, the American manufacturers believe that import restrictions must be AUTHORIZEd (as opposed to negotiated) by the U.S. government. Thus, the conflict between the American and Japanese manufacturers and its proposed resolution can be represented in terms of the IMPOSED-LIMIT triangle. This representation is illustrated in figure 2.3.

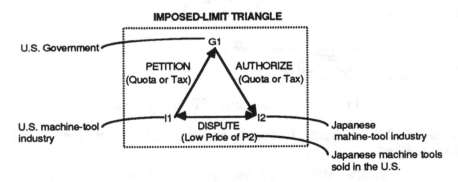

Figure 2.3. Representation of a Trade Conflict in ED-RESTRICTIONS.

In contrast to ED-RESTRICTIONS, the conflict in international trade in ED-JOBS can be modeled as an instance of the NEGOTIATED-LIMIT triangle. To illustrate this fact, consider the fragment of ED-JOBS:

> Recent protectionist measures by the Reagan administration ...
> Voluntary limits on Japanese automobiles ...

In ED-JOBS, the DISPUTE between the American automobile industry and the Japanese automobile industry has been RESOLVEd through the negotiations INVOKEd by the Reagan administration. Those negotiations resulted in a limit on Japanese cars AUTHORIZEd by the Japanese government. Clearly, the conflict settled through the use of "voluntary limits" can be modeled as an instance of the NEGOTIATED-LIMIT triangle, as shown in figure 2.4.

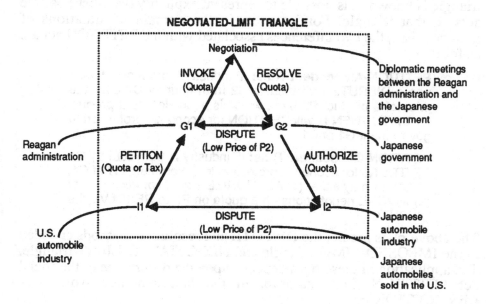

Figure 2.4. Representation of a Trade Conflict in ED-JOBS.

The main advantage of using authority triangles is that those constructs allow us to represent all the information associated with conflicts in international trade. As indicated in figure 2.2, both the IMPOSED-LIMIT triangle and the NEGOTIATED-LIMIT triangle organize general information about: (1) who may be the actors in a trade conflict; (b) what may be the object of the conflict; and (3) who may be the actors that settle the conflict. Therefore, if that information is implicit in an editorial, it will be made explicit in the triangle representations. For example, the diagram in figure 2.4 represents explicitly the following missing relationships in ED-JOBS: (a) the actors of the DISPUTE are the American automobile industry and the Japanese automobile industry; (b) the object of the DISPUTE is the low price of Japanese automobiles sold in the U.S.; and (c) the actors of the negotiation that have RESOLVEd the DISPUTE are the Reagan administration and the Japanese government.

In addition to the above inferences, each basic social act in a triangle has a set of associated inferences that indicate the acts that may have happened or may happen according to that triangle configuration (Schank and Carbonell, 1979). As a result, if one of the acts in a triangle is known, it is possible to represent explicitly the other possible acts in that triangle. For instance, in the domain of situations of protectionism, the two inferences associated with the PETITION act are as follows:

PETITION-Antecedent Rule: IF industry I1 from country C1 has a DISPUTE with industry I2 from country C2 over the price of a product P2 by I2 which is equivalent to a product P1 by I1, THEN I1 will PETITION for economic protection to government G1 of C1.

PETITION-Consequent Rule: IF industry I1 from country C1 PETITIONs for economic protection to government G1 of C1, THEN G1 may either (1) AUTHORIZE a quota or tax on P2 or (2) INVOKE negotiations on a quota on P2 to RESOLVE the DISPUTE.

The above rules predict the DISPUTE and resolution methods encoded in the IMPOSED-LIMIT triangle and NEGOTIATED-LIMIT triangle. The application of these rules depends upon the occurrence of the social act PETITION. For example, in the last sentence from ED-RESTRICTIONS:

... those [American] manufacturers would demand protection against foreign competition.

the above rules provide the basis for representing the events that may have caused and may result from the U.S. manufacturers' PETITION, namely:

- American manufacturers will PETITION for economic protection because of their DISPUTE with foreign manufacturers over import prices; and

- The U.S. government may AUTHORIZE import restrictions or INVOKE negotiations to settle the DISPUTE.

2.2.3. Beliefs and Goals Associated With Situations of Protectionism

In addition to representing conflict situations, authority triangles can be integrated with the beliefs and goals of the actors involved in such situations (Carbonell, 1981). In the case of the IMPOSED-LIMIT triangle and NEGOTIATED-LIMIT triangle, knowledge of goals and beliefs is organized by the basic social acts that characterize the methods for settling conflicts in international trade. Two main rules encode such knowledge in OpEd's politico-economic model:

Economic-Protection Rule 1: IF government G1 of country C1 has the active goals of preserving jobs in C1 and helping industry I1 from C1 preserve earnings and attain profitability, AND G1 believes those goals will be achieved by implementing economic protection P, THEN G1 will AUTHORIZE P or INVOKE negotiations to implement P.

Economic-Protection Rule 2: IF industry I1 from country C1 has the active goals of preserving earnings and attaining profitability, AND I1 believes that those goals will be achieved by economic protection P from government G1 of C1, THEN I1 will PETITION G1 to implement P.

The above rules summarize the goals and beliefs of: (1) governments that impose or negotiate economic protection; and (2) industries that PETITION for economic protection. These rules can be applied to represent relationships that are implicitly stated in editorial text. For example, in ED-JOBS, the first rule can be used to infer the Reagan administration's goals and beliefs associated with the "voluntary limits on Japanese automobiles," namely: (a) the administration's goals of preserving jobs in the U.S. and helping the American automobile industry attain profitability; and (b) the administration's belief that negotiating "voluntary limits" will achieve its goals. Similarly, the second rule can be used in ED-RESTRICTIONS to represent explicitly the connections between: (a) the American machine-tool industry's act of PETITIONing for "protection from foreign competition"; (b) the industry's active preservation goal of not being "hurt" by cheaper imports; and (c) the industry's belief that "import restrictions must be imposed so that the industry can survive." The representation of those relationships is shown in figure 2.5.

Representation:

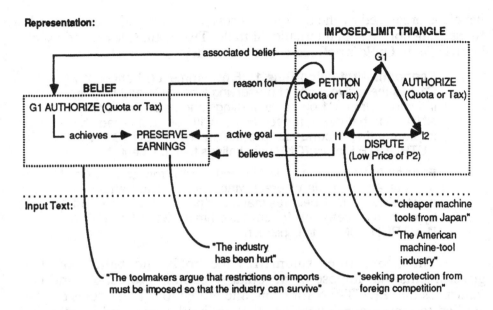

Figure 2.5. Goals and Beliefs Associated With a PETITION for
Economic Protection.

As the above diagram indicates, representing a PETITION for economic
protection requires representing: (a) the DISPUTE that precedes the
PETITION; (b) the course of action being PETITIONed to government;
(c) the goals of the actor of the PETITION; and (b) his/her belief that
those goals will be achieved by the government's action. Thus, the
representation of a conflict in international trade must include the
conflict's triangle configuration and the beliefs and goals of the actors
involved in that conflict.

2.2.4. Organizing Conflict-Resolution Events With Planboxes

From the perspective of goals and plans, the courses of action
that a government can take to protect an industry can also be represented
as *planboxes*. As originally defined by Schank and Abelson (1977),
planboxes are possible sets of actions that can be executed to achieve
delta goals, i.e., goals involving desires for a change in state. For
example, three planboxes associated with the goal of gaining control of
an object are: asking, bargaining, and stealing. Similarly, the actions of
imposing and negotiating limits on imports are the two planboxes
associated with a government's economic goals of: (a) preserving jobs;

and (b) helping domestic industries preserve earnings and attain profitability. In OpEd, those two planboxes are organized by a planning structure called P-ECON-PROTECTION (package of methods for achieving economic protection). P-ECON-PROTECTION is much like Schank and Abelson's PERSUADE package, which organizes planboxes associated with delta goals. The components of P-ECON-PROTECTION are illustrated in figure 2.6.

P-ECON-PROTECTION

CONFLICT PARTICIPANTS
C1: Importing country
C2: Exporting country
G1: Government of C1
G2: Government of C2
I1: Industry from C1
I2: Industry from C2
PRODUCTS
P1: Product by I1
P2: Product by I2 equivalent to P1
GOALS
G1 wants to help I1 PRESERVE EARNINGS
G1 wants to help I1 ATTAIN PROFITABILITY
G1 wants to PRESERVE JOBS in C1
CONFLICT SOLUTIONS
Tax: An increase in price of P2 in C1
Quota: A decrease in amount of P2 in C1
IMPOSED-LIMIT PLANBOX
G1 AUTHORIZE (Tax OR Quota) to I2
NEGOTIATED-LIMIT PLANBOX
G1 INVOKE (Negotiations for Quota) —causes—>
G1 and G2 RESOLVE (Quota) —causes—>
G2 AUTHORIZE (Quota) to I2

Figure 2.6. Planboxes for Economic Protection.

What do we gain by representing methods for achieving economic goals as planboxes organized by P-ECON-PROTECTION? One of the problems of representing verbatim arguments about protectionism is dealing with descriptions of economic-protection policies. Frequently, those descriptions do not mention the specific courses of action taken by a government. For example, the following phrase from the editorial ED-JOBS:

... protectionist measures by the Reagan administration ...

does not indicate whether the protectionist policies were unilaterally imposed or resulted from negotiations with foreign countries. This phrase can be represented as an instance of P-ECON-PROTECTION in which the importing country is the U.S. and the government of the importing country is the Reagan administration. That representation serves two purposes: (1) it acts as a place holder for the unknown course of action taken by the Reagan administration; and (2) it holds expectations about possible courses of action that may have been taken by the administration, i.e., imposing limits or negotiating limits. When the specific course of action is mentioned in the editorial, the representation of Reagan administration's plans can then be refined to include an instantiation of the corresponding planbox. For instance, after reading the following phrase in ED-JOBS:

Voluntary limits on Japanese automobiles ...

it is clear that the administration's policies resulted from negotiations with Japan and, therefore, should be represented in terms of the negotiated-limit planbox. Thus, encoding conflict-resolution methods as planboxes in P-ECON-PROTECTION provides a system for dealing with unstated protectionist actions in editorials.

2.3. Politico-Economic Reasoning

A model of conflicts in international trade also requires a representation of the reasoning chains that show: (a) why economic goals become active as a result of changes in import prices and consumer spending; and (b) why economic-protection plans result in changes in the level of earnings and employment in domestic industries. Those chains are sequences of cause-effect relationships among the economic quantities associated with the activity of trade. In OpEd, reasoning about goals and plans is represented by *reasoning scripts* (Dyer, Cullingford, and Alvarado, 1987; Flowers and Dyer, 1984), memory structures that organize causal domain knowledge in the form of prespecified reasoning-chain sequences. OpEd also includes a model of the cause-effect relationships underlying reasoning scripts which is based on previous work by Riesbeck (1984). This section presents a brief overview of Riesbeck's modeling approach and discusses OpEd's model of politico-economic reasoning.

2.3.1. Graph of Economic Quantities

As proposed by Riesbeck (1984), causal knowledge in the domain of economics can be modeled in terms of a network of economic quantities. In that network, nodes represent economic quantities and links represent the effects quantities have on one another. To illustrate this modeling approach, consider the abstract graph in figure 2.7.

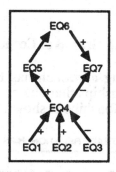

Figure 2.7. A Graph of Economic Quantities.

As the above diagram shows, two economic quantities in a graph can be connected by a signed and directed link. That link indicates whether the quantities are directly proportional or inversely proportional to one another. For example, the positive link from EQ1 to EQ4 represents the following relationships:

- If EQ1 increases, then EQ4 increases.
- If EQ1 decreases, then EQ4 decreases.
- If EQ1's level is higher than EQ1's norm, then EQ4's level is higher than EQ4's norm.
- If EQ1's level is lower than EQ1's norm, then EQ4's level is lower than EQ4's norm.

Similarly, the negative link from EQ3 to EQ4 represents the following relationships:

- If EQ3 increases, then EQ4 decreases.
- If EQ3 decreases, then EQ4 increases.
- If EQ3's level is higher than EQ3's norm, then EQ4's level is lower than EQ4's norm.
- If EQ3's level is lower than EQ3's norm, then EQ4's level is higher than EQ4's norm.

Figure 2.7 also shows that two economic quantities can be connected by a sequence of links. The sign of a sequence is positive, if: (1) all the links in the sequence are positive; or (2) there is an even number of negative links in the sequence. Otherwise, the sign of the sequence is negative. For example, EQ1 is negatively connected to EQ7 through EQ4, EQ5, and EQ6. Similarly, EQ3 is positively connected to EQ7 through EQ4.

2.3.2. Modeling Trade With Graphs of Economic Quantities

Riesbeck's modeling approach has been adopted in OpEd to represent the causal relationships that characterize the activity of trade. OpEd's graph of trade relationships is shown below.

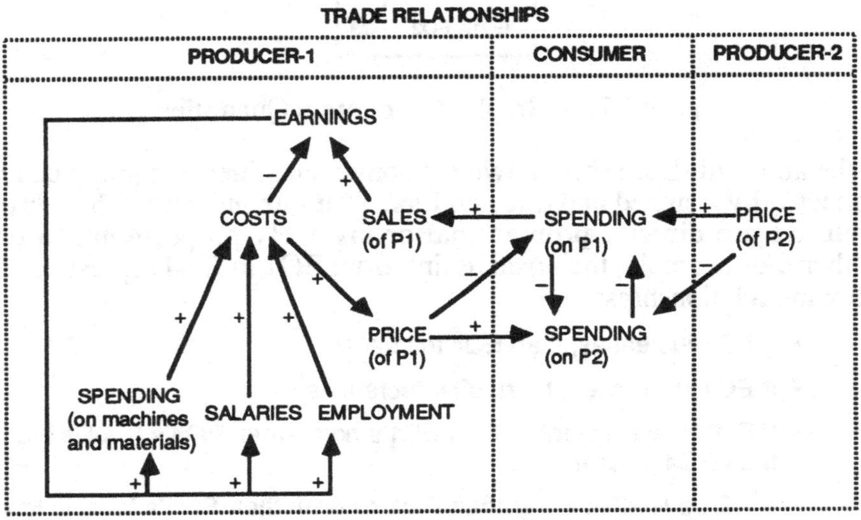

Figure 2.8. Graph of Trade Relationships.

The graph in figure 2.8 organizes causal dependencies from the perspectives of producers and consumers. From a producer's point of view, trade can be characterized in terms of that producer's level of earnings, volume of sales, production costs, and product prices:

Trade Relationship 1: The level of earnings is directly proportional to the volume of sales and inversely proportional to the level of costs.

Trade Relationship 2: The level of costs is directly proportional to: (a) the level of spending on basic machinery and production materials; (b) the level of salaries, and (c) the level of employment.

Trade Relationship 3: The volume of sales is directly proportional to the level of consumer spending on producer's products.

Trade Relationship 4: The level of prices is directly proportional to the level of costs.

Trade Relationship 5: The levels of spending, salaries, and employment are directly proportional to the level earnings.

In contrast, from a consumer's point of view, trade can be characterized in terms of product prices and level of consumer spending:

Trade Relationship 6: The level of spending on a product P1 is: (a) inversely proportional to P1's price and to the level of spending on an equivalent product P2; and (b) directly proportional to P2's price.

How is the graph of trade relationships used in OpEd? The graph provides the representational foundation for the causal chains of reasoning associated with economic goals. For instance, the graph shows that the price of product P2 is connected to the earnings of PRODUCER-1 by a positive sequence of links involving: consumer spending on P2, consumer spending on P1, and sales of P1. According to that sequence, when the price of P2 is low, the level of earnings of PRODUCER-1 is low. This causal relationship explains decreases in earnings experienced by producers whose prices are higher than its competitors'. In the domain of conflicts in international trade, this goal-based reasoning is captured by the following reasoning script:[5]

$R-LOW-IMPORT-PRICES—>LOW-DOMESTIC-EARNINGS

ROLES
C1: Importing country
I1: Industry from C1
P1: Product by I1
P2: Import equivalent to and less expensive than P1
CAUSAL CHAIN
low PRICE of P2 —causes—>
high SPENDING by C1 on P2 —causes—>
low SPENDING by C1 on P1 —causes—>
low SALES of P1 by I1 —causes—>
low EARNINGS of I1 —thwarts—>
G-PRESERVING-EARNINGS by I1

Figure 2.9. $R-LOW-IMPORT-PRICES—>LOW-DOMESTIC-EARNINGS.

---

[5]Uppercase names preceded by "$R" indicate reasoning scripts.

The above figure shows that $R-LOW-IMPORT-PRICES—>LOW-DOMESTIC-EARNINGS is an instance of the sequence of links that connects P2's price to PRODUCER-1's earnings in the graph of trade relationships. In OpEd, this script is used to represent the meaning of the following sentence from ED-RESTRICTIONS:

> **The [American machine-tool] industry has been hurt by cheaper machine tools from Japan.**

In the above sentence, the word "hurt" does not refer to the physical state of American manufacturers. Rather, it refers to the causal connection between cheap Japanese imports and the goal by American manufacturers of preserving their earnings. This causal connection is an instantiation of $R-LOW-IMPORT-PRICES—>LOW-DOMESTIC-EARNINGS:

```
low PRICE of Japanese machine tools —causes—>
  high SPENDING by U.S. on Japanese machine tools —causes—>
low SPENDING by U.S. on U.S. machine tools —causes—>
low SALES of machine tools by U.S. machine-tool industry —causes—>
low EARNINGS by U.S. machine tool industry —thwarts—>
G-PRESERVING-EARNINGS by U.S. machine-tool industry
```

Thus, the use of reasoning scripts allows OpEd to represent abstract politico-economic concepts as sequences of cause-effect relationships associated with the activity of trade.

2.3.3 Modeling Reasoning About Protectionism With Reasoning Scripts

In addition to organizing goal-based reasoning chains, the graph of trade relationships also organizes reasoning chains associated with economic-protection plans. Three instances of reasoning can be distinguished here: (1) effects of economic protections on ailing domestic industries; (2) effects of economic protections on domestic industries that use foreign materials and machinery; and (3) effects of economic protections on domestic industries that export their products.

Effects of Protectionism on Ailing Industries

Why do economic-protection plans help domestic industries? The immediate effect of such plans is to decrease domestic spending on cheap imports. This is the case because economic protections either: (a) reduce the amount of available imports through quotas; or (b) increase import prices through taxes. As indicated in the graph of trade relationships, decreasing domestic spending on imports causes an increase in domestic spending on more expensive domestic products. This increase in spending causes an increase in the volume of sales of domestic products and, consequently, an increase in the level of earnings of domestic manufacturers. In OpEd, this chain of effects on economic quantities is organized by the reasoning script shown in figure 2.10.

$R-ECON-PROTECTION—>HIGHER-DOMESTIC-EARNINGS

```
ROLES
    C1: Importing country
    G1: Government of C1
    I1: Industry from C1
    P1: Product by I1
    P2: Import equivalent to and less expensive than P1

CAUSAL CHAIN
    P-ECON-PROTECTION by G1 on P2 —causes—>
    decrease in SPENDING by C1 on P2 —causes—>
    increase in SPENDING by C1 on P1 —causes—>
    increase in SALES of P1 by I1 —causes—>
    increase in EARNINGS of I1 —achieves—>
    G-PRESERVING-EARNINGS by I1
    G-ATTAINING-PROFITABILITY by I1
```

Figure 2.10. $R-ECON-PROTECTION—>HIGHER-DOMESTIC-EARNINGS.

$R-ECON-PROTECTION—>HIGHER-DOMESTIC-EARNINGS indicates that an increase in the level of earnings of domestic manufacturers helps achieve two possible goals by domestic manufacturers: (1) the short-term goal of preserving earnings that results from sales lost to foreign competition; and (2) the long-term goal of being profitable. In OpEd, this reasoning script is used to represent the argument of American toolmakers in ED-RESTRICTIONS:

> The [American] toolmakers argue that restrictions on imports must be imposed so that the industry can survive.

Here, the word "survive" stands for the relationship of implementing a plan in order to achieve an active preservation goal. Within the context of ED-RESTRICTIONS, this goal-achievement relationship corresponds to the instantiated chain of effects shown below:

```
P-ECON-PROTECTION by U.S. on Japanese machine tools—causes—>
decrease in SPENDING by U.S. on Japanese machine tools —causes—>
increase in SPENDING by U.S. on U.S. machine tools —causes—>
increase in SALES of machine tools by U.S. machine-tool industry —causes—>
increase in EARNINGS by U.S. machine tool industry —achieves—>
G-PRESERVING-EARNINGS by U.S. machine-tool industry
```

This instantiation is another example of how reasoning scripts are used to represent abstract politico-economic concepts.

Effects of Protectionism on Industries Using Imports

Although restrictions on imports benefit ailing industries, they have negative side-effects for other domestic industries. Due to the fact that restrictions shift spending from cheap imports to expensive domestic products, industries that use those imports experience an increase their in production costs. As indicated in the graph of trade relationships, an increase in production costs results in an decrease in producer's earnings, because of a chain of effects involving an increase in product prices, a decrease in consumer spending, and a decrease in the volume of sales. This chain of reasoning is contained in $R-ECON-PROTECTION—>LOWER-DOMESTIC-EARNINGS. This reasoning script is shown below.

$R-ECON-PROTECTION—>LOWER-DOMESTIC-EARNINGS

```
ROLES
    C1: Importing country
    G1: Government of C1
    I1: Industry from C1
    I2: Industry from C1 that uses P3
    P1: Product by I1
    P2: Product by I2
    P3: Import equivalent to and less expensive than P1

CAUSAL CHAIN
P-ECON-PROTECTION by G1 on P3 —causes—>
    decrease in SPENDING by I2 on P3 —causes—>
        increase in SPENDING by I2 on P1 —causes—>
            increase in COST of P2 by I2 —causes—>
                increase in PRICE of P2 by I2 —causes—>
                    decrease in SPENDING by C1 on P2 —causes—>
                        decrease in SALES of P2 by I2 —causes—>
                            decrease in EARNINGS of I2 —thwarts—>
                                G-PRESERVING-EARNINGS by I2
```

Figure 2.11. $R-ECON-PROTECTION—>LOWER-DOMESTIC-EARNINGS.

In OpEd, $R-ECON-PROTECTION—>LOWER-DOMESTIC-EARNINGS is instantiated when reading the following excerpt from ED-RESTRICTIONS:

Restrictions on [cheaper machine tools from Japan] would mean that American manufacturers would have to make do with more expensive American machine tools. Inevitably, those American

manufacturers would produce more expensive products. They would lose sales.

The representation of this cause-effect chain is depicted in figure 2.12.

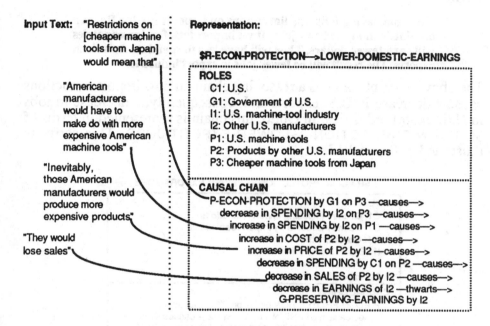

Input Text: "Restrictions on [cheaper machine tools from Japan] would mean that"

"American manufacturers would have to make do with more expensive American machine tools"

"Inevitably, those American manufacturers would produce more expensive products"

"They would lose sales"

Representation:

$R-ECON-PROTECTION—>LOWER-DOMESTIC-EARNINGS

ROLES
C1: U.S.
G1: Government of U.S.
I1: U.S. machine-tool industry
I2: Other U.S. manufacturers
P1: U.S. machine tools
P2: Products by other U.S. manufacturers
P3: Cheaper machine tools from Japan

CAUSAL CHAIN
P-ECON-PROTECTION by G1 on P3 —causes—>
decrease in SPENDING by I2 on P3 —causes—>
increase in SPENDING by I2 on P1 —causes—>
increase in COST of P2 by I2 —causes—>
increase in PRICE of P2 by I2 —causes—>
decrease in SPENDING by C1 on P2 —causes—>
decrease in SALES of P2 by I2 —causes—>
decrease in EARNINGS of I2 —thwarts—>
G-PRESERVING-EARNINGS by I2

Figure 2.12. Representation of a Causal Chain of Reasoning in ED-RESTRICTIONS.

As indicated by the above diagram, the instantiated reasoning script represents information that is implicitly stated in the editorial. Specifically, the script makes explicit: (1) why import restrictions result in an increase in spending on U.S. machine tools; (2) why the increase in spending causes an increase in prices of U.S. products; (3) why the increase in prices causes a decrease in the volume of sales by U.S. manufacturers; and (4) why the decrease in sales results in a decrease in the manufacturers' level of earnings. Thus, reasoning scripts provide a representational system for dealing with missing steps in chains of reasoning in editorials.

Effects of Protectionism on Export Industries

Another side-effect of economic-protection plans is that they may not preserve (or increase) the number of jobs in an importing country, but rather decrease it. In politico-economic editorials, this side-effect is frequently brought up in arguments against the use of import restrictions. For example, consider the following excerpt from ED-JOBS:

> **Far from saving jobs, the limitations on imports [by the Reagan administration] will cost jobs. If we import less, foreign countries will earn fewer dollars. They will have less to spend on American exports. The result will be fewer jobs in export industries.**

The above excerpt contains a reasoning chain on how import restrictions cause a decrease in U.S. exports and, consequently, a decrease in jobs in U.S. export industries. In OpEd, this chain is represented in terms of $R-ECON-PROTECTION—>LOWER-EXPORT-JOBS. This script is illustrated in figure 2.13.

```
        $R-ECON-PROTECTION—>FEWER-EXPORT-JOBS
 ┌──────────────────────────────────────────────────────┐
 │ ROLES                                                  │
 │    C1: Country imposing import restrictions            │
 │    C2: Country affected by import restrictions         │
 │    G1: Government of C1                                 │
 │    I1: Export industry from C1                         │
 │    P1: Product by I1                                   │
 │    P2: Import from C2                                  │
 ├──────────────────────────────────────────────────────┤
 │ CAUSAL CHAIN                                           │
 │  P-ECON-PROTECTION by G1 on P2 —causes—>              │
 │     decrease in SPENDING by C1 on P2 —causes—>        │
 │       decrease in SALES of P2 by C2 —causes—>         │
 │         decrease in EARNINGS of C2 —causes—>          │
 │           decrease in SPENDING by C2 on P1 —causes—>  │
 │             decrease in SALES of P1 by I1 —causes—>   │
 │               decrease in EARNINGS of I1 —causes—>    │
 │                 decrease in EMPLOYMENT in I1 —thwarts—> │
 │                   G-PRESERVING-JOBS in C1 by G1        │
 └──────────────────────────────────────────────────────┘
```

Figure 2.13. $R-ECON-PROTECTION—>FEWER-EXPORT-JOBS.

$R-ECON-PROTECTION—>FEWER-EXPORT-JOBS describes the negative feedback that results from applying restrictions to international trade. There are four major reasons for this negative feedback:

1) Import restrictions cause a decrease in sales by exporting countries and, consequently, a decrease in their level of export earnings.

2) Countries play two different roles in international trade: (a) as producers, they export their products to other countries; and (b) as consumers, they import products from other

countries. These roles depend on one another because the level of spending on imports is directly proportional to the level of export earnings.

3) The level of earnings of export industries is directly proportional to the industries' sales to importing countries.

4) The level of employment in export industries is directly proportional to the industries' level of earnings.

Therefore, import restrictions result in a decrease in the number of jobs in export industries of the countries that implement those restrictions.

Using $R-ECON-PROTECTION—>FEWER-EXPORT-JOBS also allows OpEd to represent explicitly missing cause-effect relationships in the reasoning chain in ED-JOBS. OpEd's representation of that chain is shown in figure 2.14.

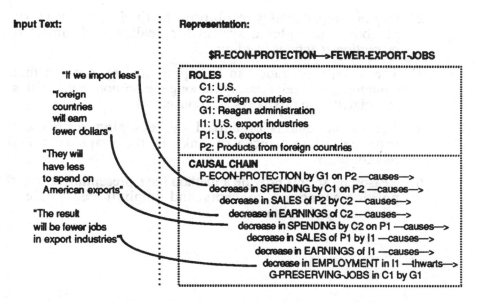

Input Text:

"If we import less",

"foreign
countries
will earn
fewer dollars",

"They will
have less
to spend on
American exports"

"The result
will be fewer jobs
in export industries"

Representation:

$R-ECON-PROTECTION—>FEWER-EXPORT-JOBS

ROLES
   C1: U.S.
   C2: Foreign countries
   G1: Reagan administration
   I1: U.S. export industries
   P1: U.S. exports
   P2: Products from foreign countries

CAUSAL CHAIN
   P-ECON-PROTECTION by G1 on P2 —causes—>
   decrease in SPENDING by C1 on P2 —causes—>
   decrease in SALES of P2 by C2 —causes—>
   decrease in EARNINGS of C2 —causes—>
   decrease in SPENDING by C2 on P1 —causes—>
   decrease in SALES of P1 by I1 —causes—>
   decrease in EARNINGS of I1 —causes—>
   decrease in EMPLOYMENT in I1 —thwarts—>
   G-PRESERVING-JOBS in C1 by G1

Figure 2.14. Representation of a Causal Chain of Reasoning in ED-JOBS.

The above diagram indicates that the following relationships are implicitly stated in ED-JOBS: (1) the relationship between import restrictions and the level of U.S. spending on imports; (2) the relationship between U.S. spending and the level of earnings by foreign countries; and (3) the relationship between foreign earnings and the number of jobs in U.S. export industries.

2.4. Summary

This chapter has presented a model of politico-economic knowledge used in OpEd for understanding editorials about protectionism. The knowledge constructs in the model constitute the foundation for representing the beliefs, belief relationships, and argument units that compose an editorial's argument graph. Five major points have been emphasized here:

1) Authority triangles represent explicitly all the information associated with conflicts in international trade, including: beliefs, goals, and conflict-resolution methods of the actors involved in the conflicts;

2) Organizing conflict-resolution methods in terms of planboxes provides a system for dealing with unstated protectionist actions in editorials.

3) The activity of trade can be represented by a graph that contains causal relationships among the economic quantities associated with producers and consumers.

4) The causal chains organized by reasoning scripts are instances of sequences of links in the graph of trade relationships.

5) Reasoning scripts provide a method for representing abstract politico-economic concepts and implicit cause-effect relationships in editorials.

Chapter 3

Beliefs and Belief Relationships

3.1. Introduction

Computer comprehension of editorial arguments in OpEd is based on the capability of modeling beliefs. Beliefs can be set apart from other conceptual structures needed to understand narrative text. As pointed out by Abelson (1973, 1979), beliefs are not goals, plans, events, or states, but rather predications about these structures and their relationships. Based on this view of beliefs, three types of predications have been characterized in OpEd:

1) <u>Evaluative Beliefs:</u> Judgements about the goodness or badness of domain-specific plans, such as: "plan P is good/bad" and "plan P should/shouldn't be implemented."

2) <u>Causal Beliefs:</u> Expectations about: (a) the possible causes for the failure or achievement of domain-specific goals; and (b) the positive or negative effects that may result from implementing domain-specific plans.

3) <u>Beliefs About Beliefs:</u> Predications about evaluative and causal beliefs, such as: "belief B1 shouldn't be held", "belief B1 does/doesn't provide evidence for belief B2" and "belief B1 contradicts belief B2."[6]

---

[6]Other predications that fall within the category of beliefs about beliefs, such as "X believes that Y believes Z," are discussed in (Wilks and Bien, 1983).

Why is it necessary to distinguish among these types of beliefs? A basic problem in editorial comprehension is to build an internal conceptual model of editorial arguments. This model, known as an *argument graph* (Flowers et al., 1982), represents explicitly whether beliefs in the editorial are involved in: (a) support relationships, because they provide evidence for one another; or (b) attack relationships, because they contradict one another. For example, consider the following excerpt from an editorial by the Los Angeles Times (1984, December 9):

ED-CONTRADICTORY-POLICIES

American negotiators are pursuing a protectionist course in efforts to control steel imports, with restrictions under consideration that would place an extraordinary burden on consumers in what seems a vain effort to protect U.S. steel makers ... This is the wrong way to go ... The American steel industry ... will be cushioned from the economic forces that alone ... hold the hope of restoring productivity and competitiveness. And consumers will be forced to pay the cost through denial of the cheaper foreign products ... This ... protectionism comes at the very moment when the U.S. government has won international agreement ... to liberalize trade in the service sector, where American companies compete so well. Washington is announcing to the world that a new wall is being built around the United States temporarily to bar the things that some foreigners do better than Americans, but that Washington wants others to pull down the walls that keep out things that U.S. industry does best.

Understanding ED-CONTRADICTORY-POLICIES requires representing the belief relationships that summarize the position of the L.A. Times, namely:

- Support Relationship Between Evaluative and Causal Beliefs: The L.A. Times believes that protectionism by the U.S. is "wrong" because: (1) import restrictions will not achieve the goals of "restoring productivity and competitiveness" for U.S. steel makers; and (2) import restrictions will force U.S. consumers "to pay the cost" of protecting the steel makers.

- Support Relationship Between Causal Beliefs: The L.A. Times believes that: (1) import restrictions will force consumers "to pay the cost" because they will result in a decrease in "cheaper foreign products" in the U.S.; and (2) import restrictions will not achieve the goals of "restoring productivity and competitiveness" because they will block the "economic forces that alone" can achieve those goals.

- <u>Attack Relationship Between Causal Beliefs Held by Different Arguers:</u> The U.S. government's belief that import restrictions will "protect U.S. steel makers" is contradicted by two of the L.A. Times' beliefs: (1) import restrictions will not achieve the goals of "restoring productivity and competitiveness" for steel makers; and (2) import restrictions will force consumers "to pay the cost."

- <u>Attack Relationship Between Evaluative Beliefs Held by the Same Arguer:</u> The L.A. Times believes that the U.S. government holds two contradictory positions with respect to international trade: (1) foreign countries should abolish the import restrictions "that keep out things that U.S. industry does best"; and (2) the U.S. should implement import restrictions "to bar the things that some foreigners do better than Americans."

As the above relationships indicate, the way in which a belief is supported or attacked in editorial arguments depends upon the nature of that belief. For instance, the evaluative belief that "a plan P shouldn't be implemented" can be supported by the causal belief that "implementing P will either fail to achieve or thwart a goal G." Similarly, the evaluative belief that "a plan P should be implemented" can be supported by the causal belief that "implementing P will achieve a goal G." Clearly, editorial comprehension requires a taxonomy of the support and attack relationships that exist among different types of beliefs.

This chapter presents a model of beliefs and belief relationships which has been developed to provide the foundation for the theory of argument units implemented in OpEd. The model characterizes attack relationships in terms of contradictions involving: (1) planning situations that cannot occur at the same time; and (2) opposite effects of a plan on goals that are interrelated. In contrast, the representation of support relationships captures the ways in which causal domain-knowledge, analogies, and examples can be used to justify: (1) why plans should/shouldn't be implemented; and (2) why plans achieve, fail to achieve, or thwart goals. The concepts described here will be illustrated using excerpts from various politico-economic editorials, including the two segments processed by OpEd (i.e., ED-JOBS and ED-RESTRICTIONS).

3.2. Belief Representation

How are beliefs represented in OpEd? The representation of a belief consists of three major components: (1) the holder of the belief; (2) the content of the belief; and (3) links that indicate whether the belief attacks, supports, or is supported by other beliefs. For example, consider figure 3.1 which illustrates the representation of four beliefs from ED-CONTRADICTORY- POLICIES.

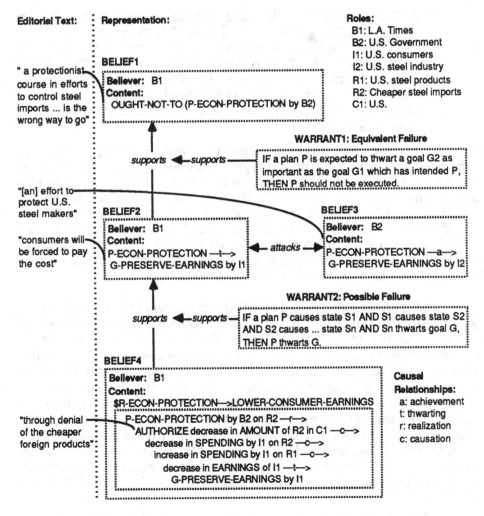

Figure 3.1. Representation of Beliefs and Belief Relationships.

The above diagram shows the attack and support relationships that contain BELIEF2, i.e., the L.A. Times' belief that import restrictions will thwart the goal of preserving earnings for U.S. consumers. Each support relationship is itself supported by a more basic belief termed *warrant* (Flowers et al., 1982; Toulmin, 1958; Toulmin et al., 1979). Warrants are inference rules that establish why conclusions can be drawn from supporting evidences (i.e., warrants are beliefs about beliefs). This explicit representation of warrants is needed because they can themselves be attacked in arguments about the use of support strategies.[7] For instance, the support relationship between BELIEF2 and the instantiation of the reasoning script $R-ECON-PROTECTION—> LOWER-CONSUMER-EARNINGS in BELIEF4 is based on the following warrant:

> **Possible-Failure Warrant:** IF plan P causes state S1 AND S1 causes state S2 AND S2 ... causes state Sn AND Sn thwarts goal G, THEN P thwarts G.

Figure 3.1 also shows that the representation of contents of beliefs involve either: (1) a causal dependency between a plan and a goal; (2) a chain of causal dependencies organized by a reasoning script; or (3) an evaluative component. Causal dependencies include intentional relationships among goals, plans, events, and states, such as: goal achievement, goal failure, goal motivation, goal suspension, plan intention, plan enablement, plan disablement, event realization, and forced events. These dependencies are represented by means of *intentional links (I-links)* (Dyer, 1983a), a representational system that encodes the motivations and intentions of narrative characters. Other non-intentional causal dependencies, such as those among states of economic quantities, are represented using a general causal link. The major causal dependencies used in OpEd are summarized in table 3.1.

---

[7]Arguments about the use of support strategies are discussed in chapter 5.

Relationship Name	Representation
Goal Achievement	STATE —achieves—> GOAL
Goal Failure	STATE —thwarts—> GOAL
Goal Motivation	STATE —motivates—> GOAL
Goal Suspension	GOAL1 —suspends—> GOAL2
Plan Intention	GOAL —intends—> PLAN
Plan Enablement	STATE —enables—> PLAN
Plan Disablement	STATE —disables—> PLAN
Event Realization	PLAN —realizes—> EVENT
Forced Event	STATE —forces—> EVENT
Consequent State	EVENT —causes—> STATE
	STATE1 —causes—> STATE2

Table 3.1. Causal Dependencies in OpEd.

The representation of causal dependencies in OpEd expands Dyer's work on intentional links. In Dyer's model, states are considered as part of events. In contrast, states and events are separated in OpEd due to the need to represent explicitly the causal relationships that exist among conflict-resolution events, states of economic quantities, economic goals, and protectionist plans. As table 2.1 indicates, in OpEd: (1) goals are motivated by desires to attain, change, or maintain given states; and (2) plans are intended in order to achieve active goals. Further interactions among plans and goals are mediated by chains of causal effects among events and states. That is, plans may achieve or thwart goals because: (1) once plans are executed, they cause events to be realized; and (2) those events result in states that may achieve or thwart goals. For example, the L.A. Times can argue that P-ECON-PROTECTION—thwarts—>G-PRESERVING-EARNINGS because of the following chain of effects:

P-ECON-PROTECTION by U.S. government on cheap steel imports—realizes—>
AUTHORIZE decrease in AMOUNT of cheap steel imports —causes—>
decrease in SPENDING by U.S. consumers on cheap steel imports—causes—>
increase in SPENDING by consumers on expensive U.S. products—causes—>
decrease in EARNINGS of U.S. consumers—thwarts—>
G-PRESERVING-EARNINGS by U.S. consumers

Therefore, dependencies of the form PLAN—achieves—>GOAL and PLAN—thwarts—>GOAL can be viewed as *condensed* causal chains of reasoning.

These plan-goal dependencies also form the representational foundation underlying evaluative components of beliefs. Evaluative components are high level abstractions that categorize and organize concepts in terms of being "good" or "bad," or leading to "good" or "bad" (Abelson, 1979). In OpEd, evaluative components are used to represent the main standpoints that argument participants hold with respect to a given plan P, i.e., whether they support or oppose the use of P. These plan evaluations are captured by the following constructs:

> **OUGHT-TO (P):** A plan P should be executed IF the following situations can be expected: (1) P will achieve the goal G1 which has intended P; AND (2) P will not thwart a goal G2 which is more important than or as important as G1.

> **OUGHT-NOT-TO (P):** A plan P should not be executed IF any of the following situations can be expected: (1) P will not achieve the goal G1 which has intended P; OR (2) P will thwart a goal G2 which is more important than or as important as G1.

For example, in the following excerpt from ED-CONTRADICTORY-POLICIES:

> ... a protectionist course in efforts to control steel imports ... is the
> wrong way to go ...

the phrase "wrong way to go" indicates that the L.A. times opposes restrictions on steel imports. This sentence is represented as an instantiation of OUGHT-NOT-TO, as indicated in figure 3.1.

OpEd's evaluative components categorize plans in terms of the possible positive or negative effects of implementing those plans.[8] Frequently, these outcomes are explicitly mentioned in editorial arguments in order to justify evaluative beliefs about plans. For instance, consider the L.A. Times' argument in ED-CONTRADICTORY-POLICIES:

> American negotiators are pursuing a protectionist course in efforts
> ... to protect U.S. steel makers ... And consumers will be forced to
> pay the cost through denial of the cheaper foreign products ...

Here the L.A. Times contrasts the following plan-goal relationships: (1) import restrictions are intended to achieve the goal of preserving earnings for U.S. steel makers; and (2) import restrictions will thwart

---

[8]The notion of evaluative components in OpEd is similar in nature to the deontic notion of *the "ought" of reasons* (Harman, 1986), which characterizes judgements that use the term "ought" to indicate reasons for doing or not doing something.

the goal of preserving earnings for U.S. consumers. These relationships refer to opposite effects on two equivalent (i.e., equally important) goals and, consequently, justify the L.A. Times' belief that the U.S. OUGHT-NOT-TO negotiate import restrictions. Thus, evaluative components provide not only a representational system for contents of beliefs, but also organize belief justifications in terms of goal achievements and goal failures.

3.3.   Attack Relationships

Contents of beliefs serve as the basis for establishing whether those beliefs attack one another. In OpEd, an *attack (A)* is modeled as a bidirectional relationship between two contradictory beliefs, i.e., if belief B1 attacks belief B2, then belief B2 attacks belief B1. Two beliefs are considered contradictory if their contents involve either: (1) planning situations that can not occur at the same time (i.e., mutually-exclusive planning situations); or (2) opposite effects of a plan P on two interrelated goals. These relationships are summarized in table 3.2 and described below.

Type of Belief Contents	Content of Belief B1	Content of Belief B2	Attack Relationship Between B1 and B2
Mutually-Exclusive Planning Situations	OUGHT-TO (P)	OUGHT-NOT-TO (P)	A-OBJECTIONABLE-PLAN
	P —achieves—> G	P —not-achieves—> G	A-UNREALIZED-SUCCESS
	P —thwarts—> G	P —not-thwarts—> G	A-UNREALIZED-FAILURE
Opposite Effects of a Plan P on Interrelated Goals	P —thwarts—> G1	P —achieves—> G2 G1 less important than G2	A-GREATER-SUCCESS
	P —achieves—> G1	P —thwarts—> G2 G1 less important than G2	A-GREATER-FAILURE
	P —achieves—> G1	P —thwarts—> G2 G1 as important as G2	A-EQUIVALENT-FAILURE
	P1 —achieves—> G1	P1 —thwarts—> G2, at time T G2 —initiates—> P2, at time T1>T G1 as important as G2 P1 instance of P P2 instance of P	A-SPIRAL-FAILURE

Table 3.2. Attack Relationships.

3.3.1. Attacks Based on Mutually-Exclusive Planning Situations

An evaluative or causal belief B1 about a plan P can be contradicted by stating a belief B2 which negates the content of B1.[9] This type of contradiction, termed *contradiction by negation* (Flowers, 1982), is the basis for three different attack structures developed within the framework of OpEd:

1) **A-OBJECTIONABLE-PLAN:** Although arguer A1 believes that plan P should be executed, arguer A2 believes that P should not be executed.

2) **A-UNREALIZED-SUCCESS:** Although arguer A1 believes that plan P achieves goal G, arguer A2 believes that P does not achieve G.

3) **A-UNREALIZED-FAILURE:** Although arguer A1 believes that plan P thwarts goal G, arguer A2 believes that P does not thwart G.

Both A-OBJECTIONABLE-PLAN and A-UNREALIZED-SUCCESS can be used to represent attacks on two beliefs associated with the execution of a plan P, namely: (1) the actor of P believes that P OUGHT-TO be implemented; and (2) the actor of P believes that P will achieve the goal G which has intended P. Frequently, these beliefs are implicitly stated in editorial arguments. For example, consider again the following fragment from ED-CONTRADICTORY-POLICIES:

> **American negotiators are pursuing a protectionist course ... in what seems a vain effort to protect U.S. steel makers ... This is the wrong way to go ...**

Here, the word "vain" stands for the negative-achievement relationship between a plan and a goal. Within the context of ED-CONTRADICTORY-POLICIES, this relationship refers to the L.A. Times' belief that import restrictions will not achieve the U.S. government's goals of helping steel makers preserve earnings and attain profitability. This belief contradicts the implicitly stated belief by the U.S. government that import restrictions will achieve its goal of helping

---

[9]At this point it is important to notice that the plan-goal relationship P—thwarts->G is not the same as the relationship P—not-achieves->G. Instead, the goal-thwarting relationship indicates one of the reasons why P can not achieve G. Similarly, the relationship P—achieves—>G is not equal to the relationship P—not-thwarts—>G, but rather a reason why P can not result in G's failure. These differences will become obvious in section 3.4, which discusses support relationships.

steel makers. Similarly, the L.A. Times' belief that import restrictions are "wrong" (i.e., OUGHT-NOT-TO be executed) attacks the implicitly stated belief by the U.S. government that import restrictions OUGHT-TO be executed. These two attacks correspond to instances of A-UNREALIZED-SUCCESS and A-OBJECTIONABLE-PLAN, respectively.

In contrast to these two attack relationships, A-UNREALIZED-FAILURE is used to represent attacks on a belief often professed by opponents of a plan P, i.e., the belief that P thwarts the goal G which has intended P. For instance, consider the following excerpt from an editorial by Lee Iacocca (1986):

ED-TOUGH-POLICY

It's time to quiet down all ... [free-trade purists] who keep telling us that getting tough on [international] trade will cost us jobs. It won't.

In ED-TOUGH-POLICY, Iacocca argues against the freetrader's belief that imposing restrictions on international trade thwarts the goal of preserving jobs. Since this goal is one of the goals that import restrictions are intended to achieve, then Iacocca's argument can be represented in terms of A-UNREALIZED-FAILURE. This representation is shown below.

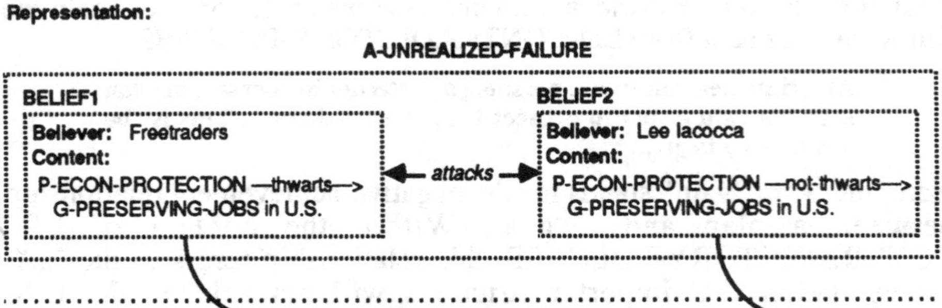

Representation:

A-UNREALIZED-FAILURE

BELIEF1		BELIEF2
Believer: Freetraders **Content:** P-ECON-PROTECTION —thwarts—> G-PRESERVING-JOBS in U.S.	← attacks →	**Believer:** Lee Iacocca **Content:** P-ECON-PROTECTION —not-thwarts—> G-PRESERVING-JOBS in U.S.

EditorialText: "[free-trade purists] ... keep telling us that   "It won't"
                      getting tough on trade will cost us jobs"

Figure 3.2. Attack Relationship in ED-TOUGH-POLICY.

3.3.2. Attacks Based on Opposite Effects on Interrelated Goals

Another way to contradict a belief about the effect a plan P has on a goal G1 is by stating that P has the opposite effect on G2, a goal more important than or equally important to G1. According to this type of contradiction by opposite effects, four attack relationships can be distinguished:

1) **A-GREATER-SUCCESS:** Although arguer A1 believes that plan P thwarts goal G1, arguer A2 believes that P achieves a more important goal G2.

2) **A-GREATER-FAILURE:** Although arguer A1 believes that plan P achieves goal G1, arguer A2 believes that P thwarts a more important goal G2.

3) **A-EQUIVALENT-FAILURE:** Although arguer A1 believes that plan P achieves goal G1, arguer A2 believes that P thwarts an equally important goal G2.

4) **A-SPIRAL-FAILURE:** Although arguer A1 believes that the instance P1 of plan P achieves goal G1, arguer A2 believes that P1 thwarts an equally important goal G2 AND G2's failure will require using P2, another instance of P.

These four attack relationships are used to represent arguments that contrast the negative and positive effects of a plan P in order to show that P should be favored or opposed. For example, A-GREATER-SUCCESS shows that the negative side-effects of a plan P are a small price to pay for P's positive effects. To illustrate this type of attack, consider the following passage taken from Greenaway and Milner (1979, pp. 18-19):

ED-REVENUE-TARIFF

If the government feels it requires additional revenue to finance higher state expenditure, tariff imposition may be viewed as a suitable source ... Since the tariff must be paid by ... domestic consumers, the government is guaranteed a yield.

The above excerpt presents an argument which Greenaway and Milner call "the argument for the revenue tariff." In this argument, the position of the government is that: (1) imposing a tariff achieves the government's the goal of attaining a higher level of spending; and (2) this goal is more important than the goal of preserving earnings by domestic consumers. Clearly, the argument for the revenue tariff amounts to an implicit attack on the belief (by protectionism opponents) that imposing tariffs will thwart the goal of preserving earnings by domestic consumers. Such an attack can be represented in terms of A-GREATER-SUCCESS, as illustrated below.

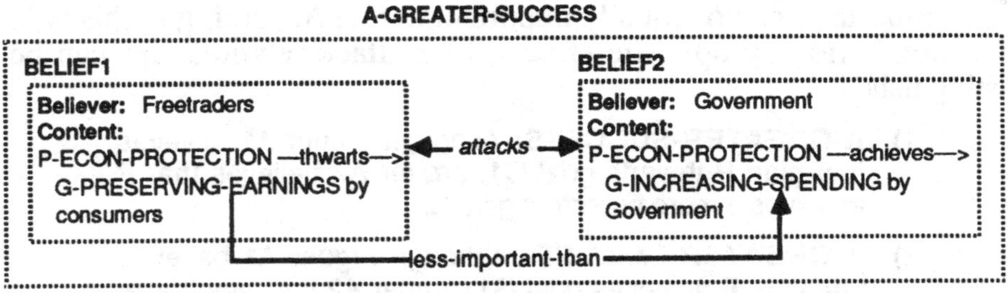

Figure 3.3. Attack Relationship in ED-REVENUE-TARIFF.

In contrast to A-GREATER-SUCCESS, the other attack relationships involving opposite effects show that the negative side-effects of a plan P do not grant the implementation of P. For example, the following excerpt from an editorial by the L.A. Times (1985, October 5):

> ... legislation to limit textile and apparel imports ... will do more harm than good ...

is an instance of A-GREATER-FAILURE. This instance contrasts: (1) the implicitly stated belief by legislators that import restrictions will lead to goal achievements; and (2) the L.A. Times' belief that those restrictions cause major goal failures. Similarly, the following excerpt from ED-CONTRADICTORY-POLICIES:

> American negotiators are pursuing a protectionist course in efforts ... to protect U.S. steel makers ... And consumers will be forced to pay the cost through denial of the cheaper foreign products ...

is an instance of A-EQUIVALENT-FAILURE. The contradictory beliefs in the above excerpt are: (1) the government's belief that import restrictions will achieve the goal of preserving earnings for steel makers; and (2) the L.A. Times' belief that those restrictions will thwart the same type of goal for consumers. (This attack relationship has already been illustrated in figure 3.1.)

Finally, A-SPIRAL-FAILURE is used to represent arguments about goal failures triggered by repeated applications of the same plan P. For instance, consider a fragment of Lance Morrow's argument in ED-RESTRICTIONS (chapter 1, page 15):

> The toolmakers argue that import restrictions must be imposed so that the industry can survive ... Restrictions on imports would mean that [other] American manufacturers would ... lose sales. Then those manufacturers would demand protection against foreign competition.

The above editorial segment contains an attack relationship between the: (1) the toolmakers' belief that import restrictions will achieve their goal of preserving the industry's level of earnings; and (2) Morrow's belief that those restrictions will thwart the same goal for other manufacturers and, consequently, motivate the use of more import restrictions. The representation of this attack relationship is shown in figure 3.4.

Representation:

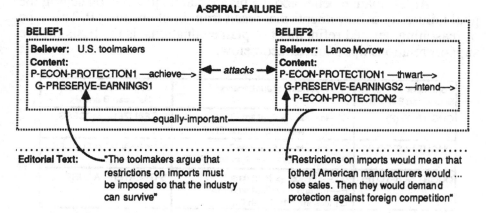

Figure 3.4. Attack Relationship in ED-RESTRICTIONS.

3.4.   Support Relationships

Beliefs can also relate to one another via relationships of support. In OpEd, a *support (S)* is a construct composed of three major elements: (1) a supported belief B; (2) a justification J that contains a single supporting belief or a conjunction of supporting beliefs; and (3) and a warrant W that grants the existence of the support relationship from J to B. Support structures are used in OpEd to represent instances of plan-based reasoning in editorial arguments, i.e., the reasoning used by arguers to justify why plans should/shouldn't be implemented or why plans will/won't cause goal achievements or failures.[10] According

---

[10]Support relationships can also be combined with attack relationships to form abstract argument configurations. Instances of these configurations are used in editorial arguments in order to: (1) justify an arguer's evaluative or causal belief B1 about a plan P; and (2) contrast B1 with a belief B2 held by the arguer's opponents. In OpEd, configurations of support and attack relationships are organized by argument units. Argument units are discussed in Chapter 4.

to the nature of these reasoning instances, four basic types of support relationships have been characterized: (1) refinements of plan evaluations; (2) refinements of plan-goal relationships; (3) analogies; and (4) examples.

3.4.1. Supports Based on Refinements of Plan Evaluations

An evaluative belief about a plan P can be justified by stating the goal failures or achievements that result from implementing P. This type of reasoning, termed refinement of plan evaluations, is the basis for the support relationships summarized below.

Content of Supported Belief B	Content of Justification J	Support Relationship Between B and J
OUGHT-TO (P)	G —intends—> P, at time T P —achieves—> G, at time T1>T	S-REALIZED-SUCCESS
OUGHT-NOT-TO (P)	G —intends—> P, at time T P —not-achieves—> G, at time T1>T	S-UNREALIZED-SUCCESS
OUGHT-NOT-TO (P)	G1 —intends—> P, at time T P —thwarts—> G2, at time T1>T G1 less important than G2	S-GREATER-FAILURE
OUGHT-NOT-TO (P)	G1 —intends—> P, at time T P —thwarts—> G2, at time T1>T G1 as important as G2	S-EQUIVALENT-FAILURE
OUGHT-NOT-TO (P1)	G1 —intends—> P1, at time T P1 —thwarts—> G2, at time T1>T G2 —intends—> P2, at time T2>T1 G1 as important as G2 P1 instance of P P2 instance of P	S-SPIRAL-FAILURE

Table 3.3. Supports Based on Refinements of Plan Evaluations.

The five support structures in table 3.3 are used to represent arguments in favor or against the use of a plan P. For example, S-REALIZED-SUCCESS embodies the following reasoning:

> 1) **S-REALIZED-SUCCESS:** Arguer A believes that plan P should be executed because A believes that P will achieve the goal G which has intended P.

To illustrate this support structure, consider the following excerpt from an editorial by the Los Angeles Times (1984, February 16):

ED-JOB-SAVING-QUOTAS

The Japanese quotas were pushed hardest by the United Auto Workers union, which touted them ... as a means of restoring American jobs ...

In ED-JOB-SAVING-QUOTAS, the position of the U.A.W. is that: (1) restrictions on Japanese automobiles should be imposed; and (2) import restrictions will achieve the goal of preserving jobs in the U.S. Clearly, ED-JOB-SAVING-QUOTAS can be represented in terms of S-REALIZED-SUCCESS, as shown in figure 3.5.

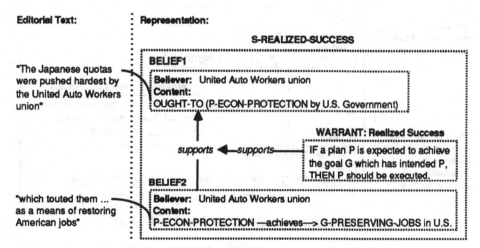

Figure 3.5. Support Relationship in ED-JOB-SAVING-QUOTAS.

In contrast to the above support relationship, S-UNREALIZED-SUCCESS involves the use of a negative achievement relationship to justify the belief that a plan P should be opposed:

2) **S-UNREALIZED-SUCCESS:** Arguer A believes that plan P should not be executed because A believes that P will not achieve the goal G which has intended P.

For instance, S-UNREALIZED-SUCCESS can be used to represent the following fragment of Milton Friedman's argument in ED-JOBS (chapter 1, page 3):

Recent protectionist measures ... have disappointed us ... They do not promote the long-run health of the [automobile and steel] industries ...

Here, the affect description "disappointed" indicates that Friedman believes that import restrictions should not be implemented. This belief is justified by the negative achievement relationship stated in the second sentence of the above editorial segment. In that sentence, the phrase "long-run health" refers to the industries' goal of attaining profitability. Since this goal is one of the goals that import restrictions are intended to achieve, then Friedman's argument can be represented as an instantiation of S-UNREALIZED-SUCCESS. This representation is shown in figure 3.6.

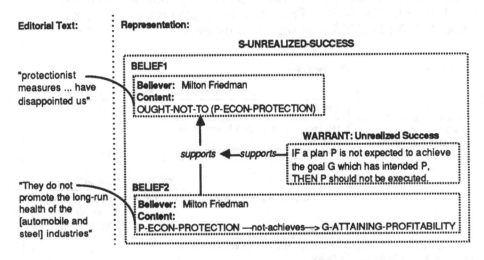

Figure 3.6. Support Relationship in ED-JOBS.

In addition to S-UNREALIZED-SUCCESS, three more support structures can be used to justify the belief that a plan P should not be implemented:

3) **S-GREATER-FAILURE:** Arguer A believes that plan P should not be executed because A believes that P will thwart a goal G2 more important than the goal G1 which has intended P.

4) **S-EQUIVALENT-FAILURE:** Arguer A believes that plan P should not be executed because A believes that P will thwart a goal G2 as important as the goal G1 which has intended P.

4) **S-SPIRAL-FAILURE:** Arguer A believes that the instance P1 of plan P should not be executed because A believes that P1 will thwart a goal G2 as important as the goal G1 which has intended P AND G2's failure will require using P2, another instance of P.

For example, in the following excerpt from an editorial by Timothy Bresnahan (1984):

> ... I think the import quotas are terrible public policy ... [P]rotecting domestic industries from foreign competition does more harm than good.

Bresnahan's argument is an instance of S-GREATER-FAILURE. Similarly, in the following excerpt from an editorial by Robert Samuelson (1984, September 12):

ED-PROTECTION-OPPONENTS

> ... In the last few months ... major retailers and farm groups have ... vigorously protested proposed new trade restrictions ... Major retailers have formed a group to resist ... restrictions on apparel, which the retailers said would have cost them ... millions of dollars ... Farm groups have joined coalitions opposing ... textile ... restrictions. About two-thirds of America's wheat, half the soybeans and a third of the corn is exported. Farm groups fear that U.S. import restrictions will cause some countries to retaliate ...

the retailers' argument and farmers' argument correspond to instances of S-EQUIVALENT-FAILURE and S-SPIRAL-FAILURE, respectively. These instances are based on the following relationships: (1) import restrictions are intended to achieve the goal of preserving earnings for the U.S. textile and apparel industries; (2) major retailers believe that import restrictions will thwart their goal of preserving earnings; and (3) farmer groups believe import restrictions will thwart foreign countries' goal of preserving earnings and, consequently, will motivate those countries to impose import restrictions on U.S. grains.[11] The representation of the supports in ED-PROTECTION-OPPONENTS is shown below.

---

[11]In ED-PROTECTION-OPPONENTS, the negative-spiral effect caused by import restrictions is indicated by the word "retaliate."

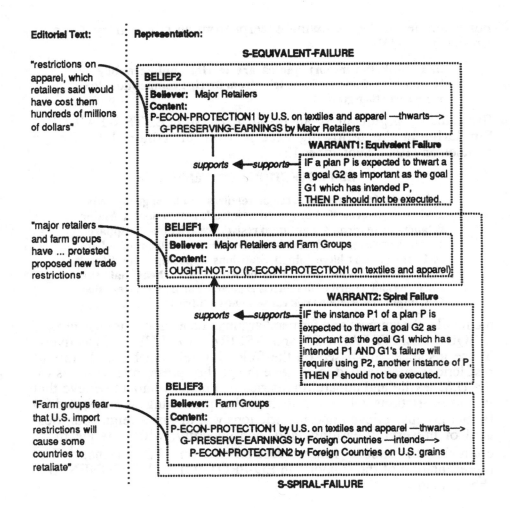

Figure 3.7. Support Relationships in ED-PROTECTION-
            OPPONENTS.

3.4.2. Supports Based on Refinements of Plan-Goal Relationships

A belief B involving a plan-goal relationship can be justified by
stating other causal beliefs that refine B and provide specific details on
why B holds. Four types of justifications can be distinguished here: (1)
causal-chain expansion; (2) consequent exclusion; (3) current-state
exclusion; and (4) antecedent exclusion. These justifications are
summarized in table 3.4 and described below.

Type of Justification	Content of Supported Belief B	Content of Justification J	Support Relationship Between B and J
Causal Chain Expansion	P —achieves—> G at time T1	P —causes—> S, at time T S —achieves—> G, at T1>T	S-POSSIBLE-SUCCESS
	P —thwarts—> G at time T1	P —causes—> S, at time T S —thwarts—> G, at T1>T	S-POSSIBLE-FAILURE
	P1 —thwarts—> G, at T1 G —intends—> P2, at T2 P1 and P2 instances of P	P1 —causes—> S, at time T S —thwarts—> G, at T1>T G —intends—> P2, at T2>T1	S-POSSIBLE-SPIRAL-FAILURE
Consequent Exclusion	P —not-achieves—> G	P —thwarts—> G	S-EXCLUDED-SUCCESS
	P —not-thwarts—> G	P —achieves—> G	S-EXCLUDED-FAILURE
Current State Exclusion	P —not-achieves—> G	S1 —thwarts—> G, at time T P —not-causes—> S2, at T S2 opposite of S1	S-UNDISTURBED-FAILURE
	P —not-thwarts—> G	S1 —achieves—> G, at time T P —not-causes—> S2, at T S2 opposite of S1	S-UNDISTURBED-SUCCESS
Antecedent Exclusion	P1 —not-achieves—> G	only P2 —achieves—> G P2 opposite of P1	S-IMPOSSIBLE-SUCCESS
	P1 —not-thwarts—> G	only P2 —thwarts—> G P2 opposite of P1	S-IMPOSSIBLE-FAILURE

Table 3.4. Supports Based on Refinements of Plan-Goal Relationships.

Supports Based on Causal-Chain Expansion

One of the ways to justify the belief that a plan P leads to a goal achievement or a goal failure is by providing a chain of causal effects that describes how those goal relationships may take place. At the abstract level, this reasoning strategy is captured by the following support structures:

1) **S-POSSIBLE-SUCCESS:** Arguer A believes that plan P will achieve goal G because A believes that P causes state S1 AND S1 causes ... state Sn AND Sn achieves G.

2) **S-POSSIBLE-FAILURE:** Arguer A believes that plan P will thwart goal G because A believes that P causes state S1 AND S1 causes ... state Sn AND Sn thwarts G.

At the level of domain-knowledge, the chains of causal effects organized by instances of the above support structures in editorials correspond to instances of reasoning scripts. For example, consider the following passage from Greenaway and Milner (1979, pp. 40-41):

ED-BENEFICIAL-TARIFF

Suppose ... policy-makers impose a tariff on low-price textiles from abroad ... Because the post-tariff price of imports is higher than their free-trade price, domestic textile producers ... can now supply more of the (diminished) market. Thus, ... domestic producers ... benefit from tariffs.

Here, the belief that tariffs achieve the goal of attaining profitability for domestic producers is supported by a causal chain on how tariffs switch domestic spending from imports to domestic products and, consequently, increase the level of earnings of domestic producers. This causal chain is an instance of $R-ECON-PROTECTION—>HIGHER-DOMESTIC-EARNINGS (chapter 2, section 2.3.3). Similarly, consider the following fragment of Milton Friedman's argument in ED-JOBS:

... the limitations on imports [by the Reagan administration] will cost jobs. If we import less, foreign countries will earn fewer dollars. They will have less to spend on American exports. The result will be fewer jobs in export industries.

In ED-JOBS, Friedman's belief that "limitations on imports will cost jobs" is supported by a reasoning chain which describes how import restrictions by the U.S. trigger a negative feedback on U.S. export jobs. This chain is an instance of the reasoning script $R-ECON-PROTECTION—>FEWER-EXPORT-JOBS. The representation of Friedman's argument is illustrated in figure 3.8.

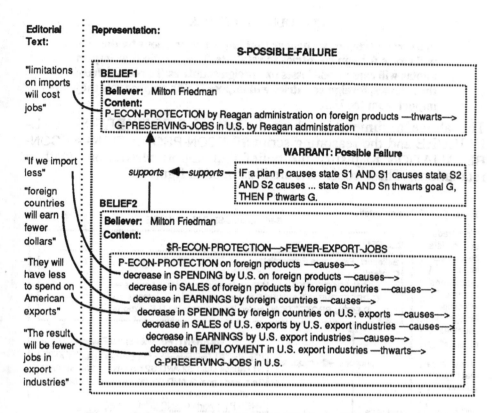

Figure 3.8. Supporting Causal Chain in ED-JOBS.

Instances of reasoning scripts can also be used to justify beliefs about the negative-spiral effects resulting from implementing a plan P. At the abstract level, those justifications are characterized by the following support structure:

3) **S-POSSIBLE-SPIRAL-FAILURE:** Arguer A believes that plan P1 (an instance of P) will thwart goal G AND G will intend plan P2 (another instance of P) because A believes that P1 causes state S1 AND S1 causes ... state Sn AND Sn thwarts G AND G's failure requires using P2.

For example, consider the following paragraph which summarizes an argument presented in Cuddington and McKinnon (1979, pp. 4-6):

ED-COUNTERATTACK

Free-trade economists believe that import restrictions by the U.S. will cause foreign countries to retaliate. They argue that import quotas will cause trade losses for foreign countries. To recover from those losses, foreign countries will impose tariffs on products they import from the U.S.

The above argument involves the use of S-POSSIBLE-SPIRAL-FAILURE and the reasoning script $R-ECON-PROTECTION—>ECON-RETALIATION to justify the belief that import restrictions lead to retaliations. These constructs are illustrated in figure 3.9.

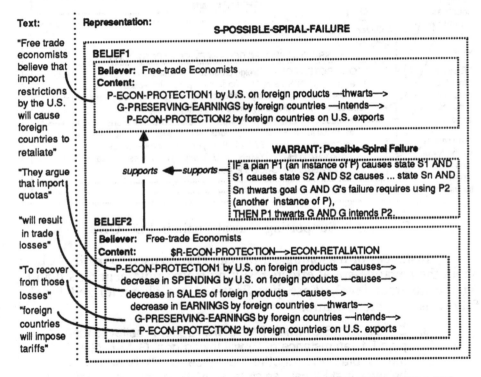

Figure 3.9. Supporting Causal Chain in ED-COUNTERATTACK.

Supports Based on Consequent Exclusion

To justify the belief that a plan P does not lead to a goal achievement or failure GS1, an arguer may claim that P leads to another goal situation GS2 which is the opposite of GS1. This reasoning strategy, termed consequent exclusion, is the basis for the following support relationships:[12]

1) **S-EXCLUDED-SUCCESS:** Arguer A believes that plan P will not achieve goal G because A believes that P will thwart G.

2) **S-EXCLUDED-FAILURE:** Arguer A believes that plan P will not thwart goal G because A believes that P will achieve G.

In the domain of international trade, S-EXCLUDED-FAILURE can be used to represent the argument by protectionist legislators that imposing import restrictions can not cost jobs because such measures are designed to save jobs. In contrast, S-EXCLUDED-SUCCESS can be used to represent arguments by opponents of import restrictions. For example, consider the following editorial fragment by economist Benjamin Zycher (1984):

ED-JOB-LOSS

... Trade ... policies cannot ... "save" jobs ... If we protect some domestic industries by imposing import restrictions, ... the net effect ... is to "save" jobs in the industries being protected but lose them in other export sectors.

Here, Zycher argues that, due to the negative feedback from import restrictions, those policies cause a decrease in the number of export jobs and, consequently, can not achieve the goal of preserving jobs in a country. Thus, Zycher's argument can be represented in terms of S-EXCLUDED-SUCCESS, as shown in figure 3.10.

---

[12]The consequent-exclusion strategy can not be used to justify the belief that a plan P leads to a goal achievement or a goal failure. That is, it is an error to present the following type of arguments: (1) plan P will achieve goal G because P can not thwart G; and (2) plan P will thwart goal G because P can not achieve G. Errors in the use of reasoning strategies are discussed in Chapter 5.

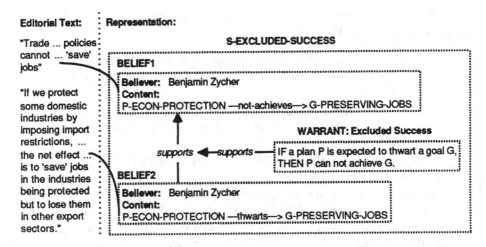

Figure 3.10. Support Relationship in ED-JOB-LOSS.

Supports Based on Current-State Exclusion

An arguer A may also claim that a plan P can not lead to a goal achievement or a goal failure GS1 if A believes that: (1) there is a state S1 which currently leads to the opposite goal situation GS2; and (2) P can not undo S1. This reasoning is characterized by the following support structures:

1) **S-UNDISTURBED-FAILURE:** Arguer A believes that plan P will not achieve goal G because A believes that G is being thwarted by a state S1 AND P can not result in S2, the opposite of S1.

2) **S-UNDISTURBED-SUCCESS:** Arguer A believes that plan P will not thwart goal G because A believes that G is being achieved by a state S1 AND P can not result in S2, the opposite of S1.

S-UNDISTURBED-FAILURE can be used to represent arguments in which the opponents of a plan P show that P will not work. For example, consider the following editorial segment by William Schneider (1985):

ED-UNBALANCED-TRADE

... [P]rotectionism is not the solution [to the U.S. balance-of-trade deficit]. The problem is [the high value of] the dollar ...

Here, Schneider argues that protectionism can not achieve the goal of attaining a balanced trade because: (1) that goal is being thwarted by the high cost of the dollar; and (2) import restrictions do not affect the cost of the dollar. Schneider's argument is represented below.

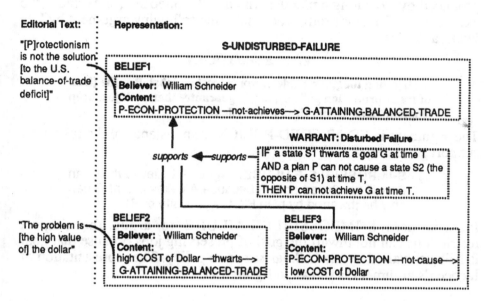

Figure 3.11. Support Relationship in ED-UNBALANCED-TRADE.

In contrast to the above support relationship, S-UNDISTURBED-SUCCESS can be used to represent arguments in which the advocates of a plan P show that P will not have negative side-effects. For instance, consider the following excerpt from an editorial by Spich and McKelvey (1985):

ED-CHEAP-CARS

... [T]he United States could put an embargo on ... all Japanese cars in the upper half of the price range. Cheap cars would still enter the U.S. market ... [and] would not raise inflation ...

The above editorial segment is an instance of S-UNDISTURBED-SUCCESS. This instance justifies the belief that an embargo on expensive Japanese cars will not thwart the U.S. goal of keeping prices from rising because: (1) importing cheap Japanese cars keeps prices down; and (2) the proposed embargo will not affect the amount of cheap Japanese cars entering the U.S.

Supports Based on Antecedent Exclusion

An arguer A may also argue that a plan P1 can not lead to a goal achievement or failure GS because A believes that GS can only be produced by executing a plan P2 which is the opposite (or excludes the execution) of P1. For example, consider the following argument by Lee Iacocca (1986):

ED-NEEDED-POLICY

... [G]etting tough on trade ... won't [cost us jobs]. But the [lack of trade-protection policies] ... will guarantee that we'll just keep shipping more ... American jobs offshore.

The argument in ED-NEEDED-POLICY is an instance of the following support structure:

1) **S-IMPOSSIBLE-FAILURE:** Arguer A believes that plan P1 will not thwart goal G because A believes that G can only be thwarted by plan P2, the opposite of P1.

Iacocca uses S-IMPOSSIBLE-FAILURE to argue that import restrictions can not thwart the goal of preserving jobs because that goal is being thwarted by the U.S. laissez-faire policy. The representation of Iacocca's argument is shown in figure 3.12.

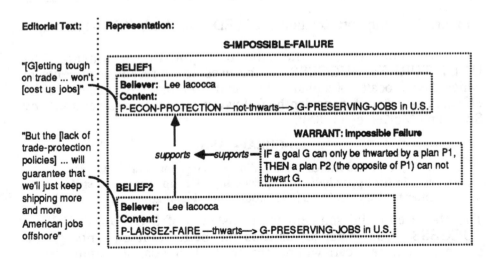

Figure 3.12. Support Relationship in ED-NEEDED-POLICY.

In contrast with Iacocca's argument, consider the following the following excerpt from an editorial by Lester Thurow (1983):

ED-LAISSEZ-FAIRE-POLICY

The Reagan administration argues that America does not need an industrial policy since all government has to do to guarantee economic success ... is keep out of the way.

The Reagan administration's argument in ED-LAISSEZ-FAIRE-POLICY is an instance of the support structure S-IMPOSSIBLE-SUCCESS, which contains the following reasoning:

> 2) **S-IMPOSSIBLE-SUCCESS:** Arguer A believes that plan P1 will not achieve goal G because A believes that G can only be achieved by plan P2, the opposite of P1.

The Reagan administration uses S-IMPOSSIBLE-SUCCESS to argue that an industrial policy (P1) can not achieve the goal (G) of attaining economic success because only a laissez-faire policy (P2) can achieve that goal.

3.4.3. Supports Based on Analogies

Another strategy used to justify causal beliefs in editorial arguments is reasoning by analogy.[13] For example, consider the following argument by Lester Thurow (1983):

ED-MOTORCYCLES

...[A] tariff on large motorcycles ... will not give America a world-class motorcycle industry ... The American steel industry has been protected since the late 1960s and is less competitive today than it was then ...

The argument in ED-MOTORCYCLES is an instance of the following support structure:

> **S-SIMILAR-UNREALIZED-SUCCESS:** Arguer A believes that plan P1 will not achieve goal G1 because A believes that a plan P2 (similar to P1) has not achieved goal G2 (similar to G1) in the past.

Thurow uses S-SIMILAR-UNREALIZED-SUCCES to argue that an import tax will not achieve the U.S. motorcycle industry's goal of becoming competitive because similar protectionist measures have not achieved that type of goal for the U.S. steel industry. This instance of S-SIMILAR-UNREALIZED-SUCCESS is illustrated in figure 3.13.

---

[13]The approach taken in this dissertation to represent the use of analogies in editorial arguments is similar to the one proposed by August and Dyer (1985a, 1985b).

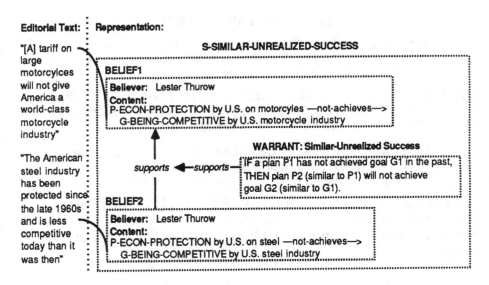

Figure 3.13. Support Relationship in ED-MOTORCYCLES.

Reasoning by analogy also serves as the basis for showing why a plan P: (1) can not achieve a goal G; (2) may achieve or thwart a goal G; or (3) may result in a negative-spiral effect. These uses of analogy are organized by the support structures shown below.

Content of Supported Belief B	Content of Justification J	Support Relationship Between B and J
P1 —not-achieves—> G1	P2 —not-achieves—> G2 P1 similar to P2 G1 similar to G2	S-SIMILAR-UNREALIZED-SUCCESS
P1 —not-thwarts—> G1	P2 —not-thwarts—> G2 P1 similar to P2 G1 similar to G2	S-SIMILAR-UNREALIZED-FAILURE
P1 —achieves—> G1	P2 —achieves—> G2 P1 similar to P2 G1 similar to G2	S-SIMILAR-SUCCESS
P1 —thwarts—> G1	P2 —thwarts—> G2 P1 similar to P2 G1 similar to G2	S-SIMILAR-FAILURE
P1 —thwarts—> G1 G1 —intends—> P2 P1 and P2 instances of P	P3 —thwarts—> G2 G2 —intends—> P4 P1 similar to P3 P2 similar to P4 G1 similar to G2	S-SIMILAR-SPIRAL-FAILURE

Table 3.5. Supports Based on Analogies.

For example, consider S-SIMILAR-SPIRAL-FAILURE. This structure embodies the following reasoning:

S-SIMILAR-SPIRAL-FAILURE: Arguer A believes that plan P1 (an instance of P) will thwart goal G1 AND G1's failure will require using P2 (another instance of P) because A believes that plan P3 (similar to P1) has thwarted goal G2 (similar to G1) in the past AND G2's failure has required using plan P4 (similar to P2).

S-SIMILAR-SPIRAL-FAILURE is used in the following segment from an editorial by Feldstein and Feldstein (1985):

ED-1930-RETALIATION

.... [A] 20% tax on imports ... could easily provoke retaliation by foreign governments ... The last major trade war [was] precipitated by our 1930 Hawley-Smoot tariff ...

Here, Feldstein and Feldstein predict the outcome of the 20% tax on imports by using a historical precedent. Specifically, their argument contain the following relationships: (1) the proposed tax on imports will thwart the goal by foreign countries of preserving earnings; (2) this goal failure will cause foreign countries to impose import restrictions on U.S. products; (3) the proposed tax is similar to the Hawley-Smoot tariff which caused trade losses for foreign countries in the 1930s; and (4) those losses caused foreign countries to impose tariffs on U.S. products. Clearly, ED-1930-RETALIATION is an instance of S-SIMILAR-SPIRAL-FAILURE.

3.4.4. Supports Based on Examples

Editorial arguments also involve the use of reasoning by example. According to this strategy, a generalization about a plan-goal relationship can be justified by presenting a prototypical instance of such a relationship. For example, consider the following excerpt from an editorial by Carl Green (1985):

ED-PUNISHMENT

... The United States can [not] inflict punishment on the Japanese by restricting imports on their manufactured products ... We have restricted imports of Japanese automobiles ... since 1981 ... But who was hurt? Certainly not the Japanese ...

At the abstract level, Green's argument is described by the following support structure:

S-PROTOTYPICAL-UNREALIZED-SUCCESS: Arguer A believes that plan P will not achieve goal G because A believes that P1 (a prototype of P) has not achieved G1 (a prototype of G) in the past.

Green uses the above structure to argue that import restrictions can not achieve the goal of lowering Japan's export earnings.[14] This generalization is justified by Green's belief that prototypic restrictions, such as those on Japanese cars, have not lowered Japan's auto export earnings. The representation of Green's argument is illustrated in figure 3.14.

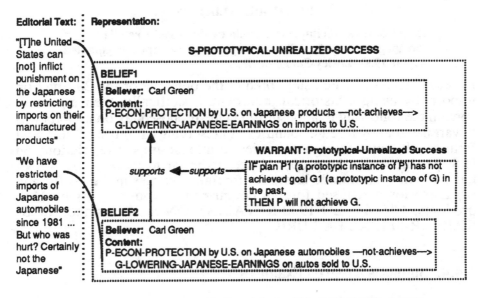

Figure 3.14. Support Relationship in ED-PUNISHMENT.

In addition to the above support structure, an arguer can also provide examples in order to justify generalizations about goal achievements, goal failures, unrealized goal failures, and negative spiral failures. These justifications are summarized below.

---

[14]In ED-PUNISHMENT, the phrase "inflict punishment" stands for the relationship of implementing a plan P to attain a state S which thwarts a preservation goal G. Within the context of international trade, P corresponds to import restrictions by an importing country, S to a decrease in earnings of an exporting country, and G to the exporting country's goal of preserving earnings.

Content of Supported Belief B	Content of Justification J	Support Relationship Between B and J
P —not-achieves—> G	P1 —not-achieves—> G1 P1 prototypic instance of P G1 prototypic instance of G	S-PROTOTYPICAL-UNREALIZED-SUCCESS
P —not-thwarts—> G	P2 —not-thwarts—> G2 P1 prototypic instance of P G1 prototypic instance of G	S-PROTOTYPICAL-UNREALIZED-FAILURE
P —achieves—> G	P1 —achieves—> G1 P1 prototypic instance of P G1 prototypic instance of G	S-PROTOTYPICAL-SUCCESS
P —thwarts—> G	P1 —thwarts—> G1 P1 prototypic instance of P G1 prototypic instance of G	S-PROTOTYPICAL-FAILURE
P1 —thwarts—> G1 G1 —intends—> P2 P1 and P2 instances of P	P3 —thwarts—> G2 G2 —intends—> P4 P3 prototypic instance of P1 P4 prototypic instance of P2 G2 prototypic instance of G1	S-PROTOTYPICAL-SPIRAL-FAILURE

Table 3.6. Supports Based on Examples.

For instance, consider following editorial segment by Lance Morrow (1983):

ED-SMOOT-HAWLEY

... What is wrong with protectionism? ... The famous Smoot-Hawley Tariff Act of 1930 set up the highest general tariff rate structure that the U.S. had ever had. One nation after another retaliated ...

Here, Morrow uses the precedent set by the Smoot-Hawley Tariff to justify his implicitly stated generalization that protectionist measures cause foreign countries to retaliate. Morrow's argument is an instance of S-PROTOTYPICAL-SPIRAL-FAILURE, which shows that a plan P will result in a negative-spiral failure if a prototypic instance of P has caused a prototypic instance of such a failure in the past.

3.5.   Summary

This chapter has presented OpEd's representational system for beliefs, attack relationships, and support relationships. The concepts described here are the basic building blocks organized by argument units in editorials. Six major points have been emphasized:

1) Every belief consists of a belief holder, the content of the belief, and links representing relationships of support or attack.

2) The content of a belief corresponds to an evaluative component, a causal relationship, or a reasoning script.

3) Evaluative components categorize plans in terms of the possible goal achievements and goal failures resulting from those plans.

4) An attack is a relationship between two beliefs whose contents involve mutually-exclusive planning situations or opposite effects of a plan on interrelated goals.

5) A support is a relationship that consists of a belief, the justification for the belief, and a warrant that connects the belief to its justification.

6) Belief justifications are based on refinements of plan evaluations, refinements of plan-goal relationships, analogies, or examples.

Chapter 4

Argument Units

4.1. Introduction

In previous chapters, it was shown that OpEd needs a model of the politico-economic domain and a model of belief relationships in order to build an editorial's argument graph. In addition to those sources of knowledge, OpEd must also know how attack and support relationships are combined to argue against an opponent. This abstract knowledge of argument structure is fundamental to the comprehension process because one-sided arguments in editorials are not instances of single attack or support relationships, but rather configurations of such relationships. Those configurations allow editorial writers to: (1) show awareness of their opponents' beliefs; (2) contradict their opponent's beliefs; and (3) provide justifications for their own beliefs.

To illustrate the importance of modeling abstract knowledge of argument structure, consider the following excerpt from an editorial by the Los Angeles Times (1984, June 14):

ED-TRADE-BARRIERS

... [M]oves to build new barriers to steel imports are [not] ... in the national interest. The International Trade Commission ... says that ... steel imports are the ... cause of ... injury to the American industry, and will offer remedies next month ... But to erect ... [trade] barriers would be a regressive step ... punishing consumers by imposing higher prices ... The jobs that tariffs and quotas may

> preserve ... are less significant than the jobs related to [American] exports ... that are imperiled by protectionism ... America invites declining economic health when it retreats behind ... trade barriers ...

Understanding ED-TRADE-BARRIERS requires representing two arguments which contain opposite views by the L.A. Times and the International Trade Commission (ITC):

Argument 1: The L.A. Times opposes the ITC's position that restrictions on steel imports are needed to protect the U.S. steel industry against foreign competition. The L.A. Times argues that import restrictions would punish consumers by imposing higher prices.

Argument 2: The L.A. Times opposes the ITC's position that restrictions on steel imports are needed to save jobs in the U.S. steel industry. The L.A. Times argues that import restrictions would cause a decline of U.S. export industries' health and, consequently, cost more jobs than it would save.

Each of the above arguments is composed of instances of several support (S) and attack (A) relationships. For example, argument 1 contains the following relationships:

- S-REALIZED-SUCCESS: The ITC believes that import restrictions should be used because they will help the steel industry preserve its level of earnings.

- A-OBJECTIONABLE-PLAN: The ITC's belief that import restrictions should be used is contradicted by the L.A. Times' belief that restrictions should not be used.

- S-EQUIVALENT-FAILURE: The L.A. Times believes that import restrictions should not be used because they will cause a decrease in consumer earnings.

- A-EQUIVALENT-FAILURE: The ITC's belief that import restrictions will help the steel industry preserve its level of earnings is contradicted by the L.A. Times' belief that restrictions will cause a decrease in consumer earnings.

- S-POSSIBLE-FAILURE: The L.A. Times believes that import restrictions will cause a decrease in consumer earnings because they will result in higher prices.

In contrast, argument 2 consists of the following relationships:

- **S-REALIZED-SUCCESS:** The ITC believes that import restrictions should be used because they will help preserve jobs in the steel industry.

- **A-OBJECTIONABLE-PLAN:** The ITC's belief that import restrictions should be used is contradicted by the L.A. Times' belief that restrictions should not be used.

- **S-GREATER-FAILURE:** The L.A. Times believes that import restrictions should not be used because they will cause a decrease in export jobs greater than the number of steel jobs saved.

- **A-GREATER-FAILURE:** The ITC's belief that import restrictions will help preserve jobs in the steel industry is contradicted by the L.A. Times' belief that restrictions will cause a decrease in export jobs.

- **S-POSSIBLE-FAILURE:** The L.A. Times believes that import restrictions will cause a decrease in export jobs because they will result in lower export earnings.

As the arguments in ED-TRADE-BARRIERS show, editorial writers may contrast their views against those held by their opponent's by using different configurations of attack and support relationships. For instance, the argument that "plan P should be implemented because P will achieve goal G1" can be opposed by stating that "P should not be used because P will result in a state S which will cause the failure of a higher level goal G2." Similarly, the argument that "a plan P should not be implemented because P will thwart goal G1" can be opposed by stating that "P should be implemented because P will result in state S which will cause the success of a higher level goal G2." Clearly, computer comprehension of editorials requires a model of abstract knowledge of argument structure.

In OpEd, configurations of attack and support relationships are represented in terms of memory structures called *argument units (AUs)* (Alvarado et al., 1985a, 1985b, 1985c, 1986, in press). When combined with domain-specific knowledge, AUs can be used to refute an opponent's argument about a plan on the basis of goal achievements and goal failures. As a result, a major task of the comprehension process in OpEd involves recognizing, accessing, instantiating, and applying AUs. This chapter presents a taxonomy of AUs which consists of a detailed description of the possible configurations of attack and support relationships. The chapter also discusses the language-independent and domain-independent nature of AUs, and illustrates their use within the framework of editorials dealing with politico-economic conflicts.

4.2.   Taxonomy of Argument Units

AUs provide a system for representing one-sided arguments about the use of plans. Such arguments are centered on two contradictory plan evaluations espoused by an arguer and the arguer's implicit opponent.[15] Each one-sided argument is represented by an AU composed of six major elements: (1) opponent's plan evaluation; (2) arguer's attack on opponent's plan evaluation; (3) arguer's justification for the attack on opponent's plan evaluation; (4) opponent's justification for his/her plan evaluation; (5) arguer's attack on opponent's justification; and (6) arguer's justification for the attack on opponent's justification. According to the nature of the arguer's attacks and justifications, four basic types of AUs have been characterized: unrealized success, realized failure, realized success, and unrealized failure.

4.2.1. Argument Units Based on Unrealized Successes

In order to rebut the argument that "a plan P should be implemented because P will achieve goal G," an arguer may use the following two-step strategy: (1) show that P will not achieve G; and (2) use that negative-achievement relationship as the reason to claim that P should not be implemented. This argumentation strategy, termed unrealized success, is the basis for five AUs summarized in table 4.1 and described below.

---

[15]One-sided arguments about the use of plans belong to a larger class of arguments termed *adversary arguments* (Flowers et al., 1982), in which arguers intend to remain adversaries and present their views for the judgement of an audience.

Opponent's Plan Evaluation and Justification	Arguer's Plan Evaluation and Justification	Arguer's Attack on Opponent's Justification and Arguer's Justification for the Attack	Argument Unit
OUGHT-TO (P) because G —intend—> P P —achieve—> G	OUGHT-NOT-TO (P) because G —intend—> P P —not-achieve—> G	P —not-achieve—> G, at time t because P —thwart—> G, at t	AU-OPPOSITE-EFFECT
		P —not-achieve—> G, at time t because S1 —thwart—> G, at t P —not-cause—> S2, at t S2 opposite of S1	AU-ACTUAL-CAUSE
		P —not-achieve—> G, at time t because only P1 —achieve—> G, at t P opposite of P1	AU-WRONG-SOLUTION
		P —not-achieve—> G, at time t because P1 —not-achieve—> G1, at t1<t P similar to P1 G similar to G1	AU-SIMILAR- UNREALIZED- SUCCESS
		P —not-achieve—> G, at time t because P1 —not-achieve—> G1, at t1<t P1 prototypic intance of P G1 prototypic instance of G	AU-PROTOTYPICAL- UNREALIZED- SUCCESS

Table 4.1. Argument Units Based on Unrealized Successes.

AU-OPPOSITE-EFFECT

AU-OPPOSITE-EFFECT is used to represent one-sided arguments in which an arguer opposes a plan P on the basis that P will thwart the goal G which has intended P. At the abstract level, those arguments can be stated as follows:

AU-OPPOSITE-EFFECT: Although opponent O believes that plan P should be used because P will achieve goal G, arguer A believes that P will not achieve G because P will thwart G. Therefore, A believes that P should not be used.

To illustrate this AU, consider Milton Friedman's argument in ED-JOBS, one of the editorial segments processed by OpEd (chapter 1, page 3):

Recent protectionist measures by the Reagan administration have disappointed us. Voluntary limits on Japanese automobiles and voluntary limits on steel by the Common Market are bad for the

> nation ... **Far from saving jobs, the limitations on imports will
> cost jobs ...**

In ED-JOBS, Friedman argues that import restrictions should not be
used because, contrary to the Reagan administration's beliefs, such
restrictions will not achieve the goal of preserving U.S. jobs but will
thwart it. Friedman's argument is an instance of AU-OPPOSITE-
EFFECT, as shown in figure 4.1.

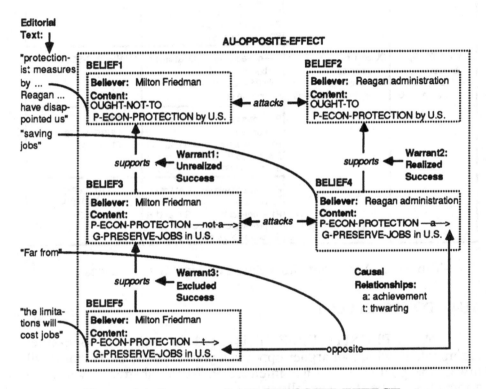

Figure 4.1. Instance of AU-OPPOSITE-EFFECT.

As indicated by the above diagram, AU-OPPOSITE-EFFECT
contains the following support and attack relationships:

- S-REALIZED-SUCCESS: Opponent O believes that plan P
  should be used because O believes that P will achieve the goal
  G which has intended P.

- A-OBJECTIONABLE-PLAN: Although opponent O believes
  plan P should be used, arguer A believes P should not be
  used.

- S-UNREALIZED-SUCCESS: Arguer A believes that plan P should not be used because A believes that P will not achieve goal G

- A-UNREALIZED-SUCCESS: Although opponent O believes plan P will achieve goal G, arguer A believes P will not achieve G.

- S-EXCLUDED-SUCCESS: Arguer A believes plan P will not achieve goal G because A believes that P will thwart G.

In addition to the above relationships, AU-OPPOSITE-EFFECT contains a declarative relationship of opposition between expected effects of a plan P on a goal G, namely: P-achieves->G and P-thwarts->G. In ED-JOBS, this relationship is signaled by the construct:

"Far from" X, Y

where the phrase "far from" indicates opposition and the elements X and Y refer to opposite effects (e.g., saving jobs and costing jobs).

AU-ACTUAL-CAUSE

Consider the following excerpt from ED-JOBS in which Friedman provides another reason to oppose the Reagan administration's use of import restrictions:

> **Recent protectionist measures by the Reagan administration have disappointed us. Voluntary limits on Japanese automobiles and voluntary limits on steel by the Common Market ... do not promote the long-run health of the industries affected. The problem of the automobile and steel industries is: in both industries, average wage rates are twice as high as the average ...**

Friedman's argument is an instance of the following argument unit:

> **AU-ACTUAL-CAUSE:** Although opponent O believes that plan P should be used because P will achieve goal G, arguer A believes that P will not achieve G because G is being thwarted by state S1 AND P can not result in S2, the opposite of S1. Therefore, A believes that P should not be used.

Friedman uses the above structure to oppose the Reagan administration's implicitly stated position that import quotas are needed to help domestic industries become profitable. Friedman argues that import quotas can not achieve the goal of attaining profitability because: (1) that goal is being thwarted by the high salaries paid to U.S. workers;

and (2) implementing import restrictions does not decrease the level of salaries in the industries being protected. That is, Friedman believes that import restrictions will not work because the actual cause of the American industries' problems is not foreign competition but high salaries. The representation of Friedman's argument is illustrated in figure 4.2.

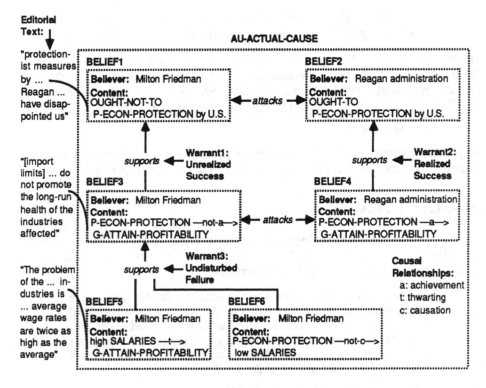

Figure 4.2. Instance of AU-ACTUAL-CAUSE.

In the domain of international trade, AU-ACTUAL-CAUSE is also used to represent rebuttals to the protectionist argument that import restrictions can save (or create) jobs. For example, consider the following excerpt from an editorial by the Los Angeles Times (1984a, December 26):

ED-ROBOTS

Those quotas on Japanese car imports that were adopted ... in 1981 are now nearing the end of their fourth year ... What has been gained? Certainly not the jobs that exponents of import restrictions once promised ... The case made for quotas four years ago was that

> they would create jobs. In fact, very few jobs have been created.
> Instead, the industry is spending more and more on robots ... rather
> than ... hiring any significant number of workers ... The quota
> system ... ought not to be extended.

In ED-ROBOTS, the L.A. Times attacks those who have endorsed car
quotas as means to create jobs in the U.S. auto industry. The L.A.
Times argues that the quotas should not be continued because: (1) an
increase in assembly-line robots has decreased jobs in car factories; and
(2) car quotas can not affect the level of automation of factories and,
consequently, can not restore the jobs lost in those factories. Clearly,
ED-ROBOTS is an instance of AU-ACTUAL-CAUSE.

AU-WRONG-SOLUTION

Another AU involving unrealized goal achievements is AU-
WRONG-SOLUTION:

> **AU-WRONG-SOLUTION:** Although opponent O believes
> that plan P should be used because P will achieve goal G,
> arguer A believes that P will not achieve G because G can
> only be achieved by plan P1, the opposite of P. Therefore, A
> believes that P should not be used.

This AU is illustrated by the following fragment of the L.A. Times'
argument in ED-CONTRADICTORY-POLICIES (chapter 3, section
3.1):

> American negotiators are pursuing a protectionist course in efforts
> to control steel imports, ... in what seems a vain effort to protect
> U.S. steel makers ... This is the wrong way to go ... The
> American steel industry ... will be cushioned from the economic
> forces that alone ... hold the hope of restoring ... competitiveness
> ...

Here, the L.A. Times argues that imposing import restrictions is the
wrong solution to the problem of turning the U.S. steel industry into a
competitive industry. The L.A. Times' justification is that
competitiveness can only be attained by a policy of non-intervention in
international markets, i.e., a laissez-faire policy. Since this policy is the
opposite of imposing import controls, then the L.A. Times argument
can be represented in terms of AU-WRONG-SOLUTION. This
representation is shown in figure 4.3.

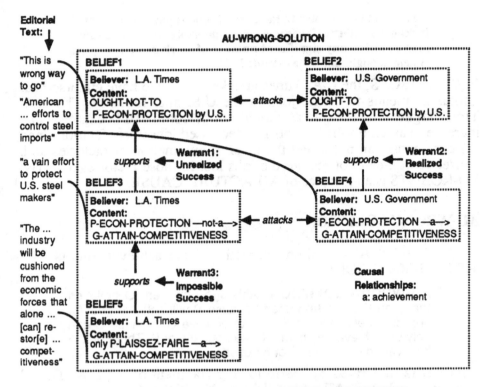

Figure 4.3. Instance of AU-WRONG-SOLUTION.

AU-SIMILAR-UNREALIZED-SUCCESS

AU-SIMILAR-UNREALIZED-SUCCESS characterizes arguments in which the effects of a plan P1 serve as the basis to justify why a similar plan P will not work:

AU-SIMILAR-UNREALIZED-SUCCESS: Although opponent O believes that plan P should be used because P will achieve goal G, arguer A believes that P will not achieve G because plan P1 (similar to P) has not achieved goal G1 (similar to G) in the past. Therefore, A believes that P should not be used.

For example, consider the following excerpt from an editorial by Lester Thurow (1983):

ED-HARLEY-DAVIDSON

... [A] tariff on large motorcycles ... will not give America a world-class motorcycle industry. And if a world-class ... industry is

not ... [achieved], we should not have ... [an] industrial policy ...
for motorcycles ... Harley-Davidson [the only U.S. producer]
argues that it needs time to become competitive ... But ... [t]he
American steel industry has been protected since the late 1960s and
is less competitive today than it was then ...

Thurow's argument is an instance of AU-SIMILAR-UNREALIZED-
SUCCESS, as shown in the figure below.

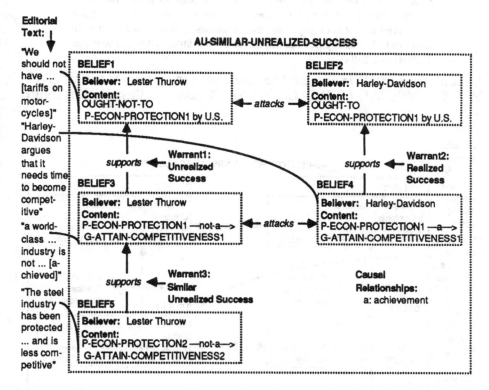

Figure 4.4. Instance of AU-SIMILAR-UNREALIZED-SUCCESS.

As figure 4.4 indicates, Thurow's refutation to Harley-
Davidson's argument is based on the historical precedent set by
restrictions on steel imports. Specifically, Thurow's argument contains
the following relationships: (1) import restrictions have been used in the
past to help the U.S. steel industry become competitive; (2) those
restrictions did not work for the steel industry; (3) the proposed tariff on
large motorcycles is similar to the import restrictions used to protect the
steel industry; and (4) the proposed tariff will also fail to help Harley-
Davidson become competitive.

AU-PROTOTYPICAL-UNREALIZED-SUCCESS

Consider the following editorial segment in which Carl Green (1985) refutes an argument to favor restrictions on Japanese imports:

ED-WRONG-PUNISHMENT

... Many senators ... believe that the United States can inflict punishment on the Japanese by restricting imports on their manufactured products. Yet experience suggests otherwise: We have restricted imports of Japanese automobiles ... since 1981. But who was hurt? Certainly not the Japanese ... [Declaring] a trade war [on Japan] is a folly ...

Green's rebuttal involves the use of the argument unit AU-PROTOTYPICAL-UNREALIZED-SUCCESS, as illustrated in figure 4.5.

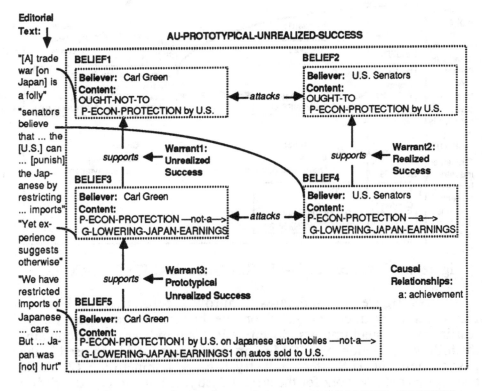

Figure 4.5. Instance of AU-PROTOTYPICAL-UNREALIZED-SUCCESS.

As the previous diagram shows, AU-PROTOTYPICAL-UNREALIZED-SUCCESS captures the use of counterexamples to refute generalizations about plan-goal relationships. At the abstract level, those rebuttals can be stated as follows:

> **AU-PROTOTYPICAL-UNREALIZED-SUCCESS**: Although opponent O believes plan that P should be used because P will achieve goal G, arguer A believes that P will not achieve G because P1 (a prototype of P) has not achieved G1 (a prototype of G) in the past. Therefore, A believes P should not be used.

In ED-WRONG-PUNISHMENT, Green uses the above AU by bringing up the case of the quotas on Japanese cars and their failure to achieve the goal of lowering Japan's car export earnings. By referring to that prototypic case, Green can show that: (1) the U.S. senators are wrong in believing that import restrictions on Japanese products will lower Japan's export earnings; and (2) restrictions on Japanese imports should not be implemented.

4.2.2. Argument Units Based on Realized Failures

Another way to rebut an opponent's argument for endorsing a plan P is by showing that P causes negative side-effects which can not be outweighed by P's benefits. Three types of negative side-effects can be distinguished here: (1) major-goal failures; (2) equivalent-goal failures; and (3) negative-spiral failures.

Rebuttals Based on Major-Goal Failures

Consider again one of the L.A. Times' arguments in ED-TRADE-BARRIERS:

> ... [M]oves to build new barriers to steel imports are [not] ... in the national interest. The International Trade Commission ... says that ... steel imports are the ... cause of ... injury to the American industry, and will offer remedies next month ... The jobs that tariffs and quotas may preserve ... are less significant than the jobs related to [American] exports ... that are imperiled by protectionism ... America invites declining economic health when it retreats behind ... trade barriers ...

The above argument is centered on the belief that imposing import restrictions costs more jobs than it saves. As such, the L.A. Times' argument is an instance of the following argument unit:

> **AU-MAJOR-FAILURE**: Although opponent O believes that plan P should be used because P will achieve goal G, arguer A believes that P will thwart a more important goal G1 because P causes state S1 AND S1 causes ... state Sn AND Sn thwarts G1. Therefore, A believes P should not be used.

The instance of AU-MAJOR-FAILURE in ED-TRADE-BARRIERS contains the following relationships: (1) the ITC believes that import restrictions should be used because they will achieve the goal of preserving jobs in the steel industry; (2) the L.A. Times believes that import restrictions should not be used because they will save steel jobs at the expense of a greater number of export jobs; and (3) the L.A. Times believes that export jobs will be lost because import restrictions will result in a decrease in the level of earnings of export industries. The representation of the L.A. Times' argument is illustrated in figure 4.6.

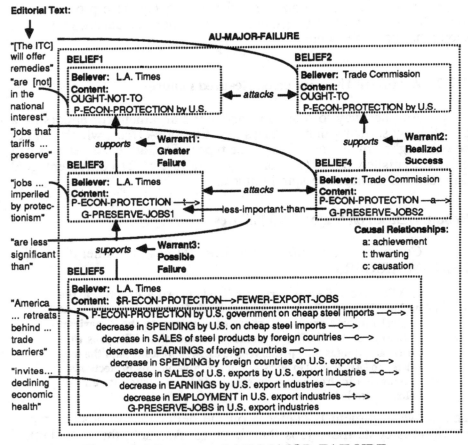

Figure 4.6. Instance of AU-MAJOR-FAILURE.

As the above figure indicates, instances of AUs may organize belief justifications based on chains of causal effects. At the level of domain knowledge, those justifications correspond to instances of reasoning scripts. For example, the L.A. Times' argument about jobs losses contains an instance of $R-ECON-PROTECTION—>FEWER-EXPORT-JOBS.

Rebuttals Based on Equivalent-Goal Failures

Another argument unit involving goal-failure rebuttals is AU-EQUIVALENCE. This AU is centered on the belief that a plan P may lead to the failure of a goal G1 equally important (or equivalent) to the goal G which has intended P:

> **AU-EQUIVALENCE**: Although opponent O believes that plan P should be used because P will achieve goal G, arguer A believes that P will thwart an equally important goal G1 because P causes state S1 AND S1 causes ... state Sn AND Sn thwarts G1. Therefore, A believes P should not be used.

To illustrate AU-EQUIVALENCE, consider an excerpt from another editorial by the L.A. Times (1985, October 4):

ED-TEXTILE-BILL

... [P]roposed legislation to limit textile and apparel imports ..., now moving ahead in both House and Senate, is ... [a] dangerous piece of legislation ... The ... bill would impos[e] on American consumers price increases for clothing and textiles ... [T]he nation ... will [not] be well served by protection that would ... burden American consumers.

In ED-TEXTILE-BILL, the L.A. Times opposes Congress' implicitly stated position that import limits are needed to achieve the goal of preserving earnings for the textile and apparel industries. The L.A. Times argues that the proposed legislation is a bad idea because: (1) it will shift consumer spending from cheap imports to expensive domestic products; (2) this shift in spending will cause a decrease in consumer's earnings; and (3) preserving consumer earnings is as important as preserving earnings of domestic industries. Clearly, ED-TEXTILE-BILL can be represented in terms of AU-EQUIVALENCE, as illustrated in figure 4.7.

Editorial Text:

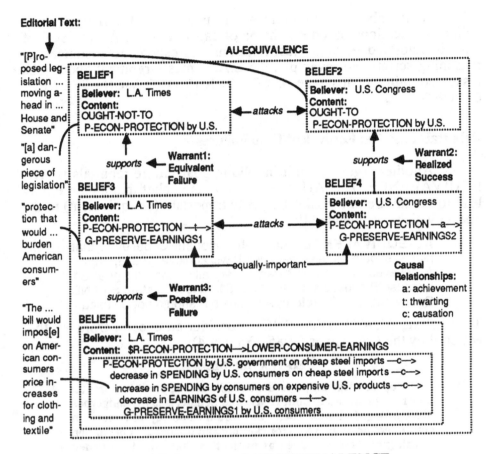

Figure 4.7. Instance of AU-EQUIVALENCE.

Rebuttals Based on Negative-Spiral Failures

An arguer can also refute an opponent's endorsement of a plan P by showing that P may cause goal failures that require repeated applications of P. For example, consider a fragment of Lance Morrow's argument in ED-RESTRICTIONS, one of the editorial segments processed by OpEd (chapter 1, page 15):

> ... American ... toolmakers argue that restrictions on imports must be imposed so that the industry can survive. It is a wrongheaded argument. Restrictions on imports would mean that American manufacturers would have to make do with more expensive American machine tools. Inevitably, those American manufacturers

**would produce more expensive products. They would lose sales.
Then those manufacturers would demand protection ...**

The above excerpt is an instance of AU-SPIRAL-EFFECT, as indicated in figure 4.8.

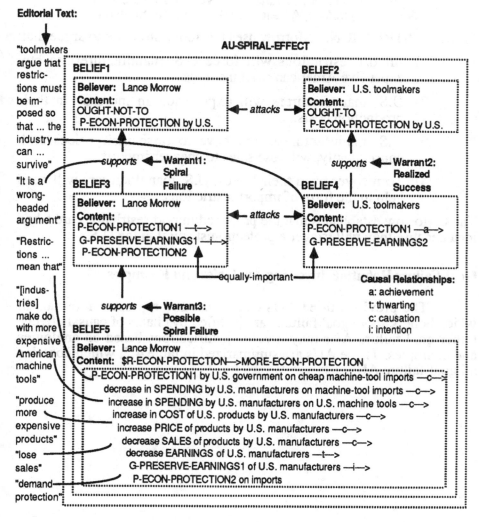

Figure 4.8. Instance of AU-SPIRAL-EFFECT.

As figure 4.8 shows, AU-SPIRAL-EFFECT organizes the following abstract configuration of attack and support relationships:

AU-SPIRAL-EFFECT: Although opponent O believes that P1 (an instance of plan P) should be used because P1 will achieve goal G, arguer A believes that P1 will thwart an equally important goal G1 which will intend P2 (another instance of P) because P1 causes state S1 AND S1 causes ... state Sn AND Sn thwarts G1 AND G1's failure requires using P2. Therefore, A believes P1 should not be used.

In ED-RESTRICTIONS, Morrow uses the above structure to argue that:

1) Import restrictions will force U.S. manufacturers to buy expensive American machine tools.

2) U.S. manufacturers will experience an increase in their production costs.

3) U.S. manufacturers will have to raise their prices and, consequently, will lose sales to cheaper imports.

4) To recover from their losses, U.S. manufacturers will need help in the form of import restrictions.

Thus, Morrow establishes that the proposed import restrictions are a bad idea because they will trigger a protectionist spiral in the U.S.

Goal-Failure Rebuttals Involving Analogies and Examples

The previous three AUs can be used to represent rebuttals in which beliefs about goal failures are justified by chains of causal effects. Other goal-failure AUs may involve justifications based on analogies and examples. Those AUs are summarized in table 4.2, which contains all goal-failure AUs.

Opponent's Plan Evaluation and Justification	Arguer's Plan Evaluation and Justification	Arguer's Attack on Opponent's Justification and Arguer's Justification for the Attack	Argument Unit
OUGHT-TO (P) because G1 —intend—> P P —achieve—> G1	OUGHT-NOT-TO (P) because G1 —intend—> P, at time t P —thwart—> G, at t2>t G1 less important than G	P —thwart—> G, at t2 because P —cause—> S, at t1>t S —thwart—> G, at t2>t1	AU-MAJOR-FAILURE
		P —thwart—> G, at t2 because P2 —thwart—> G2, t1<t P similar to P2 G similar to G2	AU-SIMILAR-MAJOR-FAILURE
		P —thwart—> G, at t2 because P2 —thwart—> G2, t1<t P2 prototypic intance of P G2 prototypic instance of G	AU-PROTOTYPICAL-MAJOR-FAILURE
OUGHT-TO (P) because G1 —intend—> P P —achieve—> G1	OUGHT-NOT-TO (P) because G1 —intend—> P, at time t P —thwart—> G, at t2>t G as important as G1	P —thwart—> G, at t2 because P —cause—> S, at t1>t S —thwart—> G, at t2>t1	AU-EQUIVALENCE
		P —thwart—> G, at t2 because P2 —thwart—> G2, t1<t P similar to P2 G similar to G2	AU-SIMILAR-EQUIVALENCE
		P —thwart—> G, at t2 because P2 —thwart—> G2, t1<t P2 prototypic intance of P G2 prototypic instance of G	AU-PROTOTYPICAL-EQUIVALENCE
OUGHT-TO (P1) because G —intend—> P1 P1 —achieve—> G1	OUGHT-NOT-TO (P1) because G —intend—> P1, at time t P1 —thwart—> G1, at t1>t G1 —intend—> P2, at t2>t1 G as important as G1 P1 instance of P P2 instance of P	P1 —thwart—> G1, at t1>t G1 —intend—> P2, at t2>t1 because P1 —cause—> S, at t0>t S —thwart—> G1, at t1>t0 G1 —intend—> P2, at t2>t1	AU-SPIRAL-EFFECT
		P1 —thwart—> G1, at t1>t G1 —intend—> P2, at t2>t1 because P3 —thwart—> G2, at t3<t4 G2 —intend—> P4, at t4<t P1 similar to P3 P2 similar to P4 G1 similar to G2	AU-SIMILAR-SPIRAL
		P1 —thwart—> G1, at t1>t G1 —intend—> P2, at t2>t1 because P3 —thwart—> G2, at t3<t4 G2 —intend—> P4, at t4<t P3 prototypic instance of P1 P4 prototypic instance of P2 G2 prototypic instance of G1	AU-PROTOTYPICAL-SPIRAL

Table 4.2. Argument Units Based on Realized Failures.

As an example of a goal-failure AU involving analogy-based justifications, consider AU-SIMILAR-SPIRAL. An arguer A1 uses AU-SIMILAR-SPIRAL when A1 states "although A2 believes plan P should be implemented to achieve goal G1, A1 believes that P should not be implemented because a similar plan P1 has caused a negative-spiral failure in the past." This abstract argument is instantiated in the following editorial segment by Feldstein and Feldstein (1985):

ED-TRADE-DEFICIT

... [A] direct approach to limiting the trade deficit by an import surcharge is ... dangerous. The 20% tax on imports that has been proposed in Congress ... could easily provoke retaliation by foreign governments ... The last major trade war [was] precipitated by our 1930 Hawley-Smoot tariff ...

In ED-TRADE-DEFICIT, Feldstein and Feldstein oppose Congress' proposal for an import tax because they believe that it will trigger a trade war just like the Hawley-Smoot tariff did in the 1930s. Clearly, ED-TRADE-DEFICIT is an instance of AU-SIMILAR-SPIRAL.

The use of examples in failure-based rebuttals is illustrated in the following editorial segment by Carl Green (1985):

ED-WRONG-VICTIM

... Many senators ... believe that the United States can inflict punishment on the Japanese by restricting imports on their manufactured products. But ... [the real victim of] restricted imports of Japanese automobiles ... was the American consumer ... [Declaring] a trade war [on Japan] is a folly ...

At the abstract level, ED-WRONG-VICTIM is characterized by the argument unit AU-PROTOTYPICAL-EQUIVALENCE:

AU-PROTOTYPICAL-EQUIVALENCE: Although opponent O believes that plan P should be used because P will achieve goal G1, arguer A believes that P will thwart an equally important goal G because P2 (a prototype of P) has thwarted G2 (a prototype of G) in the past. Therefore, A believes P should not be used.

The instance of the above structure in ED-WRONG-VICTIM contains the following beliefs by Carl Green: (1) restrictions on imports from Japan will thwart the goal of preserving consumer earnings; (2) preserving consumer earnings is as important as lowering Japan's export earnings; and (3) prototypic restrictions on Japanese automobiles have thwarted consumer earnings in the past. Thus, by presenting the negative side-effects of the car quotas, Green can refute the U.S.

senators' argument that import restrictions should be used to lower Japan's export earnings.

4.2.3. Argument Units Based on Realized Successes

Editorials may also involve rebuttals to the argument that "plan P should not be used because P will not achieve the goal G which intended P." In those rebuttals, an editorial writer may use cause-effect chains, analogies, or examples in order to demonstrate that P will achieve G. For instance, consider Lee Iacocca's (1986) response to the U.S. government's position on import restrictions:

ED-FORGOTTEN-JOBS

... A job is a ... commitment ... involving ... the government ... [T]hat's why Japanese trade policies ... [k]eep unemployment rate so low that it's even tough to measure. But the people making our trade policies ... seem to believe that [American] jobs can take care of themselves ... It's time to ... [start] getting tough on trade ...

Iacocca's argument is an instance of AU-SIMILAR-SUCCESS:

AU-SIMILAR-SUCCESS: Although opponent O believes that plan P should not be used because P will not achieve goal G, arguer A believes that P will achieve G because plan P1 (similar to P) has achieved goal G1 (similar to G) in the past. Therefore, A believes that P should be used.

Iacocca uses the above structure to present a counteranalogy to the U.S. policy maker's argument that imposing import restrictions will not save U.S. jobs. Iacocca argues that import restrictions should be imposed because: (1) Japan has imposed import restrictions in the past; (2) those restrictions have saved Japanese jobs; and (3) similar restrictions by the U.S. will also save U.S. jobs. The representation of Iacocca's argument is shown below.

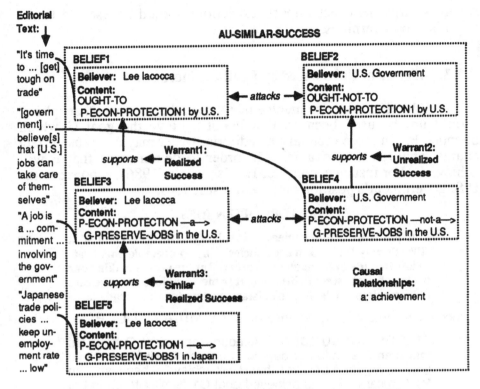

Figure 4.9. Instance of AU-SIMILAR-SUCCESS.

An arguer can also bring up the major-goal achievements resulting from a plan P to rebut the argument that "P should not be used because P will lead to a goal failure." This argumentation strategy is the basis for three of the AUs summarized in table 4.3.

Opponent's Plan Evaluation and Justification	Arguer's Plan Evaluation and Justification	Arguer's Attack on Opponent's Justification and Arguer's Justification for the Attack	Argument Unit
		P —achieve—> G, at t2 because P —cause—> S, at t1>t S —achieve—> G, at t2>t1	AU-POSSIBLE-SUCCESS
OUGHT-NOT-TO (P) because G —intend—> P P —not-achieve—> G	OUGHT-TO (P) because G —intend—> P, at time t P —achieve—> G, at t2	P —achieve—> G, at t2 because P1 —achieve—> G1, at t1<t P similar to P1 G similar to G1	AU-SIMILAR-SUCCESS
		P —achieve—> G, at t2 because P1 —achieve—> G1, at t1<t P1 prototypic instance of P G1 prototypic instance of G	AU-PROTOTYPICAL-SUCCESS
		P —achieve—> G, at t2 because P —cause—> S, at t1>t S —thwart—> G, at t2>t1	AU-MAJOR-SUCCESS
OUGHT-NOT-TO (P) because G1 —intend—> P P —thwart—> G2 G1 less important than or equally important to G2	OUGHT-TO (P) because G —intend—> P, at t P —achieve—> G, at t2 G2 less important than G	P —achieve—> G, at t2 because P3 —achieve—> G3, at t1<t P similar to P3 G similar to G3	AU-SIMILAR-MAJOR-SUCCESS
		P —achieve—> G, at t2 because P3 —achieve—> G3, at t1<t P3 prototypic instance of P G3 prototypic instance of G	AU-PROTOTYPICAL-MAJOR-SUCCESS

Table 4.3. Argument Units Based on Realized Successes.

Table 4.3 contains the AUs that characterize success-based rebuttals. For example, consider AU-MAJOR-SUCCESS. This AU embodies the following abstract argument:

AU-MAJOR-SUCCESS: Although opponent O believes that plan P should not be used because P will thwart goal G2 more important than or equally important to G1 (one of the goals which has intended P), arguer A believes that P will achieve an even more important goal G because P causes state S1 AND S1 causes ... state Sn and Sn achieves G. Therefore, A believes that P should be used.

To illustrate the above AU, consider a liberal's argument about wage controls taken from Staebler and Ross (1965, pp. 31-33):

ED-MINIMUM-WAGE

... [Conservatives have] report[ed] ... [that] [m]inimum-wage legislation ... denie[s] [employers] the prerogative of paying their workers less than $1.25 an hour, which is ... a measure of subsistence ... [A] country as affluent as ours ... [must] include the payment of wages that permit a decent standard of living ... [S]ustaining those firms which ... [can] not meet this basic cost of human labor ... [is] far less important than insuring the working man's right to support himself and his family ... I think the country has come out way ahead ...

In ED-MINIMUM-WAGE, the conservative position is that imposing a wage control is a bad idea because it will promote better living conditions for workers at the expense of a major preservation goal, i.e., the employers' right to self determination.[16] To refute the conservative position, the liberal argues that, by increasing the standard of living,[17] wage controls also lead to the achievement of a much higher level preservation goal, namely, the worker's right to be self sufficient. Clearly, ED-MINIMUM-WAGE can be represented in terms of AU-MAJOR-SUCCESS, as shown in figure 4.10.

---

[16]See Goldman et al. (1987) for a system for representing legal relationships such as *rights*.

[17]Here, standard of living is viewed as an economic quantity which is: (1) directly proportional to the level of salaries; and (2) inversely proportional to the level of spending on services and products required for daily life.

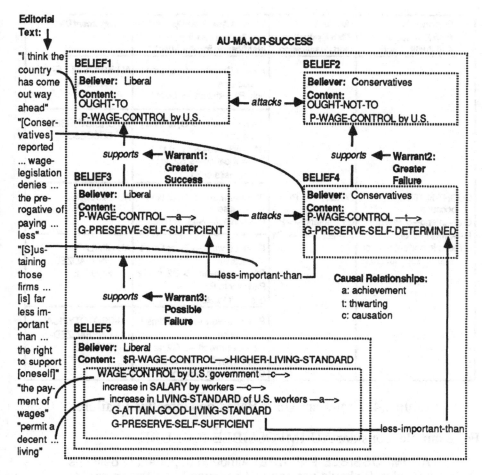

Figure 4.10. Instance of AU-MAJOR-SUCCESS.

4.2.4. Argument Units Based on Unrealized Failures

Another way to defend the use of a plan P against the claim that "P leads to goal failures" involves two steps: (1) showing that P will not cause the alleged failures; and (2) stating that P should be used because it will achieve the goal G which has intended P. This argumentation strategy, termed unrealized failure, is captured by the AUs in table 4.4.

Opponent's Plan Evaluation and Justification	Arguer's Plan Evaluation and Justification	Arguer's Attack on Opponent's Justification and Arguer's Justification for the Attack	Argument Unit
OUGHT-NOT-TO (P) because G1 —intend—> P P —thwart—> G G1 less important than or equally important to G	OUGHT-TO (P) because G1 —intend—> P P —achieve—> G1	P—not-thwart—> G, at time t because only P1 —thwart—> G, at t	AU-IMPOSSIBLE-FAILURE-
		P—not-thwart—> G, at time t because S1 —achieve—> G, at t P —not-cause—> S2, at t S2 opposite of S1	AU-UNDISTURBED-SUCCESS
		P—not-thwart—> G, at time t because P —achieve—> G, at t	AU-EXCLUDED-FAILURE
		P—not-thwart—> G, at time t because P2 —not-thwart—> G2, at t1<t P similar to P2 G similar to G2	AU-SIMILAR-UNREALIZED-FAILURE
		P—not-thwart—> G, at time t because P2 —not-thwart—> G2, at t1<t P2 prototypic instance of P G2 prototypic instance of G	AU-PROTOTYPICAL-UNREALIZED-FAILURE

Table 4.4. Argument Units Based on Unrealized Failures.

For example, consider AU-IMPOSSIBLE-FAILURE:

AU-IMPOSSIBLE-FAILURE: Although opponent O believes that plan P should not be used because P will thwart goal G more important than or equally important to G1 (the goal which has intended P), arguer A believes that P will not thwart G because G can only be thwarted by plan P1, the opposite of P. Therefore, A believes P should be used because P will achieve G1.

The above structure is illustrated by the following editorial segment from Iacocca (1986):

ED-DEFEATIST-ATTITUDE

Nothing makes me see red quicker than the defeatist attitude of some free-trade purists who say that changing America's ... trade policies would cost more jobs than it would save ... [G]etting tough on trade ... won't [cost us jobs]. But the [lack of trade-

**protection policies] ... will guarantee that we'll just keep shipping
more ... American jobs offshore.**

In ED-DEFEATIST-ATTITUDE, the affect description "see red"
indicates that Iacocca opposes the freetraders' opposition to import
restrictions. That is, Iacocca believes that import restrictions should be
used because they will achieve the goal of preserving U.S. jobs. Iacocca
further argues that import restrictions can not thwart the goal of
preserving jobs because that goal is being thwarted by the U.S. laissez-
faire policy, which is the opposite of imposing market controls. Clearly,
Iacocca's argument can be represented in terms of AU-IMPOSSIBLE-
FAILURE, as shown in figure 4.11.

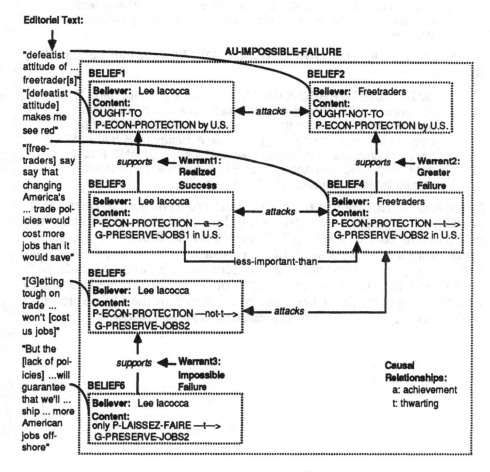

Figure 4.11. Instance of AU-IMPOSSIBLE-FAILURE.

Another argument unit from table 4.4 is AU-UNDISTURBED-SUCCESS. This AU represents rebuttals centered on the belief that a plan P will not thwart a goal G if P can not undo an existing state S1 which achieves G. For example, consider an excerpt from Spich and McKelvey (1985):

ED-ECONOMIC-DISASTER

... [F]ree-trade ... economists ... [have] raise[d] the specter of ... economic disaster ... [from] attempts to develop ... controlled access to U.S. markets ... [B]ut ... if ... the United States ... put an embargo on ... all Japanese cars in the upper half of the price range ..., [c]heap cars would still enter the U.S. ... [and] would not raise inflation ... [T]he United States ... should [use power and] approach [the trade imbalance with] the Japanese ... from a position of strength ...

At the abstract level, ED-ECONOMIC-DISASTER can be stated as follows:

AU-UNDISTURBED-SUCCESS: Although opponent O believes plan P should not be used because P will thwart goal G more important than or equally important to G1 (the goal which has intended P), arguer A believes P will not thwart G because G is being achieved by state S1 AND P can not result in S2, the opposite of S1. Therefore, A believes P should be used because P will achieve G1.

Spich and McKelvey use the above structure to refute the freetraders' position that import restrictions on Japanese cars will thwart the preservation goal of keeping U.S. prices down. Spich and McKelvey argue that the U.S. should impose restrictions on expensive cars because: (1) import restrictions will help attain a balanced trade with Japan; and (2) the proposed restrictions are not targeted to cheap Japanese imports which keep car prices down in the U.S. Spich and McKelvey's argument can be represented as shown below.

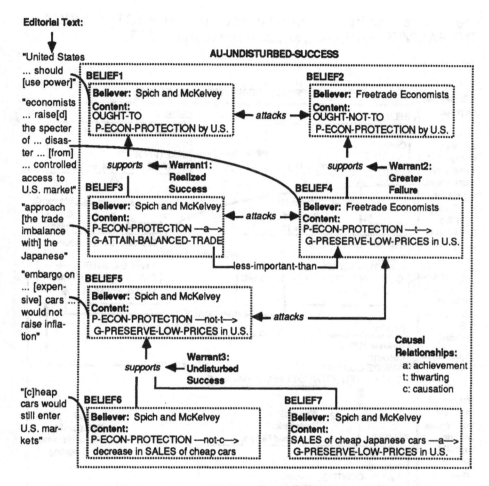

Editorial Text:

"United States ... should [use power]"

"economists ... raise[d] the specter of ... disaster ... [from] ... controlled access to U.S. market"

"approach [the trade imbalance with] the Japanese"

"embargo on ... [expensive] cars ... would not raise inflation"

"[c]heap cars would still enter U.S. markets"

AU-UNDISTURBED-SUCCESS

BELIEF1
Believer: Spich and McKelvey
Content:
OUGHT-TO
P-ECON-PROTECTION by U.S.

— *attacks* →

BELIEF2
Believer: Freetrade Economists
Content:
OUGHT-NOT-TO
P-ECON-PROTECTION by U.S.

supports ← **Warrant1: Realized Success**

supports ← **Warrant2: Greater Failure**

BELIEF3
Believer: Spich and McKelvey
Content:
P-ECON-PROTECTION —a→
G-ATTAIN-BALANCED-TRADE

— *attacks* →

BELIEF4
Believer: Freetrade Economists
Content:
P-ECON-PROTECTION —t→
G-PRESERVE-LOW-PRICES in U.S.

—less-important-than—

BELIEF5
Believer: Spich and McKelvey
Content:
P-ECON-PROTECTION —not-t→
G-PRESERVE-LOW-PRICES in U.S.

← *attacks* —

Causal Relationships:
a: achievement
t: thwarting
c: causation

supports ← **Warrant3: Undisturbed Success**

BELIEF6
Believer: Spich and McKelvey
Content:
P-ECON-PROTECTION —not-c→
decrease in SALES of cheap cars

BELIEF7
Believer: Spich and McKelvey
Content:
SALES of cheap Japanese cars —a→
G-PRESERVE-LOW-PRICES in U.S.

Figure 4.12. Instance of AU-UNDISTURBED-SUCCESS.

As a final example of rebuttals involving unrealized-goal failures, consider a liberal argument in favor of wage controls appearing in Staebler and Ross (1965, pp. 132-133):

ED-GENERAL-MOTORS

... As for ...[the conservative] charge that liberal [minimum-wage] legislation [to increase the living standard of U.S. workers] has been ... to the [great] detriment of business, it just isn't true ... [L]ook at the auto industry ... Profits are at a record high and ... there is no indication that ... [legislation] ha[s] kept GM from growing spectacularly ... Business performance and conditions have never been better. Liberals can be proud ...

The above excerpt is an instance of AU-PROTOTYPICAL-UNREALIZED-FAILURE, as illustrated in figure 4.13.

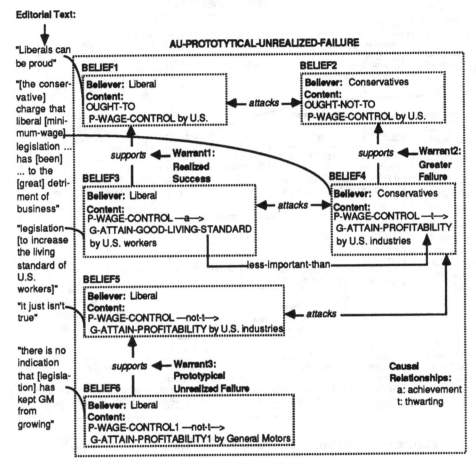

Figure 4.13. Instance of AU-PROTOTYPICAL-UNREALIZED-FAILURE.

As figure 4.13 shows, AU-PROTOTYPICAL-UNREALIZED-FAILURE embodies the following abstract argument:

> **AU-PROTOTYPICAL-UNREALIZED-FAILURE:** Although opponent O believes that plan P should not be used because P will thwart goal G more important than or equally important to G1 (the goal which has intended P), arguer A believes that P will not thwart G because P2 (a prototype of P) has not thwarted G2 (prototype of G) in the past. Therefore, A believes that P should be used because P will achieve G1.

In ED-GENERAL-MOTORS, the conservative position is that imposing wage controls is a bad idea because it thwarts businesses' goal of attaining profitability. To rebut this position, the liberal argues that: (1) wage controls help U.S. workers achieve the goal of attaining a higher standard of living; and (2) wage controls do not thwart businesses' goal of attaining profitability because that has not been the result in the prototypical case involving wage controls in General Motors. Thus, the liberal uses AU-PROTOTYPICAL-UNREALIZED-FAILURE to argue that wage controls should be continued.

4.3.   Representing Editorials With Configurations of Argument Units

The editorial segments considered so far correspond to instances of single AUs. In general, larger editorial excerpts (and editorials themselves) are composed of configurations of instantiated AUs. Two basic types of configurations can be distinguished here:

1) **Breadth-of-Support Configuration:** A one-sided argument in which two or more AUs are combined to present an arguer's evaluation of a plan from multiple perspectives.

2) **Depth-of-Support Configuration:** A one-sided argument in which an AU is concatenated with a support structure to elaborate on the goal successes or failures underlying an arguer's evaluation of a plan.

To illustrate the above configurations, consider the complete text and representation of Milton Friedman's arguments in ED-JOBS.

ED-JOBS

Recent protectionist measures by the Reagan administration have disappointed us. Voluntary limits on Japanese automobiles and voluntary limits on steel by the Common Market are bad for the nation. They do not promote the long-run health of the industries affected. The problem of the automobile and steel industries is: in both industries, average wage rates are twice as high as the average. Far from saving jobs, the limitations on imports will cost jobs. If we import less, foreign countries will earn fewer dollars. They will have less to spend on American exports. The result will be fewer jobs in export industries.

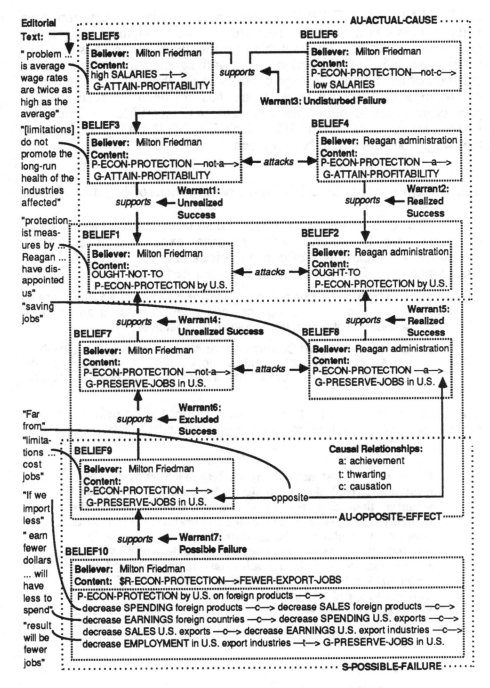

Figure 4.14. Argument Graph of ED-JOBS.

As figure 4.14 shows, ED-JOBS is composed of instances of AU-ACTUAL-CAUSE, AU-OPPOSITE-EFFECT, and S-POSSIBLE-FAILURE. These three structures form the following configurations:

- **Breadth of Support:** AU-ACTUAL-CAUSE and AU-OPPOSITE-EFFECT are combined to argue that the Reagan administration's protectionist policies are bad because they: (1) can not achieve the goal of attaining profitability for the auto and steel industries; and (2) thwart the goal of preserving U.S. jobs.

- **Depth of Support:** AU-OPPOSITE-EFFECT and S-POSSIBLE-FAILURE are combined to argue that the Reagan administration's protectionist policies are bad because they cause a decrease in U.S. export jobs and, consequently, thwart the goal of preserving U.S. jobs.

Clearly, configurations of AUs in argument graphs represent: (1) an arguer's opposition to a plan P on the basis of expected goal failures and unrealized goal successes; and (2) the arguer's reasoning on why P thwarts or fails to achieve a given goal G. Similarly, AU configurations can also represent: (1) an arguer's endorsement of a plan P on the basis of expected goal successes and unrealized goal failures; and (2) the arguer's reasoning on why P achieves or can not thwart a given goal G.

Figure 4.14 also indicates that AUs not only organize patterns of support and attack relationships in argument graphs, but also represent all the information that is implicitly stated in editorial arguments. That information includes belief contents, belief holders, and belief relationships. For example, ED-JOBS does not state explicitly: (a) Friedman's belief that import restrictions can not lower salaries in the auto and steel industries; (b) who believes that import restrictions have been implemented to save jobs; and (c) the Reagan administration's argument that import restriction should be used because they will help U.S. industries attain profitability. Thus, by representing and organizing all beliefs and belief relationships in an editorial, AUs capture the point of the editorial.

4.4.   Generality of Argument Units

In addition to organizing patterns of belief relationships in argument graphs, AUs provide a general system for representing editorials in any language or domain. That is, AU representations are based on two major axioms: (1) AUs are language independent; and (2) AUs are domain independent.[18]

4.4.1. Language-Independent Nature of Argument Units

Using AUs implies that any two editorials with the same content must be represented in the same way. For example, consider the following segments from two editorials by the Los Angeles Times:

ED-CONSUMER-ZAPPING[19]

U.S. auto manufacturers have reported record profits for 1983, an achievement that ... [can be] credit[ed] ... [to] the consumer-zapping effect ... of the quotas slapped onto Japanese car imports to the United States ... Since the "voluntary" quotas were imposed in 1981 the average retail price of all cars sold in the United States has increased ... more than the consumer price index ... The Japanese quotas were pushed hardest by the United Auto Workers union, which touted them ... as means of restoring American jobs ... What has been achieved during the period of import quotas is ... rising investment in automation ... What hasn't been achieved is any significant restoration of lost jobs ... The protectionism provided by import restrictions has proved to be a consumer punishing fiasco ... [T]he quotas ought to be ended right now.

ED-RIP-OFF[20]

... Last year the Big Three U.S. auto manufacturers had an average profit of $3,000 on each car that they sold ... But profits that are hyped by ... restraints on [Japanese] competition can reasonably be regarded as a rip-off of consumers ... The ... United Auto Workers union was the main proponent of slapping quotas on Japanese cars, figuring that it would be a sure way to restore jobs ... [F]ew jobs have in fact been reclaimed during the quota period, and more in fact are destined to be lost ... to robots on the assembly line ... What it comes down is that ... [t]he job picture has not improved under the quotas. But consumers ... have been forced to pay extraordinarily high prices for [new cars] ... [T]he quotas ought to be ... end[ed] ...

---

[18]These axioms embody basic meaning-representation requirements proposed by Schank (1973, 1975) and underlying Schank's theory of Conceptual Dependency.
[19]Los Angeles Times (1984, February 16).
[20]Los Angeles Times (1984, March 19).

It is obvious that the content of ED-RIP-OFF is identical to the content of ED-CONSUMER-ZAPPING. In both editorials, the L.A. Times uses two AUs:

- AU-ACTUAL-CAUSE: The L.A. Times refutes the argument that quotas on Japanese automobiles should be used to save jobs in the U.S. auto industry. The L.A. Times argues that import restrictions should not be continued because they can not reverse the job loss resulting from an increase in automation.

- AU-EQUIVALENCE: The L.A. Times refutes the argument that quotas on Japanese automobiles should be used to preserve earnings of the U.S. auto industry. The L.A. times argues that import restrictions should not be continued because they have increased car prices and, consequently, thwarted the goal of preserving consumer earnings.

Clearly, the representation of both editorial segments must be the same. That representation is illustrated by the breadth-of-support configuration shown in figure 4.15.

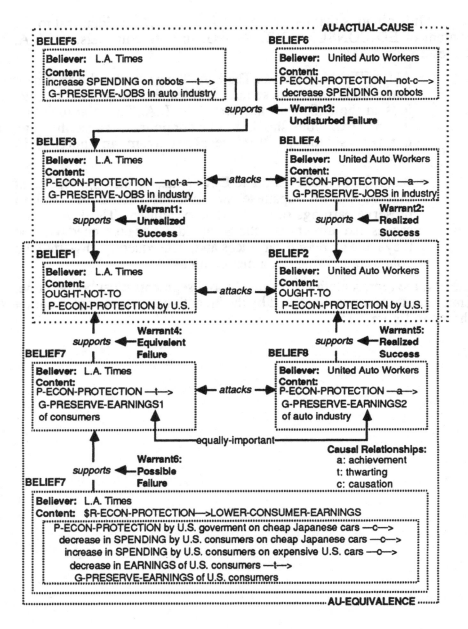

Figure 4.15. Argument Graph of ED-CONSUMER-ZAPPING and
ED-RIP-OFF.

4.4.2. Domain-Independent Nature of Argument Units

Using AUs also implies that the same abstract argument knowledge must be used to represent editorials in any domain. For example, consider three editorial segments in the domains of international trade, arms control, and drug use:

ED-TRADE-POLICY[21]

... Domestic firms grappl[ing] with greater competition from overseas ... [have] raise[d] cries for policies that will "save jobs" ... Trade policies ... cannot "save' jobs ... If we protect some domestic industries by imposing import restrictions, fewer dollars are sent overseas ... This [decrease] makes other export industries less competitive in world markets, and the net effect therefore is to "save" jobs in the industries being protected but to lose them in other export sectors ... [S]uch policy proposals ... should be met with considerable skepticism.

ED-STAR-WARS[22]

... The case is growing against programs ... which would turn outer space into a target range ... President Reagan's "Star Wars" ... is a shield ... that would shoot down Soviet missiles ... before they could reach a target ... The ... argument against "Star Wars" is that ... [it] could be overwhelmed by what the Soviet Union does best—building more missiles than the shield ... [is] designed to stop ... "Star Wars" ... works directly against Reagan's declared goal—an absolute reduction of nuclear warheads in the world. With "Star Wars," the incentive would be to build more, not to throw away any ...

ED-DRUGS[23]

... Looking at drugs ... as instruments to push the body and the mind to achieve desirable conditions difficult or even impossible to attain without—so the argument runs—the aid of chemical assistance, we can appreciate why many turn to drugs ... Why have we not floated higher and higher on an uninterrupted intake of ... [drugs]? It is because the promise of chemical achievement is betrayed by addiction ... The self preoccupation created by many chemicals blocks attainment of the goals that stimulated used in

---

[21]Benjamin Zycher (1984, April 3).
[22]Los Angeles Times (1984b, December 26).
[23]David Musto (1986, September 16).

**the first place. To the observer, if not to the confirmed drug user,
the failure of the chemical promise is evident ...**

At the abstract level, the one-sided arguments in ED-TRADE-POLICY,
ED-STAR-WARS, and ED-DRUGS are characterized by the
combination of an AU and a support structure, namely:

- AU-OPPOSITE-EFFECT: Each editorial writer refutes the
  argument that a plan P should be implemented because P
  achieves the goal G which has intended P. Each writer argues
  that P will not achieve G because P will thwart G.

- S-POSSIBLE-FAILURE: Each editorial writer argues that P
  will thwart G because P causes a state S1 which thwarts G.

Therefore, the representations of the above editorials correspond to
depth-of-support configurations in which AU-OPPOSITE-EFFECT and
S-POSSIBLE-FAILURE are instantiated in the appropriate domains.
Those instances are summarized in table 4.5.

Editorial Segment and Editorial Writer	Domain	AU-OPPOSITE-EFFECT: argument by writer (W) against opponent (O)	S-POSSIBLE-FAILURE: reasoning by writer
ED-TRADE-POLICY by B. Zycher	International Trade	O: Domestic firms believe trade policies should be used to save jobs. W: B. Zycher believes trade policies should not be used because they will cost jobs.	B. Zycher believes trade policies cost jobs because they will cause a decrease in export earnings and, consequently, a decrease in export jobs.
ED-STAR-WARS by L. A. Times	Arms Control	O: President Reagan believes "Star Wars" should be used to reduce nuclear weapons. W: The L.A. Times believes "Star Wars" should not be used because it will cause an increase in nuclear weapons.	The L.A. Times believes "Star Wars" will cause an increase in nuclear weapons because it will make the Soviet Union build more missiles than "Star Wars" can stop.
ED-DRUGS by D. Musto	Drug Use	O: Drug users believe they should use drugs to attain ideal mind and body conditions. W: D. Musto believes drug users should not use drugs because using drugs thwarts the attainment of the ideal conditions.	D. Musto believes using drugs thwarts the achievement of ideal mind and body conditions because doing drugs lead to a state of self-preoccupation and addiction.

Table 4.5. Instances of AU Configurations in Three Different Domains.

The language-independent and domain-independent axioms of
the theory of AUs give rise to three major corollaries:

1) An AU representation is extractable from any editorial about
   the use of plans.

2) A major task of the process of editorial comprehension involves recognizing AUs from input text.

3) Processes for search and retrieval must deal with the AU representation of an editorial and not with the wording used in the editorial.

As such, these three principles constitute the theoretical foundation of the process model of editorial comprehension, representation, and retrieval implemented in OpEd.[24]

4.5. Summary

This chapter has presented a taxonomy of argument units required for computer comprehension of editorial text in OpEd. The taxonomy describes the possible ways to refute an opponent's argument for endorsing or rejecting the use of a plan. Based on this AU taxonomy, argument knowledge can be characterized at four levels of abstraction:

1) Beliefs (Bs): Evaluations about plans or expectations about the effects of plans on goals.

2) Attacks (A-structures): Relationships between beliefs involving mutually exclusive planning situations or opposite effects of a plan on interrelated goals.

3) Supports (S-structures): Relationships between beliefs and belief justifications based on refinements of plan evaluations, refinements of plan-goal relationships, analogies, and examples.

4) Argument Units (AUs): Configurations of support and attack relationships that represent one-sided arguments involving unrealized successes, realized failures, realized successes, and unrealized failures.

AUs encode language-free and domain-free knowledge which can be instantiated to argue about plans in any domain. As a result, editorials can be modeled as configurations of AUs which must be recognized during editorial comprehension. The nature of these AU representations has been explored with OpEd in the domain of politico-economic editorials.

---

[24]OpEd's process model is discussed in chapters 6 through 8.

Chapter 5

Meta-Argument Units

5.1. Introduction

Editorial comprehension in OpEd requires representing arguments between editorial writers and their implicit opponents. Chapter 4 established how argument units (AUs) are used to represent one-sided arguments involving attacks on beliefs about domain-specific plans. This chapter addresses the problem of representing *meta-arguments* (Alvarado et al., in press), i.e., one-sided arguments involving attacks on warrants that grant the existence of support relationships among beliefs.

Meta-arguments occur in editorial text whenever the editorial writer shows that his/her opponent can not use a belief B1 to justify another belief B2. For example, consider the following excerpt from an editorial by the Los Angeles Times (1984, March 23):

ED-SUGAR-QUOTA

The U.S. effort to punish Marxists in Nicaragua by reducing their sugar export quota has been judged a violation of international trading rules by the council of the General Agreement on Tariffs and Trade ... Now the United States, in opposing the ... Nicaraguan leadership and its corruption of the promises and goals of ... [the anti-Somoza] revolution, finds itself abandoning the standards of law and order—a corruption of its own principles ...

Understanding ED-SUGAR-QUOTA requires realizing that the U.S. government has undermined its own argument for opposing Nicaraguan policies. Specifically, ED-SUGAR-QUOTA contains the following arguments:

1) The U.S. government believes that Nicaraguan government's policies are bad because they cause the failure of a major goal of the Nicaraguan people, i.e., preserving the principles of democracy in Nicaragua.

2) The L.A. Times believes that the U.S. can not continue using that argument because the U.S. has just imposed sugar-import restrictions that thwart a major U.S. goal, i.e., preserving the principles of democracy in foreign affairs.

As the above arguments indicate, an editorial writer may argue that his/her opponent is not allowed to use a given argument strategy to justify beliefs about a plan. For instance, if an opponent O argues that "plan P1 by X1 shouldn't be used because P1 thwarts an instance of a major goal G," then the writer can claim that O is not allowed to use that argument because O is also the actor of a plan P2 which thwarts another instance of G. Clearly, understanding editorials requires modeling arguments about the use of support strategies.

This chapter presents a taxonomy of *meta-argument units (meta-AUs)*, memory structures that organize abstract knowledge about the use of support strategies. When combined with domain-specific knowledge, meta-AUs can be used to argue against the underlying logic of an opponent's argument in the particular domain. Each meta-AU is composed of three elements: (1) opponent's belief B1 and its justification J1; (2) arguer's belief B2 that opponent should not use J1 to support B1; and (3) arguer's justification J2 for B2. According to the nature of the arguer's justification, two types of meta-AUs can be distinguished: meta-AUs based on hypocritical behavior and meta-AUs based on unsound reasoning. The first type captures meta-arguments that appear in editorials dealing with the use of plans, such as editorials on how protectionism undermines a government's professed free-trade views. The second type characterizes meta-arguments that occur in discussions about the validity of an opponent's reasoning, such as discussions about what kind of support strategies are acceptable when justifying the existence of God.

5.2. Meta-Argument Units Based on Hypocritical Behavior

One way to disallow an opponent's argument A1 for opposing the use of a plan is by showing that A1 is inconsistent with the opponent's behavior. This argumentation strategy involves the *theme of hypocrisy* (Dyer, 1983a) and is frequently used in editorials to argue that:

1) An opponent's professed opposition to using a plan P is inconsistent with that opponent's implementation of an instance of P.

2) An opponent's criticism of a plan P1 used by a third party is inconsistent with that opponent's use of a plan P2 that has the same negative side-effects of P1.

These hypocrisy-based arguments are represented in terms of the meta-AUs summarized in table 5.1 and described below.

Belief (B1) and Justification (J1) by Opponent (O)	Belief (B2) and Justification (J2) by Arguer (A)	Meta-Argument Unit

B1: OUGHT-NOT-TO (P)
because
J1: G —intend—> P
    P —not-achieve—> G
    or
    P —thwart—> G1
    G less important than or
      equally important to G1
	B2: OUGHT-NOT-TO (J1 —support—> B1)
	because
	J2: O also believes OUGHT-TO (P1 by O)
	    because
	    O believes G1 —intend—> P1 by O
	      P1 —achieve—> G1
	      P1 instance of P
	      G1 instance of G
		mAU-INCONSISTENT-ACTION

B1: OUGHT-NOT-TO (P1 by X)
because
J1: G1 —intend—> P1 by X
    P1 —thwart—> G3
    G1 less important than or
      equally important to G3
    G3 instance of G
	B2: OUGHT-NOT-TO (J1 —support—> B1)
	because
	J2: G2 —intend—> P2 by O
	    P2 —thwart—> G4
	    G2 less important than or
	      equally important to G4
	    G4 instance of G
		mAU-BACKFIRED-CRITICISM

Table 5.1. Meta-Argument Units Based on Hypocritical Behavior.

5.2.1. Inconsistencies Between Actions and Professed Beliefs

Consider the following segment from an editorial by Lester Thurow (1983):

ED-TARIFF-INCREASE

The Reagan administration argues that America does not need an industrial policy ... to guarantee economic success under capitalism. Yet, the Reagan administration has just ... increase[d] ... tariffs on large motorcycles from 4.4 percent to 49.4 percent ...

Thurow's argument in ED-TARIFF-INCREASE is an instance of the following meta-AU:

mAU-INCONSISTENT-ACTION: Although opponent O has argued that plan P should not be used because P fails to achieve G (the goal which intends P) or thwarts G0 (a goal more important than or equally important to G), arguer A believes that O should not continue arguing that way because O also believes O's plan P1 (an instance of P) should be used to achieve goal G1 (an instance of G).

Thurow uses mAU-INCONSISTENT-ACTION to attack the Reagan administration's professed position that the U.S. does not have to implement an industrial policy to help domestic industries become profitable.[25] Thurow believes that the Reagan administration can not use such an argument because: (1) the administration has just imposed tariffs on motorcycles; (2) tariffs are industrial policies to help domestic industries become profitable; and (3) the tariffs on motorcycles are inconsistent with the administration's non-intervention argument. The representation of Thurow's argument is shown in figure 5.1.

---

[25]Here, industrial policy is viewed as a class of plans including import restrictions and government loans.

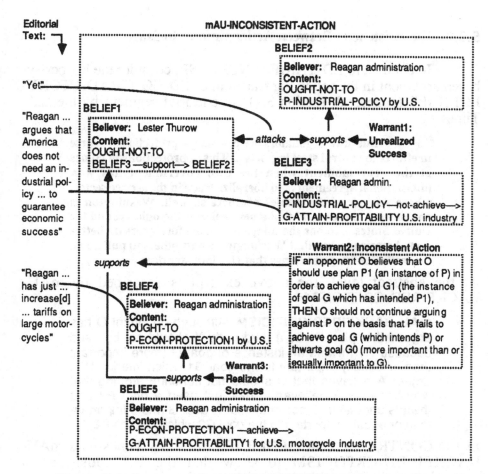

Figure 5.1. Instance of mAU-INCONSISTENT-ACTION.

As figure 5.1 shows, mAU-INCONSISTENT-ACTION organizes a configuration of supports and attacks in which an arguer's evaluation of his/her opponent's professed position is justified with the opponent's own beliefs about a plan he/she just implemented. Such plan-based beliefs are frequently unstated in editorials and are made explicit in meta-AU representations. For example, in ED-TARIFF-INCREASE, Thurow's attack on the Reagan administration's non-intervention position is justified by using the administration's implicitly stated belief that tariffs on motorcycles are needed to help the U.S. motorcycle industry attain profitability.

5.2.2. Inconsistencies Between Actions and Criticisms

In contrast to ED-TARIFF-INCREASE, consider the hypocrisy-based argument in the following fragment of ED-CONTRADICTORY-POLICIES (chapter 3, section 3.1), an editorial segment by the L.A. Times:

> **American negotiators are pursuing a protectionist course in efforts to control steel imports ... This ... protectionism comes at the very moment when the U.S. government has won international agreement ... to liberalize trade in the service sector, where American companies compete so well. Washington is announcing to the world that a new wall is being built around the United States ... to bar the things that some foreigners do better than Americans, but that Washington wants others to pull down the walls that keep out things that U.S. industry does best ...**

At the abstract level, the above excerpt is described by mAU-BACKFIRED-CRITICISM:

> **mAU-BACKFIRED-CRITICISM:** Although opponent O has argued that plan P1 by a third party X should not be used because P1 thwarts an instance of goal G (more important than or equally important to the goal G1 which intends P1), arguer A believes that O should not continue arguing that way because A believes O has just used a plan P2 that thwarts another instance of the same goal G (more important than or equally important to the goal G2 which intends P2).

In ED-CONTRADICTORY-POLICIES, the L.A. Times uses mAU-BACKFIRED-CRITICISM to show that the U.S. position on protectionism is hypocritical. Specifically, the above excerpt contains the following relationships: (1) the U.S. believes that foreign restrictions on trade in the service sector are bad because they thwart the U.S. industries' goal of preserving earnings; and (2) the L.A. Times believes the U.S. can not argue in those terms anymore because the U.S. has just negotiated steel-import restrictions that will thwart foreign industries' goal of preserving earnings. This instance of mAU-BACKFIRED-CRITICISM is illustrated in figure 5.2.

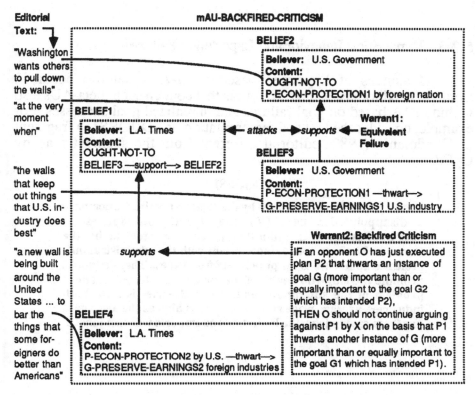

Figure 5.2. Instance of mAU-BACKFIRED-CRITICISM.

As the above diagram indicates, mAU-BACKFIRED-CRITICISM represents arguments in which an opponent O is attacked for having a "double standard" for evaluating plans. That is, O believes that: (1) a third party X should not be allowed to use a plan P1 that causes the failure of an instance of goal G; and (2) O should be allowed to use a plan P2 even though it is believed that P2 causes the failure of another instance of the same goal G.

5.2.3. Hypocritical Behavior and Expectation Failures

Instances of hypocrisy-based meta-AUs seldom occur in isolation in editorials. Rather, editorials that contain such meta-AUs also include AUs based on goal failures and unrealized goal successes. For example, consider the text and representation of ED-JOBS1, a fragment of Friedman's (1982) editorial different from the segment read by OpEd.

ED-JOBS1

Recent protectionist measures by the Reagan administration have ... disappointed ... us ... [Voluntary] limits on Japanese ... automobiles [and] ... [voluntary] limits on steel ... by the Common Market ... are ... inconsistent with the administration's professed adherence to the principle of free trade ... They do [not] ... promote the long-run health of the industries affected ... The ... problem of the automobile and steel industries is ... in both industries, average wage rates are twice as high as the average ... Far from saving jobs, the limitations on imports will cost jobs ...

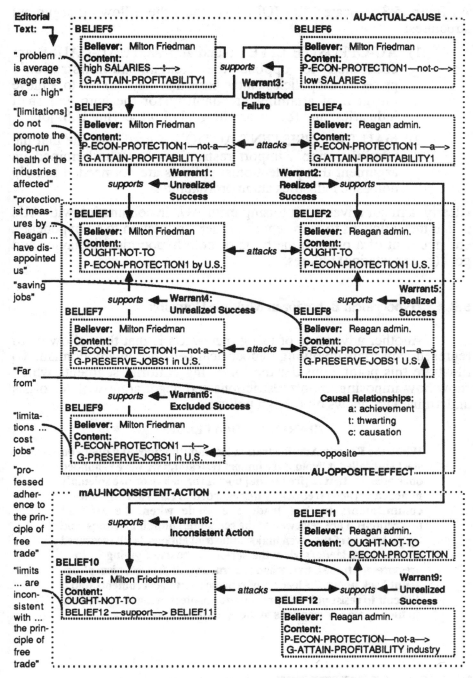

Figure 5.3. Argument Graph of ED-JOBS1.

As figure 5.3 indicates, ED-JOBS1 contains the following argument structures:

1) AU-OPPOSITE-EFFECT and AU-ACTUAL-CAUSE are combined to oppose the Reagan administration's protectionist policies on the basis that they: (a) fail to achieve the goal of attaining profitability for the auto and steel industries; and (b) thwart the goal of preserving U.S. jobs.

2) mAU-INCONSISTENT-ACTION is used to argue that the administration's import restrictions have undermined its argument that protectionist policies are not needed to help domestic industries attain profitability.

Clearly, a major advantage of using meta-AUs in conjunction with AUs is that they allow us to represent an arguer's refutation to an opponent's endorsement of a plan on the basis of both hypocritical behavior and goal (or expectation) failures.

5.2.4. Hypocritical Behavior in Multiple Domains

Another advantage of using meta-AUs is that they allow us to represent editorials involving hypocritical behavior in any domain. To illustrate this point, consider the following editorial segments which show how imposing import restrictions and negotiating with terrorists undermine U.S. views on foreign policy:

ED-FREE-TRADE-PLEDGE[26]

When the Reagan Administration last month imposed a quota on steel and called it "voluntary import restraint," we were reminded once again ... that ... [free trade] norms for behavior are solemnly honored ... [and] frequently disregarded ... Each spring, solemn commitments to free trade are made when the evils of protectionism are reviewed at the economic summit meetings held by the leaders of the seven major industrial nations. With measured alarm, those leaders view the serious ... costs of giving in to ... pressures for trade barriers and confirm an anti-protectionism pledge ... But back home, the leaders of representative governments find it difficult to resist political pressure for protection against imports. So they agree to exceptions to the open-trading system ...

---

[26]Earl Cheit (1984, October 7).

ED-ARMS-FOR-HOSTAGES[27]

The Reagan Administration, which entered office pledging that it would cut no deals with terrorists, is now seen to have indeed cut such a deal ... To win freedom for three Americans held hostage in Lebanon by a group call[ed] ... Islamic Jihad, the Administration has secretly approved and probably initiated some third-country shipments of U.S. arms to Iran, Islamic Jihad's political supporter and spiritual mentor ... The effort achieved the release of three hostages. It also leaves the United States ... open to charges of hypocritically undercutting its own policies ... [B]ecause such a deal has occurred, because ransom is seen to have been paid, further hostage-taking has been invited. This is precisely what the administration warned against the day it took office ...

At the abstract level, both editorial segments are characterized by mAU-INCONSISTENT-ACTION. In each segment, the editorial writer brings up an instance of the implementation of a plan P in order to disallow an argument for opposing the use of P. Specifically, the above editorial segments contain the following relationships:

1) In ED-FREE-TRADE-PLEDGE, Earl Cheit attacks the Reagan administration's stand on free trade. The administration has argued that protecting domestic industries from foreign competition does more harm than good. However, Cheit believes that the administration can not use that anti-protectionism argument anymore because the administration has just negotiated a quota on steel imports.

2) In ED-ARMS-FOR-HOSTAGES, the L.A. Times attacks the Reagan administration's stand on terrorism. The administration opposes negotiations with terrorists because its positive effects (i.e., achieving the release of some Americans held hostage) are outweighed by its negative side-effects (i.e., preventing the kidnapping of many more Americans). However, the L.A. Times believes that the administration can not use that argument anymore because the administration has just traded arms for three hostages.

As the above editorial segments demonstrate, hypocrisy-based arguments in editorials correspond to meta-AUs which have been instantiated with appropriate domain-specific knowledge.

---

[27]Los Angeles Times (1986, November 7).

5.3.   Meta-Argument Units Based on Unsound Reasoning

Another way to disallow an opponent's argument A1 is by showing that A1 contains reasoning errors. This strategy is the basis for meta-AUs involving attacks on the reasoning underlying an opponent's belief that a given explanation is correct. According to the nature of the errors in the opponent's reasoning, four meta-AUs have been characterized: burden of proof, plausibility, tautology, and self-contradiction. Those meta-AUs are summarized in table 5.2 and illustrated in the following sections using argument fragments from *The Atheist Debater's Handbook* (Johnson, 1981).

Belief (B1) and Justification (J1) by Opponent (O)	Belief (B2) and Justification (J2) by Arguer (A)	Meta-Argument Unit
B1: E is correct explanation of S because J1: E can not be disproved	B2: OUGHT-NOT-TO (J1 —support—> B1) because J2: O has not proved E and disproving E only causes disproof spiral	mAU-BURDEN-OF-PROOF
B1: E1 is correct explanation of S because J1: E1 is an explanation of S and E2 can not be proved E2 opposite of E1	B2: OUGHT-NOT-TO (J1 —support—> B1) because J2: E1 can not be proved	mAU-PLAUSIBILITY
B1: E1 is correct explanation of S because J1: E1 is an explanation of S and E2 can not be proved E2 opposite of E1	B2: OUGHT-NOT-TO (J1 —support—> B1) because J2: B1 is a refinement of J1	mAU-TAUTOLOGY
B1: E is correct explanation of S because J1: There is no known explanation	B2: OUGHT-NOT-TO (J1 —support—> B1) because J2: B1 contradicts J1	mAU-SELF-CONTRADICTION

Table 5.2. Meta-Argument Units Based on Unsound Reasoning.

5.3.1. Burden of Proof

The construct mAU-BURDEN-OF-PROOF represents meta-arguments in which an arguer refutes the argument that an explanation E is correct if E can not be disproved. At the abstract level, those refutations can be stated as follows:

mAU-BURDEN-OF-PROOF: Although opponent O has argued that E is the correct explanation of situation S because E can not be disproved, arguer A believes O should not argue that way because O has not proved E AND disproving E only causes an infinite disproof spiral.

For example, consider Johnson's (pp. 11-14) reply to an argument about God's existence:

ED-UNIVERSE

... Many theists insist that it is the responsibility of the atheist to offer evidence justifying his lack of belief ... [that] God ... is necessary in order to explain the existence of [the universe] ... The ... point to notice is that ... if one offers an explanation of something, one must be prepared to provide reasons for accepting the explanation ... By ... [this] token, it is incumbent upon the theist to provide reasons for his belief that God is the true explanation of the universe ... The atheist, for his part, ... need only demonstrate that the theist has failed to justify *his* position ... The reason for this procedure is fairly straightforward: ... The theist claims that the atheist must disprove God's existence. The atheist could reply that there is conclusive evidence to suggest that God does not exist and thus it is the theist who must disprove the existence of such evidence. The demand for disproof inevitably leads to an inconclusive farce ...

Johnson's argument is an instance of mAU-BURDEN-OF-PROOF, as shown below.

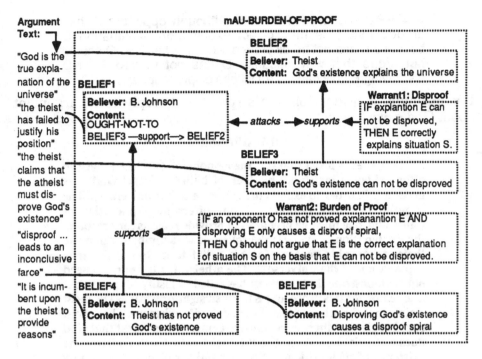

Figure 5.4. Instance of mAU-BURDEN-OF-PROOF.

As figure 5.4 indicates, Johnson does not argue against the belief that God is the explanation of the universe, but rather against the disproof-based strategy used to justify such a belief.[28] Johnson argues that the theist should not use that strategy because: (1) the theist has not provided proof of the existence of God; (2) the theist believes God's existence can not be disproved; and (3) disproof only leads to attempts to disprove evidence for prior disproof and, consequently, does not validate the theist's claim that God is the explanation of the universe. Thus, Johnson believes that the theist can not argue by shifting burden of proof of God's existence.

---

[28]In figure 5.4, the conceptual contents of beliefs involving religious concepts are described in English. Modeling religious concepts falls outside the scope of this dissertation.

5.3.2. Plausibility

Consider Johnson's (pp. 17-19) reply to another argument often used by theists:

ED-TURTLE-SHELL

There is the tendency among theists to offer, as evidence for the existence of God, phenomena which "science cannot explain." For example, neo-Darwinism has thus far been unsuccessful in explaining the development of the turtle's shell ... God, the theist claims, must therefore be the explanation of the turtle's shell ... However, the issue is not whether a particular explanation can be provided but, instead, whether the explanation is in fact correct ... The theist contends ... that since God is an adequate explanation of a puzzling phenomenon, and no other *adequate* explanation is known, then God must be the correct explanation ... But how are we to determine whether God can be used to correctly explain anything? We cannot see Him in action and no experiment ... reveals Him. Theists rely completely on God as the only adequate explanation known thus far. But this ... does not imply that God is the correct explanation ...

Johnson's argument is centered on the belief that an explanation E can not be shown to be correct solely on the basis that E is the only adequate explanation of a given situation S. As such, Johnson's argument is an instance of mAU-PLAUSIBILITY:

mAU-PLAUSIBILITY: Although opponent O has argued that E1 is the correct explanation of situation S because E1 is an explanation of S AND because it can not be proved that E2 (the opposite of E1) is the explanation of S, arguer A believes O should not argue that way because A believes that it can not be proved that E1 is the explanation of S.

The instance of mAU-PLAUSIBILITY in ED-TURTLE-SHELL contains the relationships illustrated in figure 5.5.

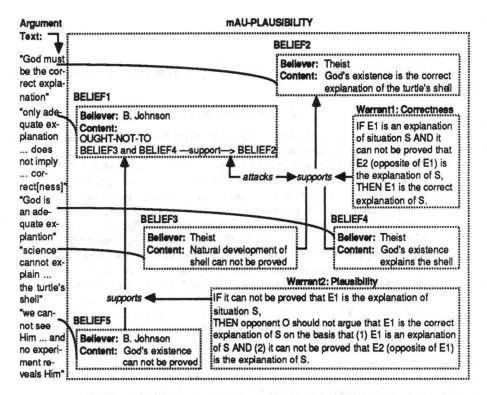

Figure 5.5. Instance of mAU-PLAUSIBILITY.

As figure 5.5. shows, Johnson attacks the argument used to justify the theist's position that God is the correct explanation of the turtle's shell. Johnson's argument involves the following beliefs: (1) correct explanations are not only adequate but also verifiable through experiments and observations; (2) God's existence can not be verified through experiments or observations; and (3) the theist argues for correctness only on the basis that God's existence is an adequate explanation of phenomena that science can not explain. Clearly, Johnson demonstrates that the theist's argument is just a plausibility argument.

5.3.3. Tautology

Another meta-AU involving attacks on unsound reasoning is mAU-TAUTOLOGY. This construct characterizes meta-arguments in which an arguer shows that a circular argument should not be used when justifying the belief that an explanation is correct:

> **mAU-TAUTOLOGY:** Although opponent O has argued that E1 is the correct explanation of situation S because E1 is an explanation of S AND because it can not be proved that E2 (the opposite of E1) is the explanation of S, arguer A believes O should not argue that way because O's belief that E is the correct explanation of S is a refinement of O's belief that E can be used to explain S.

To illustrate this meta-AU, consider another reply by Johnson (pp. 17-18, 21-22) to the turtle-shell argument:

ED-ASSUMPTION

There is the tendency among theists to offer, as evidence for the existence of God, phenomena which "science cannot explain." For example, neo-Darwinism has thus far been unsuccessful in explaining the development of the turtle's shell ... God, the theist claims, must therefore be the explanation of the turtle's shell ... The theist contends ... that since God is an adequate explanation of a puzzling phenomenon, and no other *adequate* explanation is known, then God must be the correct explanation ... But ... [i]f the theist is to use our present ignorance of an explanation grounded in natural causes as an argument for God's existence, then he must also grant present ignorance of the existence of God. For the existence of God is precisely the conclusion which the argument is set out to prove. There would be no point in providing such an argument if we already granted the existence of God ... Bearing [this] in mind ..., the turtle-shell argument ... can conclude that God exists only if it begins with that assumption ...

The above excerpt contains the instance of mAU-TAUTOLOGY shown in figure 5.6.

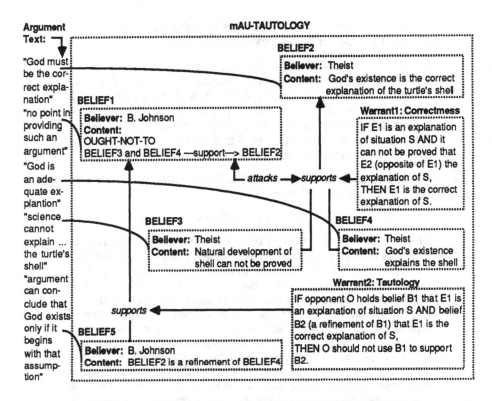

Figure 5.6. Instance of mAU-TAUTOLOGY.

As the above diagram indicates, Johnson believes that the theist can not argue that God created the turtle's shell by assuming God could have done it. Specifically, Johnson argues that: (1) an argument's conclusion should not be included among its assumptions; and (2) the theist's conclusion that "God is the correct explanation" is a refinement of the theist's assumption that "God is an adequate explanation." Clearly, Johnson believes that the turtle-shell argument is circular.

5.3.4. Self-Contradiction

An arguer can also disallow an opponent's argument A1 by showing that A1 involves a support relationship between two contradictory beliefs. This type of reasoning error occurs when the opponent argues that an explanation E is correct if E can be used to explain a situation which no one knows how to explain. For example, consider another fragment of Johnson's (pp. 22-23) argument against the turtle-shell argument:

ED-IGNORANCE

> ... [T]he use of present ignorance as an argument for God's existence will result in self-contradiction ... [C]onsider how the turtle-shell argument really performs. The theist argues: "What is the origin of the turtle's shell? I don't know. You don't know. Therefore God originated the turtle's shell." This is really saying: "What is the origin of the turtle's shell? I don't know. You don't know. Therefore we *both* know—that is, we know that God originated the it" ... To argue that we do not know how a thing was brought about is clearly not to argue that we know something concerning how it was brought about ... If we begin the argument ... by assuming a position of ignorance ..., then we cannot proceed to the conclusion that God exists ... Certainly, ... ignorance is not a good reason to believe that God exists ...

The above excerpt is an instance of mAU-SELF-CONTRADICTION, as indicated below.

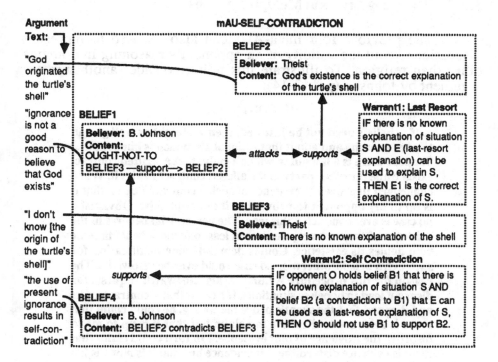

Figure 5.7. Instance of mAU-SELF-CONTRADICTION.

As figure 5.7 indicates, mAU-SELF-CONTRADICTION organizes the following abstract configuration of support and attack relationships:

mAU-SELF-CONTRADICTION: Although opponent O has argued that E1 can be used as a last-resort explanation of situation S because there is no known explanation of S, arguer A believes O should not argue that way because O's belief that E is the last-resort explanation of S contradicts O's belief that there is no known explanation.

In ED-IGNORANCE, Johnson uses the above meta-AU to argue that: (1) ignorance does not justify explanations; (2) the theist believes that there is no known explanation of the origin of the turtle's shell; and (3) the theist uses that belief as a justification for the belief that God must be the explanation of the turtle's shell. Thus, Johnson establishes that the theist's argument is self-contradictory and does not prove God's existence.

5.3.5. Reasoning Errors in Multiple Domains

The previous four meta-AUs can also be used to represent discussions about the validity of an opponent's reasoning in domains other than religion. To illustrate this point, consider another meta-argument by Johnson (pp. 12-14):

ED-CONTRACT

... If ... beliefs need not be justified, then we might as well give in to pure anarchy and admit that rational discussion is impossible ... Suppose there is a lawsuit in which I claim that a written contract exists while the other party to the alleged contract denies it. When challenged to prove the existence of such a contract I claim that it is up to my opponent to prove that it does not exist. Obviously, no case is ever conducted this way. The person who believes in the existence of the contract possesses at least one more belief than he who denies its existence. Courts demand some justification for such extra beliefs, otherwise no case could ever be resolved ... The reason for this procedure is fairly straightforward: requests for disproof lead to hopeless situations. If I claim that a contract exists and demand that the skeptic prove me wrong, he could claim that there is evidence to disprove my claim but that it is up to me to disprove the existence of *that* evidence. I in turn could claim that there is evidence discrediting his evidence but that it is now his job to disprove the existence of *my* evidence. And so it would go

**without end. Once the demand for disproof is permitted to go
unchallenged, it becomes impossible to prove any claim ...**

The meta-argument in ED-CONTRACT is an instance of mAU-BURDEN-OF-PROOF in the domain of contract law. Johnson uses this meta-AU to demonstrate that one can not argue for a contractual obligation by simply claiming that the existence of the contract can not be disproved. Johnson argues that such a disproof-based argument is incorrect because: (1) the existence of the contract has not been proved; and (2) disproving the existence of the contract causes a disproof spiral.[29] As this analysis of ED-CONTRACT shows, meta-AUs provide a system for representing one-sided arguments about the nature of valid reasoning in any domain.

5.4.   Summary

This chapter has presented a taxonomy of knowledge structures termed meta-argument units. These constructs organize abstract knowledge about the use of support strategies and can be instantiated to attack the underlying logic of an opponent's argument in any domain. Two types of meta-AUs have been characterized:

1) Meta-AUs based on hypocritical behavior, which specify argument errors that result from inconsistencies between actions and professed beliefs or from inconsistencies between actions and criticisms. These meta-AUs are used in conjunction with unrealized-success AUs and realized-failure AUs to model editorials dealing with the use of plans.

2) Meta-AUs based on unsound reasoning, which specify argument errors that result from shifting the burden of proof or from using support strategies based on plausibilities, circularities, or self-contradictions. These meta-AUs are used to model discussions about the nature of valid reasoning.

This meta-AU taxonomy extends the scope of the AU taxonomy which is required for computer comprehension of editorials in OpEd.

---

[29]In the domain of law, the meta-argument unit mAU-BURDEN-OF-PROOF also captures the reasoning underlying the following maxim of the American justice system: "innocent until proven guilty." That is, in a trial, the prosecution can not present charges against the defendant and ask the defense to disprove them. Instead, the prosecution must present the charges and "prove them beyond reasonable doubt."

However, meta-AUs are highly abstract and complex in nature, and currently beyond OpEd's processing capabilities. A real test of intelligence for computer programs will be to be able to manipulate meta-AUs, to abstract and/or learn previously unknown meta-AUs from input text, and to use this knowledge during subsequent argument comprehension.

Chapter 6

Recognizing Argument Structures

6.1.   Introduction

In previous chapters it was shown that the editorials read by
OpEd involve arguments centered on two contradictory evaluations of
plans for economic protection. Furthermore, it was established that the
conceptual representation for this type of editorials forms an argument
graph in which configurations of support and attack relationships among
beliefs are organized by instances of argument units (AUs). This chapter
examines another interrelated issue addressed within the context of
OpEd, namely: how the components of an editorial's argument graph
are recognized from the editorial text.

Parsing an editorial can be viewed as a process that involves: (1)
extracting the beliefs, belief relationships, and AUs underlying the
editorial; and (2) integrating those structures into an argument graph. A
fundamental problem that must be faced during this process is that the
editorial may not contain explicit descriptions of all the beliefs held by
the editorial writer and his/her implicit opponents. As a result, those
beliefs must be inferred from the editorial text. To illustrate the nature of
this problem, consider the following excerpt from an editorial by
Bresnaham (1984):

ED-HARMFUL-QUOTA

**... I think that the import quotas [on Japanese automobiles] are
terrible public policy ... Basic supply-and-demand analysis shows**

> that protecting domestic industries from foreign competition does
> more harm than good. Members of the protected groups (in this
> case, auto workers), stockholders in auto companies and auto
> executives clearly gain. But ... [the] quota ... on Japanese
> automobiles ... raises the price of ... cars ... [s]o [U.S.] consumers
> pay more ...

Obviously, the first sentence of ED-HARMFUL-QUOTA mentions
explicitly Bresnaham's belief that implementing import quotas on
Japanese cars is bad planning. However, other beliefs and belief
relationships are implicitly stated in ED-HARMFUL-QUOTA,
including:

- Reasoning by Actor of Plan: The U.S. government believes
  that import quotas should be implemented because they will
  help the U.S. auto industry become profitable.

- Attack Relationship Between Evaluative Beliefs: The U.S.
  government's belief that import quotas should be implemented
  is contradicted by Bresnaham's belief that implementing the
  quotas is bad planning.

- Reasoning by Editorial Writer: Bresnaham believes
  implementing import quotas is bad planning because they will
  decrease the level of consumer earnings.

- Attack Relationship Between Causal Beliefs: The U.S.
  government's belief that import quotas will help the auto
  industry become profitable is contradicted by Bresnaham's
  belief that the quotas will decrease the level of consumer
  earnings.

- Supporting Causal Chain: Bresnaham believes that import
  quotas will decrease the level of consumer earnings because:
  (1) the quotas will reduce the amount of cheap Japanese cars
  entering the U.S.; (2) this decrease in the supply of Japanese
  cars will shift consumer spending from cheap imports to
  expensive U.S. cars; and (3) this shift in spending will cause a
  decrease in consumer earnings.

As this analysis of ED-HARMFUL-QUOTA demonstrates, mapping
editorial text into conceptual representations requires making explicit the
beliefs held by editorial writers and their implicit opponents.

   This chapter presents a set of processing strategies for
recognizing beliefs, belief relationships, and AUs. The strategies allow
OpEd to recognize: (1) evaluative beliefs from descriptions of emotional

reactions and standpoints; (2) causal beliefs from evaluative beliefs; (3) reasoning scripts from causal beliefs; and (4) AUs from various linguistic constructs and from beliefs involving plan failures. The use of these strategies will be illustrated within the framework of the editorials processed by OpEd as well as other editorials in the politico-economic domain.

6.2. Recognizing Evaluative Beliefs From Explicit Standpoints

Beliefs can be inferred from explicitly stated support and opposition standpoints. For example, consider the following excerpt from an editorial by Schneider (1985):

ED-TRADE-PRACTICES

... [President] Reagan ... endorsed a new "get tough" policy against countries that subsidize exports ... or dump cheap goods in the United States ... "I will not tolerate ... unfair trade practices ...," the President told Republican Congressional leaders ...

From the above excerpt, one can infer that President Reagan believes that: (1) it is a good idea to impose sanctions against countries that subsidize exports to the U.S.; and (2) it is a bad idea to subsidize exports to the U.S. These inferences are based on the following rules:

Standpoint Rule 1: IF arguer A supports plan P, THEN A believes plan P should be executed.

Standpoint Rule 2: IF arguer A opposes plan P, THEN A believes plan P should not be executed.

As these rules indicate, descriptions of standpoints about plans can be mapped into beliefs that contain evaluations of those plans. In ED-TRADE-PRACTICES, these rules are used to infer President Reagan's beliefs from the phrases "endorsed a new ... policy" and "will not tolerate ... unfair trade practices."

Evaluative beliefs can be inferred not only from an arguer's explicit standpoint about a plan, but also from the arguer's standpoint with regard to the standpoints of other arguers. Such inferences are organized by the following rules:

Standpoint Rule 3: IF arguer A1 supports A2's support of plan P, THEN A1 believes plan P should be executed.

Standpoint Rule 4: IF arguer A1 supports A2's opposition to plan P, THEN A1 believes plan P should not be executed.

Standpoint Rule 5: IF arguer A1 opposes A2's opposition to plan P, THEN A believes plan P should be executed.

Standpoint Rule 6: IF arguer A1 opposes A2's support of plan P, THEN A believes plan P should not be executed.

For example, from the following sentence appearing in Friedman's (1982) editorial:

> ... Those of us who have ... defended [the Reagan] administration opposition to the [European] pipeline deal [with the Soviet Union] ...

one can infer (by using rule 4) that Friedman believes that the pipeline deal is a bad idea. Similarly, from the following sentence appearing in Schneider's (1985) editorial:

> ... Sen. John Glen (D-Ohio) ... castigated [Walter F.] Mondale's protectionist stance in the Democratic presidential primaries last year ...

one can infer (by using rule 6) that Sen. Glen believes that the U.S. should not implement protectionist policies. As these examples show, recognizing evaluative beliefs requires characterizing the interactions that occur between the standpoints of two arguers.

6.3.   Recognizing Evaluative Beliefs From Emotional Reactions

Beliefs can also be signaled by explicit descriptions of emotional reactions appearing in editorials. As characterized by Dyer (1983b), those descriptions capture the positive or negative states resulting from achievements or failures of goals and expectations. Based on this view of emotional reactions, two belief-inference rules have been characterized within the framework of OpEd:

Negative-Emotion Rule: IF the execution of plan P produces a negative emotional reaction for arguer A (due to A experiencing a goal or expectation failure), THEN infer that A believes plan P should not be used.

Positive-Emotion Rule: IF the execution of plan P produces a positive emotional reaction for arguer A (due to A experiencing a goal or expectation achievement), THEN infer that A believes plan P should be used.

As the above rules show, an emotional reaction associated with the execution of a plan directly reflects what an individual thinks about that plan. For example, consider a fragment of Friedman's argument in ED-JOBS, one of the editorials read by OpEd (see section 1.2):

> **Recent protectionist measures by the Reagan administration have disappointed us ...**

Here, the affect description "disappointed" indicates that Friedman believes that the Reagan administration should not implement protectionist policies. In contrast, consider the following editorial segment by the Los Angeles Times (1984, April 11):

ED-TRADE-AGREEMENT

> **Japan ... [has] agree[d] to more generous import quotas for U.S. beef and citrus ... The agreement is not by itself the answer to the U.S.-Japanese trade frictions ... [H]owever, ... [t]he Japanese concessions ... are a hopeful sign.**

In ED-TRADE-AGREEMENT, the affect description "hopeful" indicates that the L.A. Times is in favor of the new U.S.-Japanese trade agreement. As these examples demonstrate, recognizing evaluative beliefs requires applying the negative-emotion rule or the positive-emotion rule when affect descriptions are found in editorial text.

6.4. Recognizing Causal Beliefs From Evaluative Beliefs

Once OpEd has recognized an evaluative belief about a plan P1, OpEd expects to hear its justifications. Such justifications involve causal relationships that give specific details of the goal situations caused by P1. For example, if an arguer A has stated that a plan P1 should be implemented, then OpEd expects to hear that P1 will achieve the goal G1 which has intended P1. In contrast, if an arguer A has stated that a plan P1 should not be implemented, then OpEd expects to hear that either: (1) P1 will not achieve goal G1; (2) P will thwart G1; (3) P1 will thwart a goal G2 more important than or equally important to G1; or (4) P will cause goal failures that require repeated applications of P (i.e., P will cause a negative-spiral failure). These expectations are summarized in table 6.1.

Belief Triggering Expectations	Expected Input	Preconditions To Be Satisfied by Expected Input	Support Relationship Recognized When Expectation Is Fulfilled
A believe OUGHT-TO (P1)	P1 —achieve—> G1	G1 —intend—> P1	S-REALIZED-SUCCESS: A believe OUGHT-TO (P1) because A believe P1 —achieve—> G1
A believe OUGHT-NOT-TO (P1)	P1 —not-achieve—> G1	G1 —intend—> P1	S-UNREALIZED-SUCCESS: A believe OUGHT-NOT-TO (P1) because A believe P1—not-achieve—> G1
	P1 —thwart—> G1	G1 —intend—> P1	S-UNREALIZED-SUCCESS and S-EXCLUDED-SUCCESS: A believe OUGHT-NOT-TO (P1) because A believe P1—not-achieve—> G1 because A believe P1 —thwart—> G1
	P1 —thwart—> G2	G1 —intend—> P1 G1 less important than G2	S-GREATER-FAILURE: A believe OUGHT-NOT-TO (P1) because A believe P1 —thwart—> G2
	P1 —thwart—> G2	G1 —intend—> P1 G1 as important as G2	S-EQUIVALENT-FAILURE: A believe OUGHT-NOT-TO (P1) because A believe P1 —thwart—> G2
	P1 —thwart—> G2 G2 —intend—> P2	G1 —intend—> P1 G1 as important as G2 P1 instance of P P2 instance of P	S-SPIRAL-FAILURE: A believe OUGHT-NOT-TO (P1) because A believe P1 —thwart—> G2 G2 —intend—> P2

Table 6.1. Expectations Generated From Evaluative Beliefs.

Consider how OpEd uses the expectations in table 6.1 to process the following fragment of Friedman's argument in ED-JOBS:

Recent protectionist measures by the Reagan administration have disappointed us ... They do not promote the long-run health of the industries affected ...

After reading about Friedman's disappointment, OpEd infers the following belief:

BELIEF1: Friedman believes
OUGHT-NOT-TO P-ECON-PROTECTION1

where P-ECON-PROTECTION1 is an instance of the planning structure P-ECON-PROTECTION (see chapter 2, section 2.2.4) and represents the protectionist policies implemented by the Reagan administration. Based on the content of Friedman's belief, OpEd generates five expectations (Es) for belief justifications:

> E1: P-ECON-PROTECTION1 —not-achieve—> G1
>
> E2: P-ECON-PROTECTION1 —thwart—> G1
>
> E3: P-ECON-PROTECTION1 —thwart—> G2 (more important than G1)
>
> E4: P-ECON-PROTECTION1 —thwart—> G2 (equally important to G1)
>
> E5: P-ECON-PROTECTION1 —thwart—> G2 —intend—>
> P-ECON-PROTECTION2

Here, G1 represents the goal which has intended the Reagan administration's protectionist policies. This goal must be an instance of any of the goals associated with the planning structure P-ECON-PROTECTION, namely:

- G-PRESERVING-JOBS of workers.
- G-ATTAINING-PROFITABILITY by domestic industry.
- G-PRESERVING-EARNINGS by domestic industry.

In the second sentence of Friedman's argument, the word "promote" stands for a goal-achievement relationship, and the phrase "long-run health" refers to the economic well-being of the industries being protected. As a result, OpEd maps that sentence into the following causal relationship:

> P-ECON-PROTECTION1 —not-achieve—> G-ATTAINING-PROFITABILITY1

Given this relationship, OpEd tries to match it against the active expectations for belief justifications generated from BELIEF1. This match succeeds because the above relationship corresponds to the content of expectation E1. At this point, OpEd builds the following belief structures:

> BELIEF2: Friedman believes
> P-ECON-PROTECTION1 —not-achieve—>
> G-ATTAINING-PROFITABILITY1
>
> S-UNREALIZED-SUCCESS: BELIEF2 —support—> BELIEF1

As this analysis of ED-JOBS demonstrates, recognizing justifications of evaluative beliefs requires applying general knowledge of plan-based reasoning along with knowledge of domain-specific plans and goals.

6.5.   Recognizing Reasoning Scripts From Causal Beliefs

In OpEd, the process of applying reasoning scripts is based on the notion of *script headers,* a script-recognition technique originally proposed by Schank and Abelson (1977) and later developed and expanded by Cullingford (1978, 1981). Scripts headers are conceptualizations that predict the occurrence of a situational script, i.e., a script containing a sequence of actions associated with a stereotypical activity, such as eating in a fast-food restaurant. In general, script headers represent: (1) preconditions of the script; or (2) events that may precede the execution of the script. For example, the precondition "being hungry" and the action "going to the location of a fast-food restaurant" are descriptions of headers of the fast-food script ($FAST-FOOD), which organizes the following sequence of actions: a patron enters, orders a meal, pays for it, sits down, eats the meal, and leaves. When descriptions of script headers are encountered in narrative text, they trigger the expectation that the details of the associated script will also be mentioned in the text. For instance, after reading the sentence "John went to McDonald's," one may expect that the rest of the narrative will contain references to John's actions of ordering some food and eating it.

How is the notion of script headers used in OpEd? During editorial comprehension, the occurrence of reasoning scripts is signaled by beliefs involving: (a) a goal-achievement or a goal-failure relationship between a plan P and a goal G; or (b) a negative-spiral failure caused by an instance of a plan P. That is, beliefs of the form P—achieve—>G, P—thwart—>G, and P1—thwart—>G2—intend—>P2 act as headers of reasoning scripts. When one such belief is recognized, OpEd accesses the reasoning scripts organized by the given plan P and searches for the script associated with the type of plan-goal relationship contained in that belief. Once the script has been selected, OpEd attempts to understand the next input sentence from the context of that script. The representation of the sentence is matched against the conceptualizations in the script's causal chain and, if the match succeeds, the chain is instantiated up to the point referred to by the input. This process is repeated with successive input sentences until OpEd reads one that does not refer to any of the uninstantiated components of the script. At this point, it is assumed that the references to those components are implicitly stated in the editorial. As a result, OpEd instantiates the entire script and builds a support link from the instantiated script to the causal belief that triggered the application of the script in the first place. This script-application process is summarized in figure 6.1.

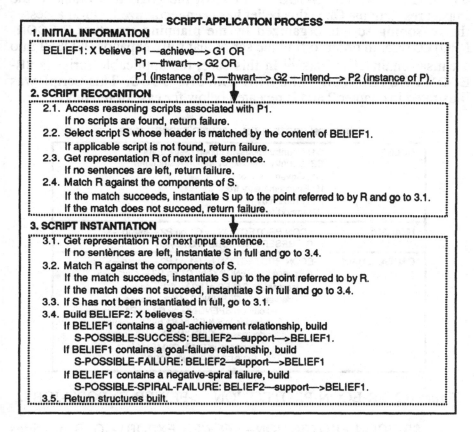

Figure 6.1. Reasoning-Script Application.

To illustrate the use of the script-application algorithm, consider how OpEd processes the following fragment of Friedman's argument in ED-JOBS:

> ... the limitations on imports will cost jobs. If we import less, foreign countries will earn fewer dollars. They will have less to spend on American exports. The result will be fewer jobs in export industries.

In the above excerpt, the word "cost" stands for a goal-failure relationship between a plan and a preservation goal. Giving this relationship, the sentence "limitations on imports cost jobs" gets mapped into the following belief:

BELIEF1: Friedman believes
          P-ECON-PROTECTION1 —thwart—> G-PRESERVING-JOBS1

where G-PRESERVING-JOBS1 is one of the goals that intended the import restrictions. Once this belief has been recognized, OpEd accesses the reasoning scripts organized by the planning structure P-ECON-PROTECTION in order to find the script that fully expands BELIEF3 into a causal chain of effects.[30] In this case, the applicable script is $R-ECON-PROTECTION—>FEWER-EXPORT-JOBS. This script was illustrated in chapter 2 and is repeated below for ease of reference.

$R-ECON-PROTECTION—>FEWER-EXPORT-JOBS

ROLES:	C1: Country imposing import restrictions
	C2: Country affected by import restrictions
	G1: Government of C1
	I1: Export industry from C1
	P1: Product by I1
	P2: Import from C2
HEADER:	P-ECON-PROTECTION by G1 on P2 —thwart—>
	G-PRESERVING-JOBS in C1 by G1
CAUSAL CHAIN:	P-ECON-PROTECTION by G1 on P2 —cause—>
	decrease in SPENDING by C1 on P2 —cause—>
	decrease in SALES of P2 by C2 —cause—>
	decrease in EARNINGS of C2 —cause—>
	decrease in SPENDING by C2 on P1 —cause—>
	decrease in SALES of P1 by I1 —cause—>
	decrease in EARNINGS of I1 —cause—>
	decrease in EMPLOYMENT in I1 —thwart—>
	G-PRESERVING-JOBS in C1 by G1

Figure 6.2. $R-ECON-PROTECTION—>FEWER-EXPORT-JOBS.

$R-ECON-PROTECTION—>FEWER-EXPORT-JOBS provides OpEd with the context for understanding why import restrictions will cause a decrease in U.S. exports and, consequently, a decrease in U.S. jobs. The process of applying this script is illustrated in table 6.2.

---

[30]In OpEd, P-ECON-PROTECTION organizes reasoning scripts in terms of the achievement and thwarting effects that import restrictions have on economic goals associated with international trade. Specifically, those scripts show how import restrictions: (1) achieve the goals of preserving earnings and attaining profitability for industries being protected; (2) thwart the goal of preserving earnings for consumers and industries that use imports; (3) thwart the goal of preserving jobs for workers in export industries; and (4) trigger protectionist spirals and economic retaliation. Those scripts are described in sections 2.3.3, 3.4.2, and 4.2.2.

Input Sentence	Representation of Input Sentence	Instantiation of $R-ECON-PROTECTION—>FEWER-EXPORT-JOBS After Processing Input Sentence
If we import less, foreign countries will earn fewer dollars	decrease SPENDING U.S. —cause—> decrease EARNINGS foreign country	P-ECON-PROTECTION U.S. —cause—> decrease SPENDING U.S. —cause—> decrease SALES foreign exports —cause—> decrease EARNINGS foreign country
They will have less to spend on American exports	decrease SPENDING foreign country	P-ECON-PROTECTION U.S. —cause—> decrease SPENDING U.S. —cause—> decrease SALES foreign exports —cause—> decrease EARNINGS foreign country —cause—> decrease SPENDING foreign country
The result will be fewer jobs in export industries	decrease EMPLOYMENT U.S.	P-ECON-PROTECTION U.S. —cause—> decrease SPENDING U.S. —cause—> decrease SALES foreign exports —cause—> decrease EARNINGS foreign country —cause—> decrease SPENDING foreign country —cause—> decrease SALES U.S. exports —cause—> decrease EARNINGS U.S. industry —cause—> decrease EMPLOYMENT U.S. —thwart—> G-PRESERVING-JOBS U.S.

Table 6.2. Script Application in ED-JOBS.

As the above table indicates, the use of reasoning scripts allows OpEd to follow belief justifications that contain structural gaps, i.e., justifications involving causal chains with implicit cause-effect relationships. Those relationships are inferred as a side-effect of the process of: (1) mapping input sentences into a reasoning script; and (2) instantiating the script with the information provided in those sentences. For example, the use of $R-ECON-PROTECTION—>FEWER-EXPORT-JOBS allows OpEd to infer the connection between the decrease in spending by foreign countries and the decrease in U.S. export jobs. That connection is described by the following cause-effect chain:

decrease in SPENDING by foreign countries on U.S. exports —causes—>
decrease in SALES of U.S. exports by U.S. export industries —causes—>
decrease in EARNINGS of U.S. export industries —causes—>
decrease in EMPLOYMENT in U.S. export industries

In ED-JOBS, the script-application process finishes after OpEd reads the sentence referring to the decrease in export jobs. At that point, OpEd builds two belief structures:

```
BELIEF2:  Friedman believes
          $R-ECON-PROTECTION—>FEWER-EXPORT-JOBS1

S-POSSIBLE-FAILURE:  BELIEF2 —support—> BELIEF1
```

where S-POSSIBLE-FAILURE represents Friedman's plan-based reasoning in ED-JOBS. Clearly, the process of recognizing the chains of causal effects that justify beliefs in editorials requires applying domain-specific knowledge in the form of reasoning scripts.

6.6.   Recognizing Argument Units From Linguistic Constructs

Beliefs and belief relationships are also recognized as a side-effect of recognizing argument units. Each AU can be cued by specific linguistic constructs that involve: (a) argument connectives such as "far from", "but", and "yet", which signal opposition and expectation failures; and (b) goal, plan, and belief relationships. As a result, following an argument involves recognizing these linguistic constructs, accessing the specific conceptualizations they refer to, and mapping from these conceptualizations into their appropriate AUs.

In editorials about the use of plans, the linguistic constructs associated with AUs conform to any of the following patterns:

1)   <Argument-Connective CONCEPT1 CONCEPT2>.

2)   <CONCEPT1 Argument-Connective CONCEPT2>.

where: (a) CONCEPT1 contains a causal belief B1 held by the editorial writer's opponent; and (b) CONCEPT2 contains the writer's justification J for an implicitly stated belief B2 that contradicts B1. According to the nature of the these concepts, three basic types of linguistic constructs have been characterized: contradictory-effect, expectation-failure, and argument-evaluation.

6.6.1. Contradictory-Effect Construct

The *contradictory-effect construct* is associated with AUs that involve opposite effects of a plan P on a goal G or on two interrelated goals G1 and G2. This linguistic construct combines the argument connective "far from" or the connective "although" with the plan-goal relationships summarized in table 6.3.

Argument Unit	Contradictory-Effect Construct Associated With Argument Unit
AU-OPPOSITE-EFFECT	"Far from" P by O —achieve—> G1, P —thwart—> G.
AU-EQUIVALENCE	"Although" P by O —achieve—> G1, P —cause—> S —thwart—> G2 (as important as G1).
AU-SPIRAL-EFFECT	"Although" P1 (instance of P) by O —achieve—> G1, P1—cause—> S —thwart—> G2 (as important as G1)—intend—> P2 (instance of P).
AU-MAJOR-FAILURE	"Although" P by O —achieve—> G1, P —cause—> S —thwart—> G2 (more important than G1).
AU-MAJOR-SUCCESS	"Although" P by O —thwart—> G1, P —cause—> S —achieve—> G2 (more important than G1).

Table 6.3. Contradictory-Effect Construct.

As an example of the contradictory-effect construct, consider the following excerpt from an editorial by Samuelson (1984, March 7):

ED-CAR-PRICES

... [A]lthough trade protection [by the U.S.] has raised auto industry profits by permitting higher new-car prices (up about 40% between 1980 and 1983), the same high prices [have] dampen[ed] consumer [purchasing power] ...

Samuelson argues against import restrictions by the U.S. on the basis that: (1) import restrictions cause an increase in car prices; (2) this price increase causes a decrease in consumer earnings; and (3) preserving consumer earnings is as important as helping the U.S. auto industry preserve its level of earnings. As such, Samuelson's argument is an instance of the argument unit AU-EQUIVALENCE which has been expressed in terms of the following construct:

"Although"   P by O —achieve—> G1,
             P —cause—> S —thwart—> G2 (as important as G1).

In ED-CAR-PRICES, P is the import restrictions, O is the U.S., G1 is the goal of preserving auto industry earnings, and G2 is the goal of preserving consumer earnings. In addition, the chain of causal effects containing the price increase (S) is an instance of the reasoning script $R-ECON-PROTECTION—>LOWER-CONSUMER-EARNINGS.

Another example of the contradictory-effect construct is provided by the following fragment of Friedman's argument in ED-JOBS:

Far from saving jobs, the limitations on imports [by the Reagan administration] will cost jobs ...

When processing ED-JOBS, OpEd must understand that the above sentence is an instance of the construct:

"Far from" P by O —achieve—> G,
    P —thwart—> G.

which signals the occurrence of AU-OPPOSITE-EFFECT. In order to recognize this AU from Friedman's argument, it is necessary to disambiguate the phrase "far from." In general, this phrase can introduce:

1) A space relationship (i.e., "far from" location L).

2) A relationship of opposition associated with AU-OPPOSITE-EFFECT.

After reading the phrase "far from," OpEd expects either a location or two cause-effect relationships in which a plan both achieves and thwarts the same goal. In the context of ED-JOBS, the latter expectation matches the meanings of "saving" and "cost." As a result, the second meaning of "far from" is selected and the following structures are instantiated:

OPPOSITE: Success: P-ECON-PROTECTION1 —achieve—>
                        G-PRESERVING-JOBS1
           Failure: P-ECON-PROTECTION1 —thwart—>
                        G-PRESERVING-JOBS1

AU-OPPOSITE-EFFECT:
    Arguer: Friedman
    Opponent: Reagan administration
    Plan: P-ECON-PROTECTION1
    Goal: G-PRESERVING-JOBS1

The above instance AU-OPPOSITE-EFFECT contains the following beliefs, support (S) relationships, and attack (A) relationships:

BELIEF1: Reagan administration believes
          OUGHT-TO P-ECON-PROTECTION1

BELIEF2: Reagan administration believes
          P-ECON-PROTECTION1 —achieve—> G-PRESERVING-JOBS1

BELIEF3: Friedman believes
          OUGHT-NOT-TO P-ECON-PROTECTION1

BELIEF4: Friedman believes
          P-ECON-PROTECTION1 —not-achieve—>
          G-PRESERVING-JOBS1

BELIEF5: Friedman believes
          P-ECON-PROTECTION1 —thwart—> G-PRESERVING-JOBS1

S-REALIZED-SUCCESS: BELIEF2 —support—> BELIEF1

S-UNREALIZED-SUCCESS: BELIEF4 —support—> BELIEF3

S-EXCLUDED-SUCCESS: BELIEF5 —support—> BELIEF4

A-OBJECTIONABLE-PLAN: BELIEF3 <—attack—> BELIEF1

A-UNREALIZED-SUCCESS: BELIEF4 <—attack—> BELIEF2

As this analysis of ED-JOBS shows, the process of recognizing AUs from linguistic constructs relies on expectations generated after an argument connective is found. These expectations involve specific information about the type of conceptualizations that may follow and/or may precede the argument connective. When an expectation is fulfilled, the appropriate AU is instantiated and, consequently, the beliefs and belief relationships organized by that AU are represented explicitly.

6.6.2. Expectation-Failure Construct

Many AUs characterize one-sided arguments in which an arguer attacks his/her opponent's expectation that a plan P will lead to a goal achievement or goal failure GS. In editorial text, those AUs are often cued by instances of the *expectation-failure construct*. This linguistic construct uses the argument connectives "but", "yet", or "however" to contrast a given expectation with the reason why that expectation will fail. For example, consider the following segment from an editorial by the Los Angeles Times (1984, May 3):

ED-AUTOMATION

... [Q]uotas were put on Japanese auto imports in 1981 ... because ... the UAW argued that without them the [auto] industry might face a collapse [and jobs would be lost] ... [H]owever, ... much of [the industry investment in the last three years] ... has been in worker-eliminating automation ...

In the above excerpt, the L.A. Times uses the argument unit AU-ACTUAL-CAUSE to refute the UAW's argument that import quotas on Japanese cars must be used to save jobs in the U.S. auto industry. The L.A. Times argues that import restrictions can not save jobs because: (1) an increase in spending on automation has decreased jobs in the auto industry; and (2) import quotas can not affect the level of spending on automation. This instance of AU-ACTUAL-CAUSE is conveyed in ED-AUTOMATION by the following construct:

O believes P —achieve—> G at time t.
"However" S —thwart—>G at time t.

Here, O corresponds to the UAW, P to the import quotas, G to the goal of preserving jobs, and S to the increase in spending on automation.

In addition to AU-ACTUAL-CAUSE, nine other AUs can be signaled by instances of the expectation-failure construct. Those AUs are summarized in the following table.

Argument Unit	Expectation-Failure Construct Associated With Argument Unit
AU-ACTUAL-CAUSE	O believes P —achieve—> G at time t. "But" S1 —thwart—> G at time t.
AU-OPPOSITE-EFFECT	O believes P —achieve—> G at time t. "But" P —thwart—> G at time t.
AU-WRONG-SOLUTION	O believes P —achieve—> G at time t. "But" only P1 —achieve—> G at time t.
AU-SIMILAR-UNREALIZED-SUCCESS	O believes P1 (instance of P) —achieve—> G1 (instance of G) at time t. "But" P2 (instance of P) —not-achieve—> G2 (instance of G) at time t1 <t.
AU-PROTOTYPICAL-UNREALIZED-SUCCESS	O believes P —achieve—> G at time t. "But" P1 (instance of P) —not-achieve—> G1 (instance of G) at time t1 <t.
AU-UNDISTURBED-SUCCESS	O believes P —thwart—> G at time t. "But" S1 —achieve—> G at time t.
AU-EXCLUDED-FAILURE	O believes P —thwart—> G at time t. "But" P —achieve—> G at time t.
AU-IMPOSSIBLE-FAILURE	O believes P —thwart—> G at time t. "But" only P1 —thwart—> G at time t.
AU-SIMILAR-UNREALIZED-FAILURE	O believes P1 (instance of P) —thwart—> G1 (instance of G) at time t. "But" P2 (instance of P) —not-thwart—> G1 (instance of G) at time t1 <t.
AU-PROTOTYPICAL-UNREALIZED-FAILURE	O believes P —thwart—> G at time t. "But" P1 (instance of P) —not-thwart—> G1 (instance of G) at time t1 <t.

Table 6.4. Expectation-Failure Construct.[31]

During editorial comprehension, these AUs are recognized by matching the components of the constructs in table 6.4 against the conceptualizations underlying the sentences that precede and follow an expectation-failure connective in the editorial. For example, consider how AU-SIMILAR-UNREALIZED-SUCCESS may be recognized when processing the following segment from an editorial by Lester Thurow (1983):

---

[31]The constructs in table 6.4 can also be used with other expectation-failure connectives, such as "yet" and "however."

ED-FOREIGN-COMPETITION

... [T]he only American [motorcycle] producer, Harley-Davidson, ... argues that it needs [a tariff on large motorcycles] ... to [help the industry] become competitive ... But ... [t]he American steel industry has been protected since the late 1960s and is less competitive today than it was then ...

In ED-FOREIGN-COMPETITION, Thurow brings up the failure of the steel-import restrictions in order to contradict the protectionist belief held by Harley-Davidson (H-D). This contradiction can be described as follows:

```
H-D believes
     P-ECON-PROTECTION1—achieve—>G-ATTAIN-COMPETITIVENESS1.
"But"
P-ECON-PROTECTION2—not-achieve—>G-ATTAIN-COMPETITIVENESS2.
```

The conceptualizations that precede and follow the connective "but" in the above construct match the components of the following pattern:

```
O believes P1 (instance of P) —achieve—> G1 (instance of G) at time t.
"But" P2 (instance of P) —not-achieve—>G2 (instance of G) at time t1<t.
```

As a result of this match, Thurow's argument can be recognized as an instance of AU-SIMILAR-UNREALIZED-SUCCESS:

```
AU-SIMILAR-UNREALIZED-SUCCESS:
    Arguer: Thurow
    Opponent: Harley-Davidson
    Plan: P-ECON-PROTECTION1
    Goal: G-ATTAIN-COMPETITIVENESS1
    Similar Plan: P-ECON-PROTECTION2
    Similar Goal: G-ATTAIN-COMPETITIVENESS2
```

This instantiated AU contains the following beliefs and belief relationships:

```
BELIEF1:  Harley Davidson believes
          OUGHT-TO P-ECON-PROTECTION1

BELIEF2:  Harley Davidson believes
          P-ECON-PROTECTION1 —achieve—>
          G-ATTAIN-COMPETITIVENESS1

BELIEF3:  Thurow believes
          OUGHT-NOT-TO P-ECON-PROTECTION1

BELIEF4:  Thurow believes
          P-ECON-PROTECTION1 —not-achieve—>
          G-ATTAIN-COMPETITIVENESS1
```

BELIEF5: Thurow believes
P-ECON-PROTECTION2 —not-achieve—>
G-ATTAIN-COMPETITIVENESS2

S-REALIZED-SUCCESS: BELIEF2 —support—> BELIEF1

S-UNREALIZED-SUCCESS: BELIEF4 —support—> BELIEF3

S-SIMILAR-UNREALIZED-SUCCESS: BELIEF5 —support—> BELIEF4

A-OBJECTIONABLE-PLAN: BELIEF3 <—attack—> BELIEF1

A-UNREALIZED-SUCCESS: BELIEF4 <—attack—> BELIEF2

As this analysis of Thurow's argument shows, linguistic constructs provide a method for for encoding the conceptualizations that can be used to uniquely identify AUs.

6.6.3. Argument-Evaluation Construct

The *argument-evaluation construct* is associated with AUs in which an arguer shows that his/her opponent should not endorse or reject a plan P solely on the basis of how P affects a goal G. This linguistic construct consists of three major components: (1) the opponent's argument A for endorsing or rejecting P; (2) a phrase, such as "is unwise" or "is wrongheaded," which is used to indicate that A is not appropriate; and (3) a chain of causal effects that describes how P affects other goals related to G. According to the nature of these components, the argument-evaluation construct can be used to characterize the four AUs summarized in table 6.5.

Argument Unit	Argument-Evaluation Construct Associated With Argument Unit
AU-EQUIVALENCE	O's argument OUGHT-TO P because P —achieve—> G1 "is wrongheaded." P —cause—> S —thwart—> G2 (as important as G1).
AU-SPIRAL-EFFECT	O's argument OUGHT-TO P1 because P1 —achieve—> G1 "is wrongheaded." P1 (instance of P) —cause—> S —thwart—> G2 —intend—> P2 (instance of P).
AU-MAJOR-FAILURE	O's argument OUGHT-TO P because P —achieve—> G1 "is wrongheaded." P —cause—> S —thwart—> G2 (more important than G1).
AU-MAJOR-SUCCESS	O's argument OUGHT-NOT-TO P because P —thwart—> G1 "is wrongheaded." P —cause—> S —achieve—> G2 (more important than G1).

Table 6.5. Argument-Evaluation Construct.

How are the above AUs recognized from instances of the argument-evaluation construct in editorial text? To illustrate this process, consider a simplified, annotated trace of the major inferences OpEd makes when reading a fragment of Morrow's argument in ED-RESTRICTIONS (see section 1.3):

The toolmakers argue that restrictions on imports must be imposed so that the industry can survive.

===> BELIEF1: Machine-tool industry believes
OUGHT-TO P-ECON-PROTECTION1

BELIEF2: Machine-tool industry believes
P-ECON-PROTECTION1 —achieve—>
G-PRESERVING-EARNINGS1

S-REALIZED-SUCCESS: BELIEF2 —support—> BELIEF1

Morrow mentions explicitly that the U.S. machine-tool industry favors imposing import restrictions. The industry argues for those restrictions on the basis that they will help protect the industry's economic well-being. This argument is represented in terms of the support relationship S-REALIZED-SUCCESS.

It is a wrongheaded argument.

===> BELIEF3: Morrow believes
OUGHT-NOT-TO P-ECON-PROTECTION1

A-OBJECTIONABLE-PLAN: BELIEF3 <—attack—> BELIEF1

=expect=> CHAIN: P-ECON-PROTECTION1—cause—>S—thwart—> G2
(G2 more important than G-PRESERVING-EARNINGS1)

CHAIN: P-ECON-PROTECTION1—cause—>S—thwart—> G2
(G2 as important as G-PRESERVING-EARNINGS1)

CHAIN: P-ECON-PROTECTION1—cause—>S—thwart—>
G2—intend—>P2
(G2 as important as G-PRESERVING-EARNINGS1)
(P2 instance of P-ECON-PROTECTION)

The text introduces the construct <ARGUMENT "is wrongheaded." CAUSAL-CHAIN>, where ARGUMENT refers to the toolmakers' position. Given that the toolmakers have argued for import restrictions, OpEd recognizes that Morrow is against such policies. At this point, OpEd expects that Morrow's position will be justified by chains of causal effects involving: (1) failures of goals more important than or equivalent to G-PRESERVING-EARNINGS1; or (2) negative-spiral failures. Furthermore, OpEd expects that those causal chains will conform to the goal-failure scripts organized by the planning structure P-ECON-PROTECTION.

Restrictions on Imports would mean that American manufacturers would have to make do with more expensive American machine tools.

===> P-ECON-PROTECTION1 by U.S. —cause—>
      increase SPENDING by U.S. manufacturers

=recognize=> $R-ECON-PROTECTION—>LOWER-DOMESTIC-EARNINGS
             $R-ECON-PROTECTION—>MORE-ECON-PROTECTION

=refine=> $R-ECON-PROTECTION—>LOWER-DOMESTIC-EARNINGS
          —imbedded-in—>
          $R-ECON-PROTECTION—>MORE-ECON-PROTECTION

=activate=> $R-ECON-PROTECTION—>MORE-ECON-PROTECTION

OpEd tries to match the causal relationship underlying the input sentence against the conceptualizations in the goal-failure scripts organized by P-ECON-PROTECTION. This match succeeds for two scripts:

1) $R-ECON-PROTECTION—>LOWER-DOMESTIC-EARNINGS
   (see section 2.3.3).

2) $R-ECON-PROTECTION—>MORE-ECON-PROTECTION
   (see section 4.2.2).

Since the information in $R-ECON-PROTECTION—>LOWER-DOMESTIC-EARNINGS is imbedded in $R-ECON-PROTECTION—>MORE-ECON-PROTECTION, the latter script is selected and instantiated up to the point referred to by the input. Thus, OpEd introduces the most inclusive script to attempt to: (1) understand Morrow's justifications; and (2) recognize the AUs that compose the editorial.[32]

Inevitably, those American manufacturers would produce more expensive products.

===> increase PRICE of U.S. products

=infer=> increase SPENDING by U.S. manufacturers —cause—>
         increase COST for U.S. manufacturers —cause—>
         increase PRICE of U.S. products

The text does not explicitly state what the connection is between the increase in spending on U.S. machine tools and the increase in prices of other U.S. products. This connection is made explicit when $R-ECON-PROTECTION—>MORE-ECON-PROTECTION is instantiated up to the point referred to by the conceptualization underlying the input. Based on this instantiation, OpEd infers that: (1) an increase in spending

---

[32]The method of applying the most inclusive script during text comprehension has been proposed by Cullingford (1978, 1981).

causes an increase in production costs; and (2) this increase in production costs leads to an increase in product prices.

They would lose sales.

===> decrease SALES of U.S. products —thwart—>
     G-PRESERVING-EARNINGS2 of U.S. manufacturers

=infer=> increase PRICE of U.S. products —cause—>
     decrease SPENDING on U.S. products —cause—>
     decrease SALES by U.S. manufacturers

=activate=> AU-EQUIVALENCE:
     Arguer: Morrow
     Opponent: Machine-tool industry
     Plan: P-ECON-PROTECTION1
     Goal: G-PRESERVING-EARNINGS1
     Equivalent Goal: G-PRESERVING-EARNINGS2
     Reasoning Script: $R-ECON-PROTECTION—>
          LOWER-DOMESTIC-EARNINGS

=infer=> BELIEF4: Morrow believes
          P-ECON-PROTECTION1 —thwart—>
          G-PRESERVING-EARNINGS2

     BELIEF5: Morrow believes
          $R-ECON-PROTECTION—>
          LOWER-DOMESTIC-EARNINGS

     S-EQUIVALENT-FAILURE: BELIEF4 —support—> BELIEF3

     S-POSSIBLE-FAILURE: BELIEF5 —support—> BELIEF4

     A-EQUIVALENT-FAILURE: BELIEF4 <—attack—> BELIEF2

Here, a decrease in the volume of sales thwarts the goal of preserving earnings of industries using U.S. machine tools. This thwarting relationship matches the last component of the script $R-ECON-PROTECTION—>LOWER-DOMESTIC-EARNINGS, which is imbedded in the active script $R-ECON-PROTECTION—>MORE-ECON-PROTECTION. Since $R-ECON-PROTECTION—>LOWER-DOMESTIC-EARNINGS involves a goal equivalent to the goal which has intended the import restrictions, AU-EQUIVALENCE is instantiated.

Then those manufacturers would demand protection against foreign competition.

===> G-PRESERVE-EARNINGS2 of U.S. manufacturers —intend—>
     P-ECON-PROTECTION2 by U.S.

```
=activate=>  AU-SPIRAL-EFFECT:
             Arguer: Morrow
             Opponent: Machine-tool industry
             Plan: P-ECON-PROTECTION1
             Goal: G-PRESERVING-EARNINGS1
             Spiral Plan: P-ECON-PROTECTION2
             Spiral Goal: G-PRESERVING-EARNINGS2
             Reasoning Script: $R-ECON-PROTECTION—>
                                      MORE-ECON-PROTECTION

=infer=>   BELIEF6:  Morrow believes
                     P-ECON-PROTECTION1 —thwart—>
                     G-PRESERVING-EARNINGS1 —intend—>
                     P-ECON-PROTECTION2

           BELIEF7:  Morrow believes
                     $R-ECON-PROTECTION—>
                     MORE-ECON-PROTECTION

           S-SPIRAL-FAILURE:  BELIEF6 —support—> BELIEF3

           S-POSSIBLE-SPIRAL-FAILURE: BELIEF7 —support—> BELIEF6

           A-SPIRAL-FAILURE:   BELIEF6 <—attack—> BELIEF2
```

The last sentence of ED-RESTRICTIONS involves a causal relationship in which the goal of preserving earnings of U.S. industries intends another instance of the planning structure P-ECON-PROTECTION. This relationship matches the last component of the active script $R-ECON-PROTECTION—>MORE-ECON-PROTECTION and, consequently, indicates that AU-SPIRAL-EFFECT must be instantiated. This analysis of how OpEd processes ED-RESTRICTIONS shows that applying expectations generated from linguistic constructs requires tracing the evolution of plan-goal situations in editorials.

6.7.   Recognizing Argument Units From Plan-Failure Beliefs

AUs can also be recognized as a side-effect of recognizing justifications of plan-failure beliefs, i.e., beliefs of the form <Plan P by Opponent O —not-achieve—> Goal G>. These beliefs amount to implicit attacks on the reasoning associated with the execution of plans, namely: the actor of a plan P believes that P should be used to achieve the goal G which has intended P. For example, consider the following fragment of the L.A. Times' argument in ED-CONTRADICTORY-POLICIES (chapter 3, section 3.1):

American negotiators are pursuing a protectionist course ... in what seems a vain effort to protect U.S. steel makers ... The American

> **steel industry ... will be cushioned from the economic forces that
> alone ... hold the hope of restoring ... competitiveness ...**

In the above excerpt, the L.A. Times refutes the U.S. government's implicitly stated position that import restrictions should be used to help the steel industry become competitive. The L.A. Times argues that import restrictions will not work because competitiveness can only be attained by a laissez-faire policy (i.e., the opposite of import restrictions). As such, the L.A. Times' argument is an instance of the argument unit AU-WRONG-SOLUTION, which is signaled by the following support relationship:

> A believes P1 by O —not-achieve—> G1
> because only P2 (opposite of P1) —achieve—> G1

In ED-CONTRADICTORY-POLICIES, A is the L.A. Times, P1 is the import restrictions, O is the U.S. government, G1 is the goal of restoring competitiveness, and P2 is a laissez-faire policy.

During editorial comprehension, the process of recognizing AUs relies on expectations generated after a plan-failure belief is found. These expectations involve specific information about: (1) the possible ways to justify plan-failure beliefs; and (2) the AUs that organize those justifications. Five AUs can be characterized by these expectations, as shown in table 6.6.

Belief Triggering Expectations	Expected Input	Preconditions To Be Satisfied by Expected Input	Argument Unit Recognized When Expectation Is Fulfilled
	P1 —thwart—> G1	G1 —intend—> P1	AU-OPPOSITE-EFFECT
	S1 —thwart—> G1	G1 —intend—> P1	AU-ACTUAL-CAUSE
A believe P1 by O —not-achieve—> G1	only P2 —achieve—> G1	G1 —intend—> P2 P2 opposite of P1	AU-WRONG-SOLUTION
	P2 —not-achieve—> G2	G2 —intend—> P2 P2 instance of P P1 instance of P G2 instance of G G1 instance of G	AU-SIMILAR-UNREALIZED-SUCCESS
	P2 —not-achieve—> G2	G2 —intend—> P2 P2 instance of P1 G2 instance of G1	AU-PROTOTYPICAL-UNREALIZED-SUCCESS

Table 6.6. Expectations Generated From Plan-Failure Beliefs.

Consider how OpEd uses the expectations in table 6.6 to processes the following fragment of Friedman's argument in ED-JOBS:

> **Recent protectionist measures by the Reagan administration have disappointed us ... They do not promote the long-run health of the industries affected. The problem of the automobile and steel industries is: in both industries, average wage rates are twice as high as the average ...**

Briefly, an analysis of the first two sentences of Friedman's argument yields the following belief structures (see section 6.4):

BELIEF1: Friedman believes
          OUGHT-NOT-TO P-ECON-PROTECTION1

BELIEF2: Friedman believes
          P-ECON-PROTECTION1 —not-achieve—>
          G-ATTAIN-PROFITABILITY1

S-UNREALIZED-SUCCESS: BELIEF2 —support—> BELIEF1

Based on the content of BELIEF2, OpEd generates five expectations (Es) for belief justifications:

E1: P-ECON-PROTECTION1 —thwart—> G-ATTAIN-PROFITABILITY1

E2: STATE1 —thwart—> G-ATTAIN-PROFITABILITY1

E3: P-LAISSEZ-FAIRE —achieve—> G-ATTAIN-PROFITABILITY1

E4: PLAN3 —not-achieve—> GOAL3
     (PLAN3 instance of P-ECON-PROTECTION1)
     (GOAL3 instance of G-ATTAIN-PROFITABILITY1)

E5: PLAN4 —not-achieve—> GOAL4
     (PLAN4 instance of P-ECON-PROTECTION)
     (GOAL4 instance of G-ATTAIN-PROFITABILITY)

Given these expectations, OpEd tries to match them against the representation of the sentence:

> **The problem of the automobile and steel industries is: in both industries, average wage rates are twice as high as the average ...**

In the above sentence, the word "problem" stands for a goal-failure relationship involving an active goal of the industries being protected. Since the only active goal known for those industries is G-ATTAIN-PROFITABILITY1, OpEd represents the above sentence as follows:

high SALARIES —thwart—> G-ATTAIN-PROFITABILITY1

This causal relationship matches the content of expectation E2. As a result, the argument unit AU-ACTUAL-CAUSE is instantiated as follows:

```
AU-ACTUAL-CAUSE:
   Arguer: Friedman
   Opponent: Reagan administration
   Plan: P-ECON-PROTECTION1
   Goal: G-ATTAIN-PROFITABILITY1
   Actual State: High SALARIES
   Opposite State: Low SALARIES
```

This instance of AU-ACTUAL-CAUSE contains not only the structures BELIEF1, BELIEF2, and S-UNREALIZED-SUCCESS, but also the following beliefs and belief relationships:

```
BELIEF3:   Friedman believes
           high SALARIES —thwart—> G-ATTAIN-PROFITABILITY1

BELIEF4:   Friedman believes
           P-ECON-PROTECTION1 —not-cause—> low SALARIES

BELIEF5:   Reagan administration believes
           OUGHT-TO P-ECON-PROTECTION1

BELIEF6:   Reagan administration believes
           P-ECON-PROTECTION1 —achieve—>
           G-ATTAIN-PROFITABILITY1

S-REALIZED-SUCCESS:   BELIEF6 —support—> BELIEF5

S-UNDISTURBED-FAILURE: BELIEF3 AND BELIEF4 —support—> BELIEF2

A-OBJECTIONABLE-PLAN:  BELIEF1 <—attack—> BELIEF5

A-UNREALIZED-SUCCESS:  BELIEF2 <—attack—> BELIEF6
```

As this analysis of Friedman's argument demonstrates, recognizing AUs requires applying general knowledge of how to reason about plan failures.

6.8.   Summary

This chapter has presented techniques for recognizing beliefs, belief relationships, and argument units (AUs). These techniques have been implemented in OpEd to understand short-politico-economic editorials dealing with the use of protectionist policies. Six major points have been emphasized here:

1) Beliefs can be recognized from explicit standpoints and from descriptions of emotional reactions.

2) In order to follow belief justifications, it is necessary to trace the evolution of plan-goal situations by applying: knowledge

of plan-based reasoning, knowledge of domain-specific plans and goals, and reasoning scripts.

3) Beliefs that contain goal-achievement and goal-failure relationships between a plan and a goal act as headers of reasoning scripts.

4) Following an argument requires recognizing specific linguistic constructs that signal the occurrence of AUs in editorial text.

5) Plan-failure beliefs signal AUs that characterize attacks on the reasoning associated with the execution of plans.

6) Instantiating AUs helps recognize implicitly stated beliefs, support relationships, and attack relationships.

Chapter 7

Memory Search and Retrieval

7.1. Introduction

In order to demonstrate its understanding of an editorial, OpEd must be able to answer questions about the issues addressed in that editorial. Chapter 1 established that question answering in OpEd is characterized in terms of three processes: (1) understanding questions from the perspective of the editorial's memory representation, or argument graph; (2) retrieving conceptual answers from the argument graph; and (3) generating conceptual answers in natural language. Furthermore, Chapter 1 indicated that question comprehension is performed by the same conceptual parser used for editorial comprehension, and answer generation is performed by a recursive-descent, English generator. This chapter examines the techniques used in the process of retrieving information from conceptual representations of editorials.

Retrieving answers to questions about an editorial requires dealing with two major processing issues: (1) how to gain initial entry to the editorial's argument graph; and (2) how to locate appropriate beliefs, belief relationships, or argument units (AUs) in that graph. To illustrate the nature of these issues, consider a segment from an editorial by Schneider (1985) and a question about its content:

ED-PROTECTIONIST-BILLS

Members of Congress came back to Washington this month in an unusually combative mood ... [after] they spent their summer vacations ... [l]istening to people complain about foreign trade ... More than 400 bills have been introduced in Congress to protect American products from import competition ... [This] protectionism is not the solution [to the U.S. balance-of-trade deficit] ... The problem is [the high value of] the dollar ...

Q: What does Schneider believe?
A: Schneider believes that import restrictions should not be imposed to balance the U.S. trade deficit. Schneider argues that such policies will not work because the actual cause of the deficit is the high value of the dollar. Schneider also believes that members of Congress are wrong to believe that import restrictions will balance the U.S. trade deficit.

Answering question Q1 involves retrieving the AU underlying Schneider's argument in ED-PROTECTIONIST-BILLS. In that editorial, Schneider uses AU-ACTUAL-CAUSE to refute Congress' implicitly stated position that import restrictions are needed to balance the U.S. trade deficit. Schneider argues that import restrictions can not achieve the goal of attaining a balanced trade because: (1) that goal is being thwarted by the high value of the dollar; and (2) import restrictions can not decrease the value of the dollar. In order to retrieve this instance of AU-ACTUAL-CAUSE as the answer to question Q1, it is necessary to have:

1) An index from argument participants to their professed beliefs.

2) Access links between beliefs and associated AUs.

3) A retrieval function that takes an argument participant (in this case, Schneider), accesses the professed beliefs of that participant, traverses the links from those beliefs to their associated AUs, and retrieves each of those AUs (in this case, the instance of AU-ACTUAL-CAUSE used by Schneider).

As this analysis of Q1 indicates, a question of the type "What does X believe?" may be answered by accessing the representation of X's beliefs and retrieving the AUs that contain those beliefs. Clearly, retrieving answers to questions about an editorial requires the use of: (1) indexing structures and access links that provide initial entry to the editorial's argument graph; and (2) search and retrieval functions that select indices and traverse access and memory links in order to locate appropriate conceptualizations in the graph.

This chapter presents a model of memory search and retrieval implemented in OpEd to answer questions about editorials that contain arguments for/against protectionism (Alvarado et al., 1985a). The model has been developed as an extension to the question-categorization scheme proposed by Lehnert (1978) and the retrieval heuristics proposed by Dyer and Lehnert (1982). Two main techniques are used in OpEd's search and retrieval model: (1) an indexing scheme based on argument units, belief relationships, argument participants, plans, and goals; and (2) a set of search and retrieval functions associated with conceptual categories of questions that request belief holders, evaluative beliefs, causal beliefs, belief justifications, and argument units. The use of the model will be illustrated using ED-JOBS, an editorial segment from Friedman (1982) read by OpEd.

7.2. Organizing and Indexing Editorial Memory

The memory representation of an editorial forms a graph of conceptual constructs instantiated during editorial comprehension. Within this argument graph, instantiated constructs are connected by memory links that indicate knowledge dependencies such as: causal relationships, support/attack relationships, containment relationships, and indexing relationships. Five major elements compose the editorial's argument graph:

1) <u>Domain-Specific Constructs:</u> Instantiations of goals, plans, events, and states underlying the issues addressed in the editorial.

2) <u>Argument Participants:</u> Instantiations of the editorial writer and his/her implicit opponents.

3) <u>Beliefs:</u> Instantiations of the argument participants' evaluations about plans and expectations about the success or failure of goals.

4) <u>Belief Relationships:</u> Instantiations of support (S) and attack (A) structures that represent relationships among evaluative and causal beliefs.

5) <u>Argument Units:</u> Instantiations of configurations of support and attack structures that represent the editorial writer's one-sided arguments.

For example, consider the text and representation of Friedman's argument in ED-JOBS.

ED-JOBS

Recent protectionist measures by the Reagan administration have disappointed us. Voluntary limits on Japanese automobiles and voluntary limits on steel by the Common Market are bad for the nation. They do not promote the long-run health of the industries affected. The problem of the automobile and steel industries is: in both industries, average wage rates are twice as high as the average. Far from saving jobs, the limitations on imports will cost jobs. If we import less, foreign countries will earn fewer dollars. They will have less to spend on American exports. The result will be fewer jobs in export industries.

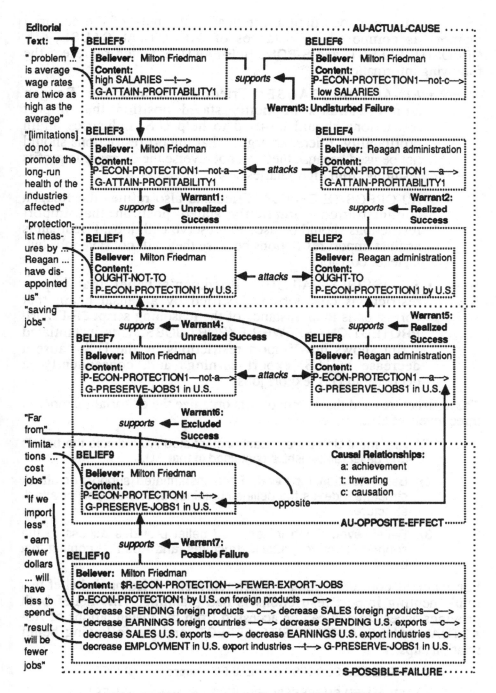

Figure 7.1. Argument Graph of ED-JOBS.

As the previous diagram indicates, the bulk of the editorial memory is composed of instances of AU-ACTUAL-CAUSE, AU-OPPOSITE-EFFECT, and S-POSSIBLE-FAILURE which represent the following information:

- AU-ACTUAL-CAUSE: Friedman refutes the Reagan administration's implicitly stated position that import restrictions should be used to help U.S. industries attain profitability. Friedman argues that import restrictions should not be used because they can not reverse the decrease in profits resulting from high salaries.

- AU-OPPOSITE-EFFECT: Friedman also refutes the Reagan administration's implicitly stated position that import restrictions should be used to preserve U.S. jobs. Friedman is against import restrictions because they will not save jobs but, instead, cost jobs.

- S-POSSIBLE-FAILURE: Friedman's belief that import restrictions cost jobs is justified by a causal chain that corresponds to an instance of the reasoning script $R-ECON-PROTECTION—>FEWER-EXPORT-JOBS. This instantiated script shows how import restrictions by the U.S. cause a decrease in U.S. export earnings and, consequently, a decrease in U.S. export jobs.

These structures and their components organize the editorial memory at three levels of abstraction:

1) **Argument-Unit Level:** Each instantiated AU indexes the beliefs and belief relationships contained in that AU.

2) **Belief-Relationship Level:** Each instantiated support or attack structure indexes the beliefs contained in that support or attack structure.

3) **Belief Level:** Each instantiated belief provides access to the support structures, attack structures, and AUs that contain that belief.

For example, consider BELIEF1 which represents Friedman's belief that implementing import restrictions is bad planning. This belief both provides access to and can be accessed from the instantiations of AU-ACTUAL-CAUSE, AU-OPPOSITE-EFFECT, and the following belief relationships:

S-UNREALIZED-SUCCESS1:   BELIEF3 —support—> BELIEF1

S-UNREALIZED-SUCCESS2:   BELIEF7 —support—> BELIEF1

A-OBJECTIONABLE-PLAN: BELIEF1 <—attack—> BELIEF2

Here, BELIEF2 is the Reagan administration's belief that import restrictions should be used, BELIEF3 is Friedman's belief that import restrictions can not help U.S. industries attain profitability, and BELIEF7 is Friedman's belief that import restrictions can not save jobs. As this example indicates, the memory representation of an editorial can be viewed as a belief network in which complex argument structures can be accessed from basic belief structures, and basic belief structures can be accessed from complex argument structures.

The indices and access links organized by AUs, belief relationships, and beliefs are not sufficient to provide initial entry to the argument graph during question answering. For example, consider the following questions:

Q1: What is the result of the limitations on imports?

Q2: What does the Reagan administration think about the limitations on imports?

Although question Q1 requests beliefs involving plan-goal relationships and question Q2 requests the beliefs of an argument participant, those questions do not supply any AU, belief relationship, or belief to serve as an index for memory search. To handle such questions, OpEd imposes two additional indexing levels on the argument graph created during editorial comprehension: (1) indexing by domain-specific constructs; and (2) indexing by argument participants.

(1) Indexing by Domain-Specific Constructs: Each goal or plan indexes the beliefs that contain instantiations of that goal or plan. For example, both the goal G-ATTAIN-PROFITABILITY and the planning structure P-ECON-PROTECTION (see section 2.2.4) index the following beliefs from ED-JOBS:

BELIEF3: Milton Friedman believes
          P-ECON-PROTECTION1 —not-achieve—>
          G-ATTAIN-PROFITABILITY1

BELIEF4: Reagan administration believes
          P-ECON-PROTECTION1 —achieves—>
          G-ATTAIN-PROFITABILITY1

Similarly, the following beliefs from ED-JOBS:

BELIEF7: Milton Friedman believes
          P-ECON-PROTECTION1 —not-achieve—>
          G-PRESERVE-JOBS1

BELIEF8: Reagan administration believes
P-ECON-PROTECTION1 —achieves—>
G-PRESERVE-JOBS1

BELIEF9: Milton Friedman believes
P-ECON-PROTECTION1 —thwart—>
G-PRESERVE-JOBS1

BELIEF10: Milton Friedman believes
$R-ECON-PROTECTION—>FEWER-EXPORT-JOBS

are indexed by both the goal G-PRESERVE-JOBS and the planning structure P-ECON-PROTECTION.

(2) **Indexing by Argument Participants:** Each instantiated argument participant indexes the participant's *top beliefs,* i.e., beliefs that do not support other beliefs. Within the framework of editorials about the use of plans, the top beliefs of an argument participant correspond to his/her evaluative beliefs about those plans. For example, the following beliefs:

BELIEF1: Friedman believes
OUGHT-NOT-TO P-ECON-PROTECTION1

BELIEF2: Reagan administration believes
OUGHT-TO P-ECON-PROTECTION1

represent the plan evaluations presented in ED-JOBS and can be accessed through the instantiations of Friedman and the Reagan administration, respectively.

These two levels of indexing along with the indexing information organized by AUs, belief relationships, and beliefs provide a system for accessing and locating the components of the argument graph to be retrieved during question answering. For example:

1) The AUs used by an editorial writer can be accessed through the top beliefs indexed by the instantiation of the writer.

2) The reasoning used by the editorial writer's implicit opponent, to endorse or reject the use of a plan, can be accessed through the top beliefs indexed by the instantiation of that opponent.

3) The justifications of an argument participant for his/her beliefs about the effects of a plan P can be accessed through the representation of P.

4) The justifications of an argument participant for his/her beliefs about the success or failure of a goal G can be accessed through the representation of G.

Clearly, the constructs that compose an editorial's argument graph not only represent the conceptual content of the editorial, but also provide the means to organize and access that information.

7.3. Retrieving Information From Editorial Memory

OpEd's model of memory search and retrieval is based on techniques developed for answering questions about narratives involving stereotypical situations, goal and planning situations, and complex interpersonal relationships. According to Lehnert (1978), answering a question requires analyzing the conceptual content of the question into one of a number of conceptual question categories. Lehnert has identified thirteen categories:

1) **Causal Antecedent:** Questions that ask for the states that cause a given event.

2) **Goal Orientation:** Questions that ask for the goals behind a given plan.

3) **Enablement:** Questions that ask for the state that enables a plan.

4) **Causal Consequent:** Questions that ask for the states that result from a given event.

5) **Verification:** Questions that ask whether an event has happened or not.

6) **Disjunctive:** Questions that give two disjunctive events and ask which one occurred.

7) **Instrumental:** Questions that ask for the events that are instrumental for a given event.

8) **Concept Completion:** Questions that seek a component (e.g., the actor) of an event.

9) **Expectational:** Questions that ask for the states that prevent an event from occurring.

10) **Judgemental:** Questions that solicit a judgement on the part of the listener.

11) **Quantification:** Questions that ask for a quantity or for a relative value on a finite scale.

12) **Feature Specification:** Questions that ask about a feature of a person or a thing.

13) **Request:** Questions that solicit the execution of a specific action by the listener.

This categorization scheme has been expanded by Dyer (1983a) to include two more question categories:

14) **Affect:** Questions that ask for the goal situations underlying an emotional reaction.

15) **Event Specification:** Questions that ask for events that occur in a given setting.

When answering questions about a narrative, each conceptual question category leads to the selection of different search and retrieval processes. As established by Dyer and Lehnert (1982), those search and retrieval processes do not depend on the specific contents of the narrative memory, but rather on the knowledge dependencies that exist among the constructs that organize the narrative memory. As such, the process of retrieving answers to questions about a narrative involves: (1) accessing instantiated goals, plans, and events; and (2) traversing appropriate memory links that encode causal dependencies, such as goal achievement, goal failure, goal motivation, goal suspension, plan intention, plan enablement, plan disablement, event realization, and forced events. For example, in order to answer the following goal orientation question:

Q: For what purpose did John hire a chauffeur?

in the context of a story such as:

John was tired of driving to work everyday. He decided to hire a chauffeur.

it is necessary to: (1) access the representation of John's plan for hiring a chauffeur; (2) traverse the links between John's plan and the goal that plan is intended to achieve (i.e., to avoid driving); and (3) retrieve that goal.

How have these techniques been adapted in OpEd to retrieve answers to questions about editorials? Once an editorial's argument graph and indexing structures have been built in memory, OpEd demonstrates its comprehension by answering questions that involve retrieving instantiated beliefs, belief relationships, and AUs from the argument graph. This retrieval process relies on expectations that are generated after a question word (e.g., "who", "what", "why", "how", etc.) is found at the beginning of a question. These expectations perform two specific tasks: (1) determining the question's conceptual category based on the information provided in the question and the information requested by the question; and (2) activating appropriate search and retrieval processes based on the question's conceptual category. Five conceptual categories have been characterized within the framework of OpEd:

1) **Belief Holder:** Questions that ask for the holder of a given belief, such as "Who believes that the limitations on imports will cost jobs?" These questions are much like the concept-completion questions identified by Lehnert.

2) **Causal Belief:** Questions that ask for causal beliefs involving goals, plans, events, and states, such as "What does Milton Friedman think the result of the limitations on imports will be?" These questions form a meta-category for five question types identified by Lehnert: causal antecedent, causal consequent, goal orientation, enablement, and expectational.

3) **Belief Justification:** Questions that ask for the justifications of a given belief, such as "Why does Milton Friedman believe that the limitations on imports will cost jobs?"

4) **Affect/Belief:** Questions that look for beliefs associated with emotional reactions resulting from the execution of a plan, such as "Why have the limitations on imports disappointed Milton Friedman?" These questions form a meta-category for the affect questions identified by Dyer.

5) **Top-Belief/AU:** Questions that seek answers involving the top beliefs or argument units associated with an argument participant, such as "What is the opinion of Milton Friedman?"

These five categories, along with the retrieval strategies used in OpEd, are summarized in table 7.1 and illustrated below using simplified traces of how OpEd answers questions about ED-JOBS.

Conceptual Question Category	Question Word	Information in Input Question	Information Requested	Search and Retrieval Process
Belief Holder	Who	Plan Evaluation or Plan-Goal Relationship	Holder of Belief About Plan	Argument-Participant Retrieval Using Plan Indexing
	Who	Goal Situation	Holder of Belief About Goal Situation	Argument-Participant Retrieval Using Goal Indexing
Causal Belief	What	Plan	Consequent Goal Situation	Causal-Belief Retrieval Using Plan Indexing
	What	Plan and Argument Participant	Consequent Goal Situation	Causal-Belief Retrieval Using Plan Indexing Limited by Argument Participant
	How or What	Goal Situation	Causal Plan or Causal State	Causal-Belief Retrieval Using Goal Indexing
	How or What	Goal Situation and Argument Participant	Causal Plan or Causal State	Causal-Belief Retrieval Using Goal Indexing Limited by Argument Participant
Belief Justification	Why	Plan Evaluation or Plan-Goal Relationship	Justification for Belief About Plan	Belief-Justification Retrieval Using Plan Indexing
	Why	Evaluative or Causal Belief of Argument Participant	Justification for Belief About Plan	Belief-Justification Retrieval Using Plan Indexing Limited by Argument Participant
Affect/Belief	What	Affect and Argument Participant	Causal Plan	Plan-Retrieval Using Argument-Participant Indexing
	Why	Affect, Plan, and Argument Participant	Plan-Goal Relationship	Belief-Justification Retrieval Using Argument-Participant Indexing
Top-Belief/AU	What	Plan and Argument Participant	Top Belief and its Justification	Top-Belief Retrieval Using Argument-Participant Indexing
	What	Argument Participant	Argument Unit or Top Belief and its Justification	Argument-Unit or Top-Belief Retrieval Using Argument-Participant Indexing

Table 7.1. OpEd's Question Categories and Retrieval Processes.

7.3.1. Belief-Holder Questions

(1) Argument-Participant Retrieval Using Plan Indexing: Given the content of an evaluative or a causal belief about a plan, OpEd retrieves the argument participant who holds that belief.

Q1: Who believes that the limitations on imports are bad?

```
===>  BELIEF:  (*H?*) believes
                OUGHT-NOT-TO P-ECON-PROTECTION

=recognize=>   Belief-Holder Question
=activate=>    Argument-Participant Retrieval Using Plan Indexing
=select=>  Index: P-ECON-PROTECTION
=access=>  Matching beliefs about negative evaluations indexed
            by P-ECON-PROTECTION:
            BELIEF1:  Friedman believes
                        OUGHT-NOT-TO P-ECON-PROTECTION1

=retrieve=>   Holder of BELIEF1: Friedman
=answer=>  MILTON FRIEDMAN.
```

Q2: Who believes that the limitations on imports will save jobs?

```
===>  BELIEF:  (*H?*) believes
                P-ECON-PROTECTION —achieve—> G-PRESERVE-JOBS

=recognize=>   Belief-Holder Question
=activate=>    Argument-Participant Retrieval Using Plan Indexing
=select=>  Index: P-ECON-PROTECTION
=access=>  Matching  beliefs about goal achievements indexed
            by P-ECON-PROTECTION:
            BELIEF8:  Reagan Administration believes
                        P-ECON-PROTECTION1 —achieve—>
                        G-PRESERVE-JOBS1

=retrieve=>   Holder of BELIEF8: Reagan Administration
=answer=>  THE REAGAN ADMINISTRATION.
```

As these examples show, answering a belief-holder question about a plan requires: (1) selecting the index associated with that plan; (2) using that index to access a belief that matches the question's information; and (3) retrieving the holder of that belief.

(2) Argument-Participant Retrieval Using Goal Indexing: Given the content of a causal belief about a goal situation, OpEd retrieves the argument participant who holds that belief.

Q: Who believes that jobs will be lost?

```
===>  BELIEF:  (*H?*) believes
                (*C?*) —thwart—> G-PRESERVE-JOBS
```

```
=recognize=>    Belief-Holder Question
=activate=>     Argument-Participant Retrieval Using Goal Indexing
=select=>       Index: G-PRESERVE-JOBS
=access=>       Matching beliefs about goal failures indexed
                by G-PRESERVE-JOBS:
                BELIEF9:   Friedman believes
                            P-ECON-PROTECTION1 —thwart—>
                            G-PRESERVE-JOBS1

=retrieve=>     Holder of BELIEF9: Milton Friedman
=answer=>       MILTON FRIEDMAN.
```

To answer a belief-holder question about a goal situation, OpEd must: (1) select the index associated with the given goal; (2) use that index to access a belief about a goal situation that matches the question's information; and (3) retrieve the holder of that belief. Thus, answering the above question requires accessing Friedman's belief that import restrictions cost jobs.

7.3.2. Causal-Belief Questions

(1) Causal-Belief Retrieval Using Plan Indexing: Given a plan, OpEd retrieves the beliefs which contain the goal situations resulting from the execution of that plan.

Q: What is the result of the limitations on imports?

```
===>  P-ECON-PROTECTION —lead-to—> (*GS?*)

=recognize=>    Causal-Belief Question
=activate=>     Causal-Belief Retrieval Using Plan Indexing
=select=>       Index: P-ECON-PROTECTION
=access=>       Beliefs about plan-goal relationships indexed
                by P-ECON-PROTECTION:
                (BELIEF3, BELIEF4, BELIEF7, BELIEF8, BELIEF9)

=refine=>       BELIEF7 —supported-by—> BELIEF9

=retrieve=>     BELIEF3:  Friedman believes
                            P-ECON-PROTECTION1 —not-achieve—>
                            G-ATTAIN-PROFITABILITY1

                BELIEF4:  Reagan administration believes
                            P-ECON-PROTECTION1 —achieve—>
                            G-ATTAIN-PROFITABILITY1
```

BELIEF8: Reagan administration believes
                 P-ECON-PROTECTION1 —achieve—>
                 G-PRESERVE-JOBS1

BELIEF9: Friedman believes
                 P-ECON-PROTECTION1 —thwart—>
                 G-PRESERVE-JOBS1

=answer=> MILTON FRIEDMAN BELIEVES THAT PROTECTIONIST
POLICIES BY THE REAGAN ADMINISTRATION DO NOT LEAD
TO THE ACHIEVEMENT OF NORMAL PROFITS OF THE STEEL
INDUSTRY AND THE AUTOMOBILE INDUSTRY.

THE REAGAN ADMINISTRATION BELIEVES THAT
PROTECTIONIST POLICIES BY THE REAGAN ADMINISTRATION
LEAD TO THE ACHIEVEMENT OF NORMAL PROFITS OF THE
STEEL INDUSTRY AND THE AUTOMOBILE INDUSTRY.

THE REAGAN ADMINISTRATION BELIEVES THAT
PROTECTIONIST POLICIES BY THE REAGAN ADMINISTRATION
ACHIEVE THE PRESERVATION OF JOBS FOR U.S.

MILTON FRIEDMAN BELIEVES THAT PROTECTIONIST
POLICIES BY THE REAGAN ADMINISTRATION WILL THWART
THE PRESERVATION OF JOBS FOR U.S.

Here, the answer to a causal-belief question about a plan is
found by: (1) selecting the index associated with that plan; and (2) using
that index to access the beliefs that contain plan-goal relationships,
namely BELIEF3, BELIEF4, BELIEF7, BELIEF8, and BELIEF9. Since
BELIEF9 supports BELIEF7, the latter belief need not be retrieved as part
of the answer. Thus, OpEd's answer consists of BELIEF3, BELIEF4,
BELIEF8, and BELIEF9, and provides details about the most specific
goal situations caused by the Reagan administration's protectionist
policies.

(2) Causal-Belief Retrieval Using Plan Indexing Limited by Argument Participant:

Given an argument participant and a plan, OpEd
retrieves the beliefs which contain the goal situations resulting from the
execution of that plan.

Q: What does the Reagan administration think the result of the
     limitations on imports will be?

===> BELIEF: Reagan administration believes
                      P-ECON-PROTECTION —lead-to—> (*GS?*)

=recognize=> Causal-Belief Question
=activate=> Causal-Belief Retrieval Using Plan Indexing Limited
                   by Argument Participant
=select=> Index: P-ECON-PROTECTION

=access=>   Matching Reagan administration's beliefs about plan-goal
             relationships indexed by P-ECON-PROTECTION:
             (BELIEF4, BELIEF8)

=retrieve=> BELIEF4: Reagan administration believes
                       P-ECON-PROTECTION1 —achieve—>
                       G-ATTAIN-PROFITABILITY1

             BELIEF8: Reagan administration believes
                       P-ECON-PROTECTION1 —achieve—>
                       G-PRESERVE-JOBS1

=answer=>   THE REAGAN ADMINISTRATION BELIEVES THAT
             PROTECTIONIST POLICIES BY THE REAGAN ADMINISTRATION
             LEAD TO THE ACHIEVEMENT OF NORMAL PROFITS OF THE
             STEEL INDUSTRY AND THE AUTOMOBILE INDUSTRY.

             THE REAGAN ADMINISTRATION BELIEVES THAT
             PROTECTIONIST POLICIES BY THE REAGAN ADMINISTRATION
             ACHIEVE THE PRESERVATION OF JOBS FOR U.S.

Finding the answer to a causal-belief question that provides an
argument participant and a plan requires: (1) selecting the index
associated with the given plan; (2) using that index to access the beliefs
of the given participant; and (3) retrieving those beliefs that contain plan-
goal relationships. Thus, using the argument-participant information
limits the beliefs accessed during memory search to the causal beliefs of
that participant.

(3) **Causal-Belief Retrieval Using Goal Indexing:** Given a goal
situation, OpEd retrieves the beliefs which contain plans or states that
cause the given goal situation.

Q: **What deteriorates the long-run health of the automobile and the
     steel industries?**

===>   (*C?*) —thwart—> G-ATTAIN-PROFITABILITY1

=recognize=> Causal-Belief Question
=activate=>   Causal-Belief Retrieval Using Goal Indexing
=select=>   Index: G-ATTAIN-PROFITABILITY
=access=>   Matching beliefs about goal failures indexed
              by G-ATTAIN-PROFITABILITY:
              (BELIEF5)

=retrieve=>   BELIEF5: Friedman believes
                        high SALARIES —thwart—>
                        G-ATTAIN-PROFITABILITY1

=answer=>   MILTON FRIEDMAN BELIEVES THAT NORMAL SALARY IN THE
              STEEL INDUSTRY AND THE AUTOMOBILE INDUSTRY HIGHER
              THAN THE NORM THWARTS THE ACHIEVEMENT OF NORMAL
              PROFITS OF THE STEEL INDUSTRY AND THE AUTOMOBILE
              INDUSTRY.

As this example shows, to answer a causal-belief question about a goal situation, OpEd has to: (1) select the index associated with the given goal; (2) use that index to access beliefs that contain the given goal situation; and (3) retrieve those beliefs.

(4) Causal-Belief Retrieval Using Goal Indexing Limited by Argument Participant: Given an argument participant and a goal situation, OpEd retrieves the beliefs which contain plans or states that cause the given goal situation.

> Q: **How does the Reagan administration think the long-run health of the automobile and steel industries will be promoted?**
>
> ===> BELIEF: Reagan administration believes
>   (*C?*) —achieve—> G-ATTAIN-PROFITABILITY1
>
> =recognize=> Causal-Belief Question
> =activate=> Causal-Belief Retrieval Using Plan Indexing Limited
>   by Argument Participant
> =select=> Index: G-ATTAIN-PROFITABILITY
> =access=> Matching Reagan administration's beliefs about goal
>   achievements indexed by G-ATTAIN-PROFITABILITY:
>   (BELIEF4)
>
> =retrieve=> BELIEF4: Reagan administration believes
>   P-ECON-PROTECTION1 —achieve—>
>   G-ATTAIN-PROFITABILITY1
>
> =answer=> THE REAGAN ADMINISTRATION BELIEVES THAT PROTECTIONIST POLICIES BY THE REAGAN ADMINISTRATION LEAD TO THE ACHIEVEMENT OF NORMAL PROFITS OF THE STEEL INDUSTRY AND THE AUTOMOBILE INDUSTRY.

Here, OpEd finds the answer to the causal-belief question by: (1) selecting the index associated with the goal G-ATTAIN-PROFITABILITY; (2) using that index to access the Reagan administration's beliefs about goal achievements; and (3) retrieving that belief.

7.3.3. Belief-Justification Questions

(1) Belief-Justification Retrieval Using Plan Indexing: Given a plan evaluation or a plan-goal relationship, OpEd retrieves the immediate justifications for beliefs which contain that plan evaluation or plan-goal relationship.

Q: Why are the limitations on imports good?

```
===>  (*B?*) —support—>
         BELIEF: (*H?*) believes
                 OUGHT-TO P-ECON-PROTECTION
```

```
=recognize=>   Belief-Justification Question
=activate=>    Belief-Justification Retrieval Using Plan Indexing
=select=>      Index: P-ECON-PROTECTION
=access=>      Matching beliefs about negative evaluations indexed
               by P-ECON-PROTECTION:
               BELIEF2:  Reagan administration believes
                         OUGHT-TO P-ECON-PROTECTION1
```

```
=select=>   Index: BELIEF2
=access=>   Justifications of BELIEF2: (BELIEF4, BELIEF8)
=retrieve=> BELIEF4:  Reagan administration believes
                      P-ECON-PROTECTION1 —achieve—>
                      G-ATTAIN-PROFITABILITY1

            BELIEF8:  Reagan administration believes
                      P-ECON-PROTECTION1 —achieve—>
                      G-PRESERVE-JOBS1
```

```
=answer=> THE  REAGAN  ADMINISTRATION  BELIEVES  THAT
          PROTECTIONIST POLICIES BY THE REAGAN ADMINISTRATION
          LEAD TO THE ACHIEVEMENT OF NORMAL PROFITS OF THE
          STEEL INDUSTRY AND THE AUTOMOBILE INDUSTRY.

          THE  REAGAN  ADMINISTRATION  BELIEVES  THAT
          PROTECTIONIST POLICIES BY THE REAGAN ADMINISTRATION
          ACHIEVE THE PRESERVATION OF JOBS FOR U.S.
```

**Q2: Why do the limitations on imports not promote the long-run
     health of the automobile and steel industries?**

```
===>  (*B?*) —support—>
         BELIEF: (*H?*) believes
                 P-ECON-PROTECTION —not-achieve—>
                 G-ATTAIN-PROFITABILITY
```

```
=recognize=>   Belief-Justification Question
=activate=>    Belief-Justification Retrieval Using Plan Indexing
=select=>      Index: P-ECON-PROTECTION
=access=>      Matching beliefs about unrealized goal achievements indexed
               by P-ECON-PROTECTION:
               BELIEF3:  Friedman believes
                         P-ECON-PROTECTION1 —not-achieve—>
                         G-ATTAIN-PROFITABILITY1
```

```
=select=>   Index: BELIEF3
=access=>   Justifications of BELIEF3: (BELIEF5, BELIEF6)
=retrieve=> BELIEF5:  Friedman believes
                      high SALARIES —thwart—>
                      G-ATTAIN-PROFITABILITY1
```

BELIEF6: Friedman believes
          P-ECON-PROTECTION1 —not-cause—>
          low SALARIES

=answer=> MILTON FRIEDMAN BELIEVES THAT NORMAL SALARY IN THE
           STEEL INDUSTRY AND THE AUTOMOBILE INDUSTRY HIGHER
           THAN THE NORM THWARTS THE ACHIEVEMENT OF NORMAL
           PROFITS OF THE STEEL INDUSTRY AND THE AUTOMOBILE
           INDUSTRY.

           MILTON FRIEDMAN BELIEVES THAT PROTECTIONIST
           POLICIES BY THE REAGAN ADMINISTRATION DO NOT CAUSE
           NORMAL SALARY IN THE STEEL INDUSTRY AND THE
           AUTOMOBILE INDUSTRY LOWER THAN THE NORM.

As these examples show, finding the answer to a belief-justification question that provides a plan relationship involves accessing the editorial memory through two levels of indexing. Specifically, OpEd must: (1) select the index associated with the given plan; (2) use that index to access beliefs whose contents match the given plan relationship; and (3) retrieve the justifications indexed by those beliefs.

(2) Belief-Justification Retrieval Using Plan Indexing Limited by Argument Participant: Given an argument participant's evaluative or a causal belief about a plan, OpEd retrieves the immediate justifications for that belief.

Q: Why does Milton Friedman believe that the limitations on imports will cost jobs?

===> (*B?*) —support—>
      BELIEF: Friedman believes
               P-ECON-PROTECTION —thwart—> G-PRESERVE-JOBS

=recognize=>   Belief-Justification Question
=activate=>   Belief-Justification Retrieval Using Plan Indexing Limited
               by Argument Participant
=select=> Index: P-ECON-PROTECTION
=access=> Matching Friedman's beliefs about goal failures indexed
           by P-ECON-PROTECTION:
           BELIEF9: Friedman believes
                     P-ECON-PROTECTION1 —thwart—>
                     G-PRESERVE-JOBS1

=select=> Index: BELIEF9
=access=> Justifications of BELIEF9: (BELIEF10)
=retrieve=> BELIEF10: Friedman believes
                      $R-ECON-PROTECTION—>
                      FEWER-EXPORT-JOBS

=answer=> MILTON FRIEDMAN BELIEVES THAT AS A CONSEQUENCE OF
          PROTECTIONIST   POLICIES   BY   THE   REAGAN
          ADMINISTRATION, U.S. IMPORTS FEWER PRODUCTS; AND IF

> U.S. IMPORTS FEWER PRODUCTS, THEN THERE IS A
> DECREASE IN PROFITS OF FOREIGN COUNTRIES; AND IF
> THERE IS A DECREASE IN PROFITS OF FOREIGN COUNTRIES,
> THEN FOREIGN COUNTRIES BUY FEWER AMERICAN
> EXPORTS; AND IF FOREIGN COUNTRIES BUY FEWER
> AMERICAN EXPORTS, THEN THERE IS A DECREASE IN
> PROFITS OF EXPORT INDUSTRIES; AND IF THERE IS A
> DECREASE IN PROFITS OF EXPORT INDUSTRIES, THEN THERE
> IS A DECREASE IN JOBS IN EXPORT INDUSTRIES; AND A
> DECREASE IN JOBS IN EXPORT INDUSTRIES THWARTS THE
> PRESERVATION OF JOBS FOR U.S.

Here, OpEd finds the answer by: (1) selecting the index
associated with P-ECON-PROTECTION; (2) using that index to access
Friedman's belief about the goal failure given in the question; and (3)
retrieving the justification indexed by that belief. Consequently, OpEd's
answer contains the instance of $R-ECON-PROTECTION—>FEWER-
EXPORT-JOBS that shows how import restrictions by the U.S. cause a
decrease in U.S. export jobs.

7.3.4. Affect/Belief Questions

(1) **Plan Retrieval Using Argument-Participant Indexing:** Given
an affect and an argument participant, OpEd retrieves the plan whose
execution has caused that affect.

Q: What has disappointed Milton Friedman?

===> NEGATIVE-AFFECT by Friedman
      —associated-belief—>
      BELIEF: Friedman believes
               OUGHT-NOT-TO ("P?")

=recognize=> Affect/Belief Question
=activate=> Plan Retrieval Using Argument-Participant Indexing
=select=> Index: Friedman
=access=> Matching top beliefs about negative evaluations indexed
           by Friedman:
           BELIEF1: Friedman believes
                     OUGHT-NOT-TO P-ECON-PROTECTION1

=retrieve=> Plan Evaluated in BELIEF1: P-ECON-PROTECTION1
=answer=> PROTECTIONIST POLICIES BY THE REAGAN
           ADMINISTRATION.

Since OpEd infers evaluative beliefs from affect descriptions
(see section 6.3), answering a question about the cause of an affect
involves: (1) accessing the top beliefs indexed by the argument
participant experiencing that affect; and (2) finding a belief that

corresponds to the affect description in the question. Once a belief has been found, OpEd retrieves the plan contained in that belief.

(2) Belief-Justification Retrieval Using Argument-Participant Indexing: Given an affect, an argument participant, and a plan, OpEd retrieves the beliefs which contain goal situations underlying the given affect and resulting from the execution of the given plan.

Q: **Why have the limitations on imports disappointed Milton Friedman?**

```
===> NEGATIVE-AFFECT by Friedman
      —associated-belief—>
      BELIEF: Friedman believes
                OUGHT-NOT-TO P-ECON-PROTECTION
      —supported-by—>
      BELIEF: Friedman believes
                P-ECON-PROTECTION —lead-to—> (*GS?*)

=recognize=>  Affect/Belief Question
=activate=>   Belief-Justification Retrieval Using
              Argument-Participant Indexing
=select=>     Index: Friedman
=access=>     Matching top beliefs about negative evaluations indexed
              by Friedman:
              BELIEF1: Friedman believes
                       OUGHT-NOT-TO P-ECON-PROTECTION1

=select=>     Index: BELIEF1
=access=>     Justifications of BELIEF1: (BELIEF3, BELIEF7)
=select=>     Index: BELIEF7
=refine=>     BELIEF7 —supported-by—> BELIEF9
=retrieve=>   BELIEF3: Friedman believes
                       P-ECON-PROTECTION1 —not-achieve—>
                       G-ATTAIN-PROFITABILITY1

              BELIEF9: Friedman believes
                       P-ECON-PROTECTION1 —thwart—>
                       G-PRESERVE-JOBS1

=answer=>  MILTON FRIEDMAN BELIEVES THAT PROTECTIONIST
           POLICIES BY THE REAGAN ADMINISTRATION DO NOT LEAD
           TO THE ACHIEVEMENT OF NORMAL PROFITS OF THE STEEL
           INDUSTRY AND THE AUTOMOBILE INDUSTRY.

           MILTON FRIEDMAN BELIEVES THAT PROTECTIONIST
           POLICIES BY THE REAGAN ADMINISTRATION WILL THWART
           THE PRESERVATION OF JOBS FOR U.S.
```

To answer the above affect/belief question, OpEd must: (1) access the top belief that corresponds to the given affect description; and (2) access recursively the justifications of that belief in order to find the most specific plan-goal relationships underlying the affect. As a result,

OpEd's answer contains Friedman's position that import quotas both cost jobs and fail to help domestic industries attain profitability.

7.3.5. Top-Belief/AU Questions

(1) Top-Belief Retrieval Using Argument-Participant Indexing: Given a plan and an argument participant, OpEd retrieves the argument participant's top beliefs and its immediate justifications.

> **Q: What does the Reagan administration think about the limitations on imports?**

```
===>   BELIEF:  Reagan administration believes
                   (*R?*) P-ECON-PROTECTION

=recognize=>   Top-Belief/AU Question
=activate=>    Top-Belief Retrieval Using Argument-Participant Indexing
=select=>      Index: Reagan administration
=access=>      Matching top beliefs about P-ECON-PROTECTION indexed
               by Reagan administration:
               BELIEF2:  Reagan administration believes
                           OUGHT-TO P-ECON-PROTECTION1

=select=>  Index: BELIEF2
=access=>  Justifications of BELIEF2: (BELIEF4, BELIEF8)
=retrieve=>  BELIEF2:  Reagan administration believes
                           OUGHT-TO P-ECON-PROTECTION1
               —supported-by—>
               BELIEF4:  Reagan administration believes
                           P-ECON-PROTECTION1 —achieve—>
                           G-ATTAIN-PROFITABILITY1

=retrieve=>  BELIEF2:  Reagan administration believes
                           OUGHT-TO P-ECON-PROTECTION1
               —supported-by—>
               BELIEF8:  Reagan administration believes
                           P-ECON-PROTECTION1 —achieve—>
                           G-PRESERVE-JOBS1
```

=answer=> THE REAGAN ADMINISTRATION BELIEVES THAT PROTECTIONIST POLICIES BY THE REAGAN ADMINISTRATION ARE GOOD BECAUSE THE REAGAN ADMINISTRATION BELIEVES THAT PROTECTIONIST POLICIES BY REAGAN ADMINISTRATION LEAD TO THE ACHIEVEMENT OF NORMAL PROFITS OF THE STEEL INDUSTRY AND THE AUTOMOBILE INDUSTRY.

THE REAGAN ADMINISTRATION BELIEVES THAT PROTECTIONIST POLICIES BY THE REAGAN ADMINISTRATION ARE GOOD BECAUSE THE REAGAN ADMINISTRATION BELIEVES THAT PROTECTIONIST POLICIES BY REAGAN

ADMINISTRATION ACHIEVE THE PRESERVATION OF JOBS
FOR U.S.

Answering the above top-belief/AU question requires: (1)
accessing the Reagan administration's top belief about import
restrictions; (2) accessing the justifications indexed by that belief; and
(3) retrieving those justifications along with the administration's top
belief. Thus, OpEd's answers contain the administration's reasoning for
negotiating the import restrictions on automobiles and steel.

**(2) Argument-Unit or Top-Belief Retrieval Using Argument-
Participant Indexing:** Given an argument participant, OpEd retrieves the
argument units that contain the participant's top belief and its
justifications. If the argument participant has not used any argument
units, OpEd retrieves the participant's top belief and its immediate
justifications.

Q: What does Milton Friedman believe?

===> BELIEF: Friedman believes (*BC?*)

=recognize=> Top-Belief/AU Question
=activate=> Argument Unit or Top-Belief Retrieval Using
             Argument-Participant Indexing
=select=> Index: Friedman
=access=> Top beliefs indexed by Friedman:
           BELIEF1: Friedman believes
                     OUGHT-NOT-TO P-ECON-PROTECTION1

=select=> Index: BELIEF1
=access=> AUs that contain BELIEF1:
           (AU-ACTUAL-CAUSE, AU-OPPOSITE-EFFECT)

=retrieve=> AU-ACTUAL-CAUSE: Arguer: Friedman
                               Opponent: Reagan administration
                               Plan: P-ECON-PROTECTION1
                               Goal: G-ATTAIN-PROFITABILITY1
                               Actual State: High SALARIES
                               Opposite State: Low SALARIES

             AU-OPPOSITE-EFFECT: Arguer: Friedman
                                  Opponent: Reagan administration
                                  Plan: P-ECON-PROTECTION1
                                  Goal: G-PRESERVE-JOBS1

=answer=> MILTON FRIEDMAN BELIEVES THAT PROTECTIONIST
           POLICIES BY THE REAGAN ADMINISTRATION ARE BAD
           BECAUSE MILTON FRIEDMAN BELIEVES THAT
           PROTECTIONIST POLICIES BY THE REAGAN ADMINISTRATION
           DO NOT LEAD TO THE ACHIEVEMENT OF NORMAL PROFITS
           OF THE STEEL INDUSTRY AND THE AUTOMOBILE INDUSTRY.
           MILTON FRIEDMAN BELIEVES THAT PROTECTIONIST

POLICIES BY THE REAGAN ADMINISTRATION DO NOT LEAD
TO THE ACHIEVEMENT OF NORMAL PROFITS OF THE STEEL
INDUSTRY AND THE AUTOMOBILE INDUSTRY BECAUSE
MILTON FRIEDMAN BELIEVES THAT NORMAL SALARY IN THE
STEEL INDUSTRY AND THE AUTOMOBILE INDUSTRY HIGHER
THAN THE NORM THWARTS THE ACHIEVEMENT OF NORMAL
PROFITS OF THE STEEL INDUSTRY AND THE AUTOMOBILE
INDUSTRY. MILTON FRIEDMAN BELIEVES THAT THE REAGAN
ADMINISTRATION IS WRONG BECAUSE THE REAGAN
ADMINISTRATION BELIEVES THAT PROTECTIONIST POLICIES
BY THE REAGAN ADMINISTRATION LEAD TO THE
ACHIEVEMENT OF NORMAL PROFITS OF THE STEEL
INDUSTRY AND THE AUTOMOBILE INDUSTRY.

MILTON FRIEDMAN BELIEVES THAT PROTECTIONIST
POLICIES BY THE REAGAN ADMINISTRATION ARE BAD
BECAUSE MILTON FRIEDMAN BELIEVES THAT
PROTECTIONIST POLICIES BY THE REAGAN ADMINISTRATION
WILL THWART THE PRESERVATION OF JOBS FOR U.S.
MILTON FRIEDMAN BELIEVES THAT THE REAGAN
ADMINISTRATION IS WRONG BECAUSE THE REAGAN
ADMINISTRATION BELIEVES THAT PROTECTIONIST POLICIES
BY THE REAGAN ADMINISTRATION ACHIEVE THE
PRESERVATION OF JOBS FOR U.S.

To answer the above question, OpEd must retrieve the AUs used
by Friedman in ED-JOBS. This retrieval process involves: (1) accessing
Friedman's top belief that implementing import restrictions is a bad idea;
and (2) accessing the instances of AU-ACTUAL-CAUSE and AU-
OPPOSITE-EFFECT indexed by Friedman's top belief. Clearly, the
answer to a top-belief/AU question about the writer of an editorial
contains the points of that editorial.

7.4.   Summary

This chapter has presented techniques for organizing and
retrieving information from editorial memory. These techniques have
been implemented in OpEd to understand and answer questions about
editorials that contain arguments for/against protectionism. Five major
points have been emphasized here:

1) The memory representation of an editorial forms an
   argument graph organized in terms of beliefs, belief
   relationships, and argument units (AUs).

2) Initial entry to the editorial's argument graph is provided by
   indexing structures associated with argument participants,
   plans, and goals.

3) To answer a question about the editorial, it is necessary to analyze the contents of the question into one of five conceptual question categories: belief holder, causal belief, belief justification, affect/belief, and top-belief/AU.

4) Each conceptual question category leads to the selection of search and retrieval processes which use indexing structures to gain access to the argument graph.

5) Search and retrieval processes make use of the knowledge dependencies that exist among the constructs that organize the argument graph.

Chapter 8

Annotated Example of the OpEd System

8.1. Introduction

The theory of argument comprehension described in previous chapters has been developed from the perspective of natural language understanding. Because of this approach, argument comprehension in OpEd is not considered as an isolated task but rather as an integral aspect of language comprehension. As such, OpEd's process model involves the use of techniques for mapping input editorial text into an argument graph that represents and maintains the context of the editorial for subsequent question answering. This chapter illustrates those techniques by analyzing a detailed example of OpEd's input/output behavior.

In OpEd, editorial comprehension and question answering are performed using the parsing techniques provided by DYPAR (Dyer, 1983a), an expectation-based, conceptual parser designed for in-depth understanding of narrative text.[33] OpEd reads input editorial text and questions in a left-to-right manner, one word or phrase at a time. As each word and/or phrase is read, OpEd's lexicon is accessed in order to identify the conceptualization underlying that word or phrase. Associated with entries in the lexicon are knowledge structures, and associated with those structures are processing strategies called *demons*.

---

[33]For a description of OpEd's components see section 1.4.

Demons are delayed procedures that implement test/action rules, where tests and actions may involve tasks such as: disambiguating word senses, resolving pronoun and concept references, searching and retrieving information, matching and binding conceptualizations, and recognizing beliefs and argument structures. When a lexical item is recognized, an instance of the associated knowledge structure is placed in OpEd's working memory, and instances of the associated demons are placed in a demon agenda (i.e., demons are "spawned"). Then, OpEd tests all demons in the agenda and executes those whose test portions are satisfied. After demons are executed, they are removed from the agenda (i.e., demons are "killed").

To illustrate how lexical items are declared in OpEd's lexicon, consider a simplified representation of the word "hurt":

```
(DEFINE-WORD HURT
    DEMONS ((PHYSICAL-INJURY? M1) (ECONOMIC-INJURY? M2))
    M1 (LEAD-TO ANTE (DO ACTOR H1 <== (EXPECT HUMAN BEFORE))
                CONSE (GOAL-SITUATION
                          GOAL (GOAL TYPE (PRESERVATION)
                                     ACTOR H2 <== (EXPECT HUMAN AFTER)
                                     OBJECT (STATE TYPE (PHYSICAL)
                                                   OBJECT H2
                                                   SCALE (NORM)))
                          STATUS (THWARTED)))
    M2 ($R-LOW-IMPORT-PRICES-->LOW-DOMESTIC-EARNINGS
        IMPORT M1 <== (EXPECT (PHYS-OBJ FOOD) BEFORE)
        INDUSTRY N1 <== (EXPECT INSTITUTION AFTER)))
```

The above entry contains two meanings of "hurt" that correspond to the following patterns:

- Physical-Injury Pattern: Human H1 "hurt" human H2. For example, "John, the bully of the neighborhood, hurt Bill."

- Economic-Injury Pattern: Import M1 "hurt" industry N1 (see section 2.3). For example, "Imports of Japanese machine tools have hurt U.S. toolmakers."

These meanings are encoded in terms of hierarchical data structures called *frames* (Charniak 1977, 1978; Minsky 1975, 1977). Those frames are of the form:

```
CONCEPT = (HEAD SLOT-1 VARIABLE-1 <== (DEMON-1 ARGUMENT-1)
                ...
                SLOT-N VARIABLE-N <== (DEMON-N ARGUMENT-N))
```

Here, HEAD is the type of the CONCEPT, SLOTS are the components of that CONCEPT, VARIABLES are place holders for the values of those

SLOTS, and DEMONS are the processes that find instantiated constructs in working memory based on the descriptions provided in the given ARGUMENTS. The lexical entry for "hurt" also has two disambiguation demons (i.e., PHYSICAL-INJURY? and ECONOMIC-INJURY?) that select the appropriate meaning of "hurt" by matching the components of the physical-injury and economic-injury patterns against the conceptualizations of phrases that precede and follow "hurt" in a given sentence. As this example indicates, processes involving language analysis, knowledge application, and knowledge interactions are implemented in OpEd in terms of demons.

This chapter presents annotated traces of how OpEd reads a segment from an editorial by Friedman (1982) and answers questions about its content. The traces include information on memory instantiations and bindings that result from the execution of demons. Because the complete, unannotated traces are over 200 pages long, only highlights of OpEd's input/output behavior are shown here. In addition, the following changes have been made to the original traces: (1) messages involving test/action rules associated with demons are shown only for the first instance of each type of demon; and (2) portions of the internal structure of conceptualizations and demon instances have been omitted and marked by ellipses. The chapter also describes the current status of OpEd's implementation, including computer systems and programming tools used, number of demons implemented, and computer time and memory requirements.

8.2.   Editorial-Comprehension Trace

```
==> (OPED 'ED-JOBS)
```

Editorial: ED-JOBS
Writer: MILTON FRIEDMAN
Country: U.S.

Initialization: The initial information provided to the program involves the author of the editorial and the country where it was written. As a result, OpEd creates instantiations of Friedman and the U.S. in episodic memory. OpEd also creates the global variables WRITER and COUNTRY, which contain access links to the instantiations of Friedman and the U.S., respectively. These links may be used to resolve concept and pronoun references.

8.2.1. First Sentence

Processing Sentence:
RECENT PROTECTIONIST MEASURES BY THE REAGAN
ADMINISTRATION HAVE DISAPPOINTED US *PERIOD*

RECENT ==>
```
    Adding to *working-memory*:
        #{^WEB.6403} = ()
    Spawning demon: #{^WEB.6405: ^FIND-REFERENCE …}
        ((HEAD ^FIND-REFERENCE)
         (ARGUMENTS ^WEB.6403 (PLAN EVENT)…))
        If PLAN or EVENT follows and a matching PLAN or
        EVENT exists,
        Then return matching PLAN or EVENT.
        Otherwise, ignore word RECENT.
```

Slot-Filler Objects: The basic slot-filler representation object used in OpEd is called *web* (Mueller and Zernik, 1984). Webs implement frames that correspond to: (1) instances of concepts in working memory and episodic memory; and (2) instances of active demons in the demon agenda. Each demon instance contains the name of the demon and the arguments to be used by that demon. The first argument of a demon always corresponds to a web that represents the instance of the concept in working memory or episodic memory associated with that demon.

Concept Reference: The word "recent" introduces the patterns <"recent" PLAN> and <"recent" EVENT>. These patterns indicate that OpEd's episodic memory must be searched in order to find a matching plan or event. This memory search is restricted to the constructs instantiated during editorial comprehension because OpEd does not maintain a historical memory for politico-economic beliefs, goals, plans, and events. If a matching plan or event is not found in the representation of the current context of the editorial, OpEd ignores the word "recent."

PROTECTIONIST ==>
```
    Adding to *working-memory*:
        #{^WEB.6406} = ()
    Spawning demon: #{^WEB.6408: ^PROTECTIONIST-BELIEF …}
        ((HEAD ^PROTECTIONIST-BELIEF)
         (ARGUMENTS ^WEB.6406 (HUMAN INSTITUTION AUTHORITY)…))
        If HUMAN, INSTITUTION, or AUTHORITY follows,
        Then HUMAN, INSTITUTION, or AUTHORITY favors
```

```
          P-ECON-PROTECTION.
    Spawning demon: #{^WEB.6409: ^REINTERPRET-CONCEPT …}
      ((HEAD ^REINTERPRET-CONCEPT)
        (ARGUMENTS ^WEB.6406 PLAN P-ECON-PROTECTION …))
      If PLAN follows,
      Then reinterpret PLAN as P-ECON-PROTECTION.
```

Ambiguous Word: Ambiguous words have demons that disambiguate them according to the active context. The word "protectionist" has at least two meanings: (1) it indicates that HUMANS, INSTITUTIONS, and AUTHORITIES believe that it is a good idea to implement import restrictions (e.g., "a protectionist congressman"); or (2) it indicates that general PLANS are of the type P-ECON-PROTECTION (e.g., "protectionist policies"). As a result, after reading the word "protectionist" OpEd expects a HUMAN, an INSTITUTION, an AUTHORITY, or a general PLAN.

MEASURES ==>
```
    Recognized word: MEASURE
    Recognized suffix: S
    Adding to *working-memory*:
        #{^WEB.6410} = ()
    Spawning demon: #{^WEB.6416: ^PLURAL …}
        ((HEAD ^PLURAL)
         (ARGUMENTS ^WEB.6410))
        If content of ^WEB.6410 is known,
        Then modify ^WEB.6410 with GROUP-INSTANCES = *MULTIPLE*.
    Spawning demon: #{^WEB.6412: ^DISAMBIGUATE-USING-WORD …}
        ((HEAD ^DISAMBIGUATE-USING-WORD)
         (ARGUMENTS ^WEB.6410 OF (FOOD LIQUID) AFTER QUANTITY …))
        If FOOD or LIQUID found AFTER and modified by word OF,
        Then ^WEB.6410 is QUANTITY.
    Spawning demon: #{^WEB.6413: ^DISAMBIGUATE …}
        ((HEAD ^DISAMBIGUATE)
         (ARGUMENTS ^WEB.6410 HUMAN BEFORE P-MEASURING …))
        If HUMAN found BEFORE,
        Then ^WEB.6410 is P-MEASURING.
    Spawning demon: #{^WEB.6414: ^DISAMBIGUATE-USING-WORD …}
        ((HEAD ^DISAMBIGUATE-USING-WORD)
         (ARGUMENTS ^WEB.6410 TO LEAD-TO AFTER PLAN …))
    Spawning demon: #{^WEB.6415: ^DISAMBIGUATE-USING-WORD …}
        ((HEAD ^DISAMBIGUATE-USING-WORD)
         (ARGUMENTS ^WEB.6411 BY (HUMAN AUTHORITY) AFTER PLAN …))
```

Morphological Endings: If OpEd cannot recognize a word or phrase directly in the lexicon, it applies morphological analysis to decompose that word or phrase into a recognizable ROOT and a SUFFIX. This analysis is done by using a decision tree implemented as a *discrimination net* (Charniak et al., 1980), where each path in the net represents a particular SUFFIX. When a ROOT is recognized, a copy of its associated conceptualization is placed in working memory. Copies of the demons associated with that conceptualization and the SUFFIX are placed in the demon agenda. If the word is ambiguous, its disambiguation demons, along with the SUFFIX demons, are placed in the demon agenda. For example, the word "measure" has demons that account for three different meanings: (1) a QUANTITY of a FOOD or LIQUID, such as "two measures of sugar"; (2) a plan P-MEASURING, such as "the gardener measures the tree every day"; (3) a general PLAN, such as "measures to lower the trade deficit" or "measures by the U.S. Congress."

```
Executing demon: #{^WEB.6409: ^REINTERPRET-CONCEPT …}
    #{^WEB.6410} = ((HEAD ^P-ECON-PROTECTION)
                    (ACTOR (*VAR* 'ACTOR.6419)))
                   (IMPORTING-COUNTRY (*VAR* 'IC.5016.6424))
                   (EXPORTING-COUNTRY (*VAR* 'EC.5017.6425))
                   (IMPORT (*VAR* 'I.5018.6426))
                   (PROTECTED-INDUSTRY (*VAR* 'PI.5019.6427))
                   (ACTIONS (*OR* #{^WEB.6453: ^AUTHORIZE …}
                                  #{^WEB.6440: ^RESOLVE …})))…)
Spawning demon: #{^WEB.6496: ^FIND-P-ECON-PROTECTION …}
    ((HEAD ^FIND-P-ECON-PROTECTION)
     (ARGUMENTS ^WEB.6410 …))
    If matching P-ECON-PROTECTION exists,
    Then return P-ECON-PROTECTION found.
    Otherwise, create a new instance of P-ECON-PROTECTION.
Spawning demon: #{^WEB.6493: ^FILLER …}
    ((HEAD ^FILLER)
     (ARGUMENTS ^WEB.6410 (IMPORT NATION) (EXPORTING-COUNTRY …))
    If filler of the path (IMPORT NATION) in ^WEB.6410 is known,
    Then return it as the value of the path (EXPORTING-COUNTRY).
Spawning demon: #{^WEB.6491: ^FILLER …}
    ((HEAD ^FILLER)
     (ARGUMENTS ^WEB.6410 (ACTOR NATION) (IMPORTING-COUNTRY …))
Spawning demon: #{^WEB.6490: ^INFER-PROTECTED-INDUSTRY …}
    ((HEAD ^INFER-PROTECTED-INDUSTRY)
     (ARGUMENTS ^WEB.6410 …))
    If IMPORTING-COUNTRY and IMPORT are known,
    Then infer PROTECTED-INDUSTRY.
Spawning demon: #{^WEB.6420: ^EXPECT-USING-WORD …}
    ((HEAD ^EXPECT-USING-WORD)
     (ARGUMENTS ^WEB.6410
                ACTOR.6419 BY (AUTHORITY COUNTRY) AFTER …)
    If AUTHORITY or COUNTRY found AFTER and modified by word BY,
    Then bind ACTOR.6419 to AUTHORITY or COUNTRY found.
Killing demon: #{^WEB.6409: ^REINTERPRET-CONCEPT …}
Executing demon: #{^WEB.6416: ^PLURAL …}
```

```
#{^WEB.6410: ^P-ECON-PROTECTION...} <--((HEAD ^P-ECON-PROTECTION)
                                        (GROUP-INSTANCES
                                         *MULTIPLE*)...)
Killing demon: #{^WEB.6416: ^PLURAL ...}
Killing demon: #{^WEB.6415: ^DISAMBIGUATE-USING-WORD ...}
Killing demon: #{^WEB.6414: ^DISAMBIGUATE-USING-WORD ...}
Killing demon: #{^WEB.6413: ^DISAMBIGUATE ...}
Killing demon: #{^WEB.6412: ^DISAMBIGUATE-USING-WORD ...}
Killing demon: #{^WEB.6408: ^PROTECTIONIST-BELIEF ...}
```

Bottom-Up Disambiguation and Top-Down Disambiguation:
There are two ways of disambiguating a word: bottom-up and top-down. Bottom-up disambiguation occurs when the expectation encoded in a demon associated with an ambiguous word is satisfied and, consequently, the appropriate meaning of that word is selected. In contrast, top-down disambiguation occurs when one of the meanings of an ambiguous word satisfies the expectation encoded in an active demon that was not spawned by that word. For example, the instance of the demon REINTERPRET-CONCEPT associated with the word "protectionist" expects a general PLAN. This expectation matches one of the meanings of the word "measures." As a result, the word "protectionist" is disambiguated in a bottom-up manner, the word "measures" is disambiguated in a top-down manner, and the phrase "protectionist measures" is represented as an instance of the planning structure P-ECON-PROTECTION (see section 2.2.4).

BY THE REAGAN ADMINISTRATION ==>
```
    Recognized phrase: REAGAN ADMINISTRATION
    Adding to *working-memory*:
        #{^WEB.6564} = ((HEAD ^AUTHORITY)
                        (TYPE EXECUTIVE-BRANCH)
                        (NAME REAGAN-ADMINISTRATION)
                        (NATION ^WEB.6572)...)
    Spawning demon: #{^WEB.6576: ^FIND-AUTHORITY ...}
        ((HEAD ^FIND-AUTHORITY)
         (ARGUMENTS ^WEB.6564 ...))
        If matching AUTHORITY exists,
        Then return AUTHORITY found.
        Otherwise, create a new instance of AUTHORITY.
    Executing demon: #{^WEB.6576: ^FIND-AUTHORITY ...}
        #{^WEB.6564: AUTHORITY ...} = #{^AUTHORITY.1136 ...}
    Killing demon: #{^WEB.6576: ^FIND-AUTHORITY ...}
    Executing demon: #{^WEB.6420: ^EXPECT-USING-WORD ...}
        ACTOR.6419 <-- #{^AUTHORITY.1136 ...}
    Killing demon: #{^WEB.6420: ^EXPECT-USING-WORD ...}
    Killing demon: #{^WEB.6405: ^FIND-REFERENCE ...}
    Executing demon: #{^WEB.6491: ^FILLER ...}
        IC.5016.6424 <-- ((HEAD ^COUNTRY)
```

```
                              (NAME U.S.) …)
          Killing demon: #{^WEB.6491: ^FILLER …}
```

Articles: The words "the", "a", and "an" are ignored since OpEd searches episodic memory every time it creates an instance of a concept in working memory. The result of this search indicates whether an instance of the concept already exists episodic memory. If that is the case, a referent to that instance is returned. Otherwise, a new instantiation of the concept is created in episodic memory. The task of searching for matching instances in episodic memory is handled by demons of the type FIND (e.g., FIND-AUTHORITY).

Slot-Filling Demons and Prepositions: EXPECT demons implement expectations for the class of concepts that can be used to fill in slots in other concepts. These expectations include information regarding the direction of search (i.e., before or after a conceptualization) and word precedence. In addition, EXPECT demons may use the syntactic information provided by prepositions. For example, the following demon instance:

```
#{^WEB.6420: ^EXPECT-USING-WORD …} =
    ((HEAD ^EXPECT-USING-WORD)
     (ARGUMENTS ^WEB.6410
              ACTOR.6419 BY (AUTHORITY COUNTRY) AFTER …)
```

searches for a concept of the class AUTHORITY or COUNTRY that follows the phrase "protectionist measures" and is preceded by the word "by." If such a concept is found, then it is bound to the variable ACTOR.6419 associated with the actor slot the structure P-ECON-PROTECTION. This expectation is satisfied when the conceptualization of the phrase "Reagan administration" is created in working memory.

HAVE DISAPPOINTED ==>
```
    Recognized word: DISAPPOINT
    Recognized suffix: ED
    Adding to *working-memory*:
        #{^WEB.6615} = ((HEAD ^AFFECT)
                       (TYPE NEGATIVE)
                       (ACTOR (*VAR* 'A.2617))
                       (CAUSE (*VAR* 'C.2619))…)
    Spawning demon: #{^WEB.6623: ^PAST …}
        ((HEAD ^PAST)
         (ARGUMENTS ^WEB.6615))
        If ^WEB.6615 is not preceded by the word HAVE,
        HAS, AM, IS, or ARE,
        Then modify ^WEB.6615 with TIME = PAST.
    Spawning demon: #{^WEB.6616: ^EXPECT …}
        ((HEAD ^EXPECT)
```

```
        (ARGUMENTS ^WEB.6615 A.2617 HUMAN AFTER …))
    If HUMAN found AFTER,
    Then bind A.2617 to HUMAN found.
Spawning demon: #{^WEB.6618: ^EXPECT …}
    ((HEAD ^EXPECT)
     (ARGUMENTS ^WEB.6615 C.2619 (PLAN EVENT) BEFORE …))
Spawning demon: #{^WEB.6619: ^BIND-MEANING …}
    ((HEAD ^BIND-MEANING)
     (ARGUMENTS ^WEB.6615 C.2619 HUMAN BEFORE DO …))
    If HUMAN found BEFORE,
    Then create an instance of event DO and bind it to C.2619.
Spawning demon: #{^WEB.6620: ^INFER-BELIEF-FROM-AFFECT …}
    ((HEAD ^INFER-BELIEF-FROM-AFFECT)
     (ARGUMENTS ^WEB.6615 …))
    If the CAUSE and ACTOR of the AFFECT are known,
    Then infer appropriate BELIEF from AFFECT.
Killing demon: #{^WEB.6623: ^PAST …}
Executing demon: #{^WEB.6618: ^EXPECT …}
    C.2619 <-- ((HEAD ^P-ECON-PROTECTION)
                (ACTOR ^AUTHORITY.1136)
                (IMPORTING-COUNTRY ^COUNTRY.587)
                (GROUP-INSTANCES *MULTIPLE*) …)
Killing demon: #{^WEB.6618: ^EXPECT …}
Killing demon: #{^WEB.6619: ^BIND-MEANING …}
```

Emotional Reactions Associated With the Execution of Plans:
The demons that search for the cause of "disappointment" account for
the following cases:

- <HUMAN1 "disappoint" HUMAN2>. For example, the
  sentence "The Reagan administration disappointed Milton
  Friedman" indicates that an action by the Reagan
  administration causes Friedman's disappointment. This case is
  handled by the demon instance #{^WEB.6619: ^BIND-
  MEANING …}.

- <PLAN or EVENT "disappoint" HUMAN>. For example,
  "U.S. import restrictions disappointed Friedman." This case is
  handled by the demon instance #{^WEB.6616: ^EXPECT …}.

In ED-JOBS, the second demon is executed and P-ECON-PROTECTION
is recognized as the cause of the given negative emotion.

```
US *PERIOD* ==>
    Adding to *working-memory*:
        #{^WEB.6628} = ()
    Spawning demon: #{^WEB.6630: ^GROUP-REFERENCE-1 …}
        ((HEAD ^GROUP-REFERENCE-1)
         (ARGUMENTS ^WEB.6628 …))
        If a GROUP containing the WRITER was previously mentioned,
```

```
    Then bind ^WEB.6628 to the GROUP found.
    Otherwise, bind ^WEB.6628 to the WRITER.
Executing demon: #{^WEB.6630: ^GROUP-REFERENCE-1 …}
    #{^WEB.6628} = ((HEAD ^HUMAN)
                    (FIRST-NAME MILTON)
                    (LAST-NAME FRIEDMAN)
                    (GENDER MALE)
                    (ROLE-THEME EDITORIAL-WRITER)
                    (NATION ^COUNTRY.587)…)
Killing demon: #{^WEB.6630: ^GROUP-REFERENCE-1 …}
Executing demon: #{^WEB.6616: ^EXPECT …}
    A.2617 <-- ((HEAD ^HUMAN)
                (FIRST-NAME MILTON)
                (LAST-NAME FRIEDMAN)
                (GENDER MALE)
                (ROLE-THEME EDITORIAL-WRITER)
                (NATION ^COUNTRY.587)…)
Killing demon: #{^WEB.6616: ^EXPECT …}
```

Pronoun Reference: The reference for the pronoun "us" is found by the demon demon GROUP-REFERENCE-1. This demon searches working memory for a previously mentioned GROUP that includes the writer of the editorial (in this case, Friedman). Since that search fails, then the demon binds "us" to the value of the global variable WRITER. This binding allows OpEd to recognize that Friedman is the individual experiencing the negative emotional reaction.

```
Executing demon: #{^WEB.6620: ^INFER-BELIEF-FROM-AFFECT …}
Inferring BELIEF:
    #{^WEB.6640: ^BELIEF …} =
        ((HEAD ^BELIEF)
         (CONTENT ((HEAD ^OUGHT-NOT-TO)
                   (OBJECT ((HEAD ^P-ECON-PROTECTION)
                            (ACTOR ^AUTHORITY.1136)
                            (IMPORTING-COUNTRY ^COUNTRY.587)…))))
          (BELIEVER ((HEAD ^HUMAN)
                     (FIRST-NAME MILTON)
                     (LAST-NAME FRIEDMAN)…)))
Spawning demon: #{^WEB.6651: ^FIND-BELIEF …}
    ((HEAD ^FIND-BELIEF)
     (ARGUMENTS ^WEB.6640))
    If matching BELIEF exists,
    Then return BELIEF found.
    Otherwise, create a new instance of BELIEF.
Killing demon: #{^WEB.6620: ^INFER-BELIEF-FROM-AFFECT …}
Executing demon: #{^WEB.6651: ^FIND-BELIEF …}
    #{^WEB.6640: ^BELIEF …} = #{^BELIEF.6664 …}
Spawning demon: #{^WEB.6670: ^EXPECT-UNREALIZED-SUCCESS …}
    ((HEAD ^EXPECT-UNREALIZED-SUCCESS)
                (ARGUMENTS ^BELIEF.6664))
```

```
        If a matching UNREALIZED-SUCCESS RELATIONSHIP follows,
        Then reinterpret it as a justification for BELIEF.6664.
   Spawning demon: #{^WEB.6671: ^EXPECT-REALIZED-FAILURE …}
     ((HEAD ^EXPECT-REALIZED-FAILURE)
      (ARGUMENTS ^BELIEF.6664))
        If a matching REALIZED-FAILURE RELATIONSHIP follows,
        Then reinterpret it as a justification for BELIEF.6664.
   Killing demon: #{^WEB.6651: ^FIND-BELIEF …}
   Killing demon: #{^WEB.6693: ^FILLER …}
   Executing demon: #{^WEB.6496: ^FIND-P-ECON-PROTECTION …}
     #{^WEB.6410: ^P-ECON-PROTECTION…} =
         #{^P-ECON-PROTECTION.6682…}
   Killing demon: #{^WEB.6496: ^FIND-P-ECON-PROTECTION …}
```

Recognizing Evaluative Beliefs and Expecting Justifications:
From Friedman's disappointment, OpEd infers that Friedman believes
that the Reagan administration should not implement protectionist
policies (see section 6.3). Once OpEd has instantiated Friedman's
evaluative belief, OpEd expects to hear Friedman's justifications (see
section 6.4). These expectations involve unrealized successes and
failures of the goals associated with import restrictions, namely: (1) a
short-term goal of preserving earnings by domestic industries; (2) a
long-term goal of achieving profitability by domestic industries; and (3)
a goal of preserving jobs in the country imposing the restrictions. These
expectations are encoded in the instances of the demons EXPECT-
UNREALIZED-SUCCESS and EXPECT-REALIZED-FAILURE.

Result of parse:
```
   ((HEAD ^AFFECT)
    (TYPE NEGATIVE)
    (ACTOR ((HEAD ^HUMAN)
            (FIRST-NAME MILTON)
            (LAST-NAME FRIEDMAN)
            (GENDER MALE)
            (ROLE-THEME EDITORIAL-WRITER)
            (NATION ((HEAD ^COUNTRY) (NAME U.S.)…))…))
    (CAUSE ((HEAD ^P-ECON-PROTECTION)
            (ACTOR ((HEAD ^AUTHORITY)
                    (TYPE EXECUTIVE-BRANCH)
                    (NAME REAGAN-ADMINISTRATION)
                    (NATION ((HEAD ^COUNTRY) (NAME U.S.)…)…))
            (IMPORTING-COUNTRY ((HEAD ^COUNTRY)
                                (NAME U.S.)…))
            (GROUP-INSTANCES *MULTIPLE*)…))
    (ASSOCIATED-BELIEF ^BELIEF.6664))
```

```
Inferred BELIEF:
    ((HEAD ^BELIEF)
    (CONTENT ((HEAD ^OUGHT-NOT-TO)
              (OBJECT ((HEAD ^P-ECON-PROTECTION)
                       (ACTOR ^AUTHORITY.1136)
                       (IMPORTING-COUNTRY ^COUNTRY.587)…))))
                       (GROUP-INSTANCES *MULTIPLE*)…))))
    (BELIEVER ((HEAD ^HUMAN)
               (FIRST-NAME MILTON)
               (LAST-NAME FRIEDMAN)
               (GENDER MALE)
               (ROLE-THEME EDITORIAL-WRITER)
               (NATION ((HEAD ^COUNTRY) (NAME U.S.))))))
```

End of Sentence: Lexical demons which have not been executed by the end of the sentence are removed from the demon agenda. As a result, only knowledge application demons (e.g., those responsible for recognizing belief justifications) remain active at the end of each sentence. At this point, OpEd traverses working memory and displays the conceptualizations which are not contained in other conceptualizations. In addition, OpEd displays instances of beliefs, belief relationships, cause-effect chains, or AUs that have been inferred during sentence comprehension.

8.2.2. Second Sentence

Processing Sentence:
VOLUNTARY LIMITS ON JAPANESE AUTOMOBILES AND VOLUNTARY LIMITS ON STEEL BY THE COMMON MARKET ARE BAD FOR THE NATION *PERIOD*

VOLUNTARY LIMITS ==>
```
    Recognized phrase: VOLUNTARY LIMITS
    Adding to *working-memory*:
        #{^WEB.6722} = ((HEAD ^P-ECON-PROTECTION)
                        (ACTOR (*VAR* 'A.5015.6075))
                        (IMPORTING-COUNTRY (*VAR* 'IC.5016.6076))
                        (PROTECTED-INDUSTRY (*VAR* 'PI.5019.6079))
                        (ACTIONS #{^WEB.6730: ^RESOLVE…})
                        (IMPORT (*VAR* 'I.6035))
                        (EXPORTING-COUNTRY (*VAR* 'EC.6033))…)
    Spawning demon: #{^WEB.6723: ^EXPECT-USING-WORD …}
        ((HEAD ^EXPECT-USING-WORD)
         (ARGUMENTS ^WEB.6722
                    EC.6033 BY (COUNTRY INSTITUTION) AFTER …)
    Spawning demon: #{^WEB.6736: ^EXPECT-USING-WORD …}
        ((HEAD ^EXPECT-USING-WORD)
```

```
        (ARGUMENTS ^WEB.6722 I.6035 ON (PHYS-OBJ FOOD) AFTER …))
Spawning demon: #{^WEB.6761: ^INFER-PROTECTED-INDUSTRY …}
    ((HEAD ^INFER-PROTECTED-INDUSTRY)
    (ARGUMENTS ^WEB.6722 …))
Spawning demon: #{^WEB.6762: ^FILLER …}
    ((HEAD ^FILLER)
    (ARGUMENTS ^WEB.6722 (ACTOR NATION) (IMPORTING-COUNTRY)…))
Spawning demon: #{^WEB.6764: ^FILLER …}
    ((HEAD ^FILLER)
    (ARGUMENTS ^WEB.6722 (IMPORT NATION) (EXPORTING-COUNTRY)…))
Spawning demon: #{^WEB.6767: ^FIND-P-ECON-PROTECTION …}
    ((HEAD ^FIND-P-ECON-PROTECTION)
    (ARGUMENTS ^WEB.6722 …))
```

Lexical Items for Economic Protection Plans: "Voluntary limits" is processed as a phrase. It is represented as an instance of the planning structure P-ECON-PROTECTION in which the selected action is RESOLVE through negotiations (see section 2.2). The slot-filling expectations generated by the phrase "voluntary limits" account for the following cases:

- <"Voluntary limits" "on" PHYS-OBJ or FOOD>. For example, "voluntary limits on motorcycles" and "voluntary limits on French wine."

- <"Voluntary limits" "by" COUNTRY>. Here COUNTRY is the country that limits its exports to another country. For example, "voluntary limits by Japan."

```
ON JAPANESE ==>
    Adding to *working-memory*:
        #{^WEB.6819} = ()
    Spawning demon: #{^WEB.6820: ^MODIFY-CONCEPT …}
    ((HEAD ^MODIFY-CONCEPT)
    (ARGUMENTS ^WEB.6819
                  (HUMAN PHYS-OBJ INSTITUTION AUTHORITY FOOD)
                  NATION
                  (COUNTRY NAME (JAPAN))…))
    If HUMAN, PHYS-OBJ, INSTITUTION, AUTHORITY, or FOOD follows,
    Then modify it with NATION = (COUNTRY NAME (JAPAN)).
    Spawning demon: #{^WEB.6821: ^DISAMBIGUATE …}
    ((HEAD ^DISAMBIGUATE)
    (ARGUMENTS ^WEB.6819 (EVENT PLAN) AFTER HUMAN …))
    Spawning demon: #{^WEB.6822: ^DISAMBIGUATE …}
    ((HEAD ^DISAMBIGUATE-LANGUAGE)
    (ARGUMENTS ^WEB.6822
                  IN (LANGUAGE TYPE (JAPANESE)) …))
    If an MTRANS is found BEFORE and the word
    JAPANESE is modified by the word IN,
    Then the word JAPANESE refers to:
```

```
    (LANGUAGE TYPE (JAPANESE)).
```

AUTOMOBILES ==>
```
    Recognized word: AUTOMOBILE
    Recognized suffix: S
    Adding to *working-memory*:
        #{^WEB.6823} = ((HEAD ^PHYS-OBJ)
                       (TYPE TRANSPORTATION)
                       (NAME AUTOMOBILE)
                       (NATION (*VAR* 'NATION.2863))…)
    Spawning demon: #{^WEB.6827: ^PLURAL …}
        ((HEAD ^PLURAL)
         (ARGUMENTS ^WEB.6823))
    Spawning demon: #{^WEB.6826: ^FIND-PHYS-OBJ …}
        ((HEAD ^FIND-PHYS-OBJ)
         (ARGUMENTS ^WEB.6823 …))
        If matching PHYS-OBJ exists,
        Then return PHYS-OBJ found.
        Otherwise, create a new instance of PHYS-OBJ.
    Executing demon: #{^WEB.6827: ^PLURAL …}
        #{^WEB.6825: ^PHYS-OBJ …} <-- ((HEAD ^PHYS-OBJ)
                                       (TYPE TRANSPORTATION)
                                       (NAME AUTOMOBILE)
                                       (NATION (*VAR* 'NATION.2863))
                                       (GROUP-INSTANCES *MULTIPLE*))
    Executing demon: #{^WEB.6821: ^MODIFY-CONCEPT …}
        #{^WEB.6823: ^PHYS-OBJ …} <-- ((HEAD ^PHYS-OBJ)
                                       (TYPE TRANSPORTATION)
                                       (NAME AUTOMOBILE)
                                       (NATION ((HEAD ^COUNTRY)
                                                (NAME JAPAN) …))
                                       (GROUP-INSTANCES *MULTIPLE*))
    Killing demon: #{^WEB.6820: ^MODIFY-CONCEPT …}
    Killing demon: #{^WEB.6822: ^DISAMBIGUATE-LANGUAGE …}
    Killing demon: #{^WEB.6821: ^DISAMBIGUATE …}
    Executing demon: #{^WEB.6736: ^EXPECT-USING-WORD …}
        I.6035 <-- ((HEAD ^PHYS-OBJ)
                    (TYPE TRANSPORTATION)
                    (NAME AUTOMOBILE)
                    (NATION ^COUNTRY.604)…)
    Killing demon: #{^WEB.6736: ^EXPECT-USING-WORD …}
    Executing demon: #{^WEB.6764: ^FILLER …}
        EC.6033 <-- ((HEAD ^COUNTRY) (NAME JAPAN) …)
    Killing demon: #{^WEB.6764: ^FILLER …}
    Executing demon: #{^WEB.6826: ^FIND-PHYS-OBJ …}
        #{^WEB.6823: ^PHYS-OBJ …} = #{^PHYS-OBJ.6855 …}
    Killing demon: #{^WEB.6826: ^FIND-PHYS-OBJ …}
    Killing demon: #{^WEB.6723: ^EXPECT-USING-WORD …}
```

Simple Modifiers and Slot Filling: The word "Japanese" has three possible meanings:

1) It indicates that a HUMAN, PHYS-OBJ, INSTITUTION, AUTHORITY, or FOOD is from Japan. For example, "Japanese steel industry."

2) It refers to the actor of a PLAN or EVENT. For example, "The Japanese have agreed to more generous import quotas for U.S. computer components"

3) It refers to the language used to transfer mental information . For example, "Bill told John a story in Japanese." (Transfer of mental information information is represented in terms of an MTRANS, i.e., one of eleven primitives of Schank's (1973, 1975) Conceptual Dependency theory.)

In ED-JOBS, the first meaning is selected after the conceptualization underlying the word "automobiles" is placed in working memory. As a result, the slot:

```
NATION = (COUNTRY NAME (JAPAN)).
```

is added to the representation of "automobiles." After this modification takes place, the representation of "Japanese automobiles" is bound to the IMPORT slot of the structure P-ECON-PROTECTION underlying the phrase "voluntary limits."

AND ==>
```
    Adding to *working-memory*:
        #{^WEB.6857} = ()
    Spawning demon: #{^WEB.6859: ^BUILD-GROUP …}
        ((HEAD ^BUILD-GROUP)
         (ARGUMENTS ^WEB.6857 …))
        If the CONCEPTS that precede and follow ^WEB.6857 are known,
        Then build a GROUP and bind it to ^WEB.6857.
    Spawning demon: #{^WEB.6860: ^GROUP-MODIFIER …}
        ((HEAD ^GROUP-MODIFIER)
         (ARGUMENTS ^WEB.6857 …))
        If a GROUP follows ^WEB.6857,
        Then modify it with information contained in ^WEB.6857.
```

VOLUNTARY LIMITS ==>
```
    Recognized phrase: VOLUNTARY LIMITS
    Adding to *working-memory*:
        #{^WEB.6861} = ((HEAD ^P-ECON-PROTECTION)
                        (ACTOR (*VAR* 'A.5015.6075))
                        (IMPORTING-COUNTRY (*VAR* 'IC.5016.6076))
                        (PROTECTED-INDUSTRY (*VAR* 'PI.5019.6079))
                        (ACTIONS #{^WEB.6869: ^RESOLVE …})
                        (IMPORT (*VAR* 'I.6035))
                        (EXPORTING-COUNTRY (*VAR* 'EC.6033))…)
    Spawning demon: #{^WEB.6862: ^EXPECT-USING-WORD …}
```

```
    ((HEAD ^EXPECT-USING-WORD)
    (ARGUMENTS ^WEB.6861
                    EC.6033 BY (COUNTRY INSTITUTION) AFTER …))
Spawning demon: #{^WEB.6875: ^EXPECT-USING-WORD …}
    ((HEAD ^EXPECT-USING-WORD)
    (ARGUMENTS ^WEB.6861 I.6035 ON (PHYS-OBJ FOOD) AFTER …))
Spawning demon: #{^WEB.6900: ^INFER-PROTECTED-INDUSTRY …}
    ((HEAD ^INFER-PROTECTED-INDUSTRY)
    (ARGUMENTS ^WEB.6861 …))
Spawning demon: #{^WEB.6901: ^FILLER …}
    ((HEAD ^FILLER)
    (ARGUMENTS ^WEB.6861 (ACTOR NATION) (IMPORTING-COUNTRY)…))
Spawning demon: #{^WEB.6903: ^FILLER …}
    ((HEAD ^FILLER)
    (ARGUMENTS ^WEB.6861 (IMPORT NATION) (EXPORTING-COUNTRY)…))
Spawning demon: #{^WEB.6906: ^FIND-P-ECON-PROTECTION …}
    ((HEAD ^FIND-P-ECON-PROTECTION)
    (ARGUMENTS ^WEB.6861 …))
Executing demon: #{^WEB.6859: ^BUILD-GROUP …}
    #{^WEB.6857} = ((HEAD ^P-ECON-PROTECTION)
                    (GROUP-INSTANCES ^WEB.6722 ^WEB.6861)…)
Spawning demon: #{^WEB.7001: ^FIND-GROUP …}
    ((HEAD ^FIND-GROUP)
    (ARGUMENTS ^WEB.6957))
    If matching GROUP of class P-ECON-PROTECTION exists,
    Then return GROUP found.
    Otherwise, create a new instance of GROUP.
Killing demon: #{^WEB.6859: ^BUILD-GROUP …}
```

Conjunctions: Associated with the word "and" is the demon BUILD-GROUP. This demon handles phrases of the form <x "and" Y> by building a GROUP structure composed of the representations of x and Y. Also associated with the word "and" is the demon GROUP-MODIFIER. This demon handles noun groups of the form <x "and" Y z> by building a GROUP structure that contains: (1) an instance of z's representation modified by the information in x; and (2) an instance of z's representation modified by the information in Y. An example of the noun groups handled by the GROUP-MODIFIER demon is the phrase "automobile and steel industries" (see section 8.2.4).

```
ON STEEL ==>
    Adding to *working-memory*:
        #{^WEB.7010} = ((HEAD ^PHYS-OBJ)
                        (TYPE MATERIAL)
                        (NAME STEEL)
                        (NATION (*VAR* 'NATION.2870)…)
    Spawning demon: #{^WEB.7013: ^FIND-PHYS-OBJ …}
        ((HEAD ^FIND-PHYS-OBJ)
        (ARGUMENTS ^WEB.7010…))
```

```
Executing demon: #{^WEB.7013: ^FIND-PHYS-OBJ …}
    #{^WEB.7010: ^PHYS-OBJ …} = #{^PHYS-OBJ.1401 …}
Killing demon: #{^WEB.7013: ^FIND-PHYS-OBJ …}
Executing demon: #{^WEB.6875: ^EXPECT-USING-WORD …}
    I.6035 <-- ((HEAD ^PHYS-OBJ)
                (TYPE MATERIAL)
                (NAME STEEL)
                (NATION (*VAR* 'NATION.2870)…)
Killing demon: #{^WEB.6875: ^EXPECT-USING-WORD …}
```

BY THE COMMON MARKET ==>
```
    Recognized phrase: COMMON MARKET
    Adding to *working-memory*:
        #{^WEB.7024} = ((HEAD ^INSTITUTION)
                        (TYPE TRADE)
                        (NAME COMMON-MARKET)…)
Spawning demon: #{^WEB.7045: ^FIND-INSTITUTION …}
    ((HEAD ^FIND-INSTITUTION)
     (ARGUMENTS ^WEB.7044)…)
    If matching INSTITUTION exists,
    Then return INSTITUTION found.
    Otherwise, create a new instance of INSTITUTION.
Executing demon: #{^WEB.7045: ^FIND-INSTITUTION …}
    #{^WEB.7045: ^INSTITUTION …} = #{^INSTITUTION.985 …}
Killing demon: #{^WEB.7045: ^FIND-INSTITUTION …}
Executing demon: #{^WEB.6862: ^EXPECT-USING-WORD …}
    EC.6033 <-- ((HEAD ^INSTITUTION)
                (TYPE TRADE)
                (NAME COMMON-MARKET)…)
Killing demon: #{^WEB.6862: ^EXPECT-USING-WORD …}
Killing demon: #{^WEB.6903: ^FILLER …}
```

ARE BAD FOR ==>
```
    Recognized phrase: BE BAD FOR
    Adding to *working-memory*:
        #{^WEB.7101} = ((HEAD ^LEAD-TO)
                        (ANTE (*VAR* 'ANTE.5640))
                        (CONSE ((HEAD ^GOAL-SITUATION)
                                (GOAL ((HEAD ^GOAL)
                                        (ACTOR (*VAR* 'C.5644))…))
                                (STATUS THWARTED)…))…)
Spawning demon: #{^WEB.7102: ^EXPECT …}
    ((HEAD ^EXPECT)
     (ARGUMENTS ^WEB.7101 ANTE.5640 (PLAN EVENT) BEFORE …))
Spawning demon: #{^WEB.7105: ^BIND-MEANING …}
    ((HEAD ^BIND-MEANING)
     (ARGUMENTS ^WEB.7101 ANTE.5640 HUMAN BEFORE DO …))
Spawning demon: #{^WEB.7106: ^EXPECT …}
    ((HEAD ^EXPECT)
     (ARGUMENTS ^WEB.7101
                C.5644
```

```
                    (HUMAN INSTITUTION COUNTRY)
                    AFTER …))
Executing demon: #{^WEB.7102: ^EXPECT …}
    ANTE.5640 <-- ((HEAD ^P-ECON-PROTECTION)
                    (GROUP-INSTANCES ^WEB.6724 ^WEB.6863)…)
Killing demon: #{^WEB.7102: ^EXPECT …}
Killing demon: #{^WEB.7105: ^BIND-MEANING …}
```

Goal Failures: The phrase "be bad for" is represented in terms of a causal relationship involving a goal failure. Appropriate demons are activated to identify the cause of this goal failure and the character experiencing it. Those demons handle the following cases:

- <PLAN or EVENT "is bad for" HUMAN, INSTITUTION, or COUNTRY>. For example, "drinking is bad for John."

- <HUMAN1 "is bad for" HUMAN2, INSTITUTION, or COUNTRY>. In this case, HUMAN1 is the ACTOR of an unstated PLAN or EVENT that causes a goal failure for HUMAN2. For example, "A protectionist president is bad for the U.S."

In Friedman's argument, the first case is satisfied by the GROUP structure that represents the policies of the Reagan administration.

```
THE NATION *PERIOD* ==>
    Adding to *working-memory*:
        #{^WEB.7125} = ()
    Spawning demon: #{^WEB.7127: ^BIND-COUNTRY …}
        ((HEAD ^BIND-COUNTRY)
         (ARGUMENTS ^WEB.7125 …))
        If a COUNTRY was previously mentioned,
        Then bind ^WEB.7125 to COUNTRY found.
        Otherwise, bind ^WEB.7125 to COUNTRY where
        the editorial was written.
    Executing demon: #{^WEB.7127: ^BIND-COUNTRY …}
        #{^WEB.7125} = ((HEAD ^COUNTRY) (NAME U.S.)…)
    Killing demon: #{^WEB.7127: ^BIND-COUNTRY …}
    Executing demon: #{^WEB.7106: ^EXPECT …}
        C.5644 <-- ((HEAD ^COUNTRY) (NAME U.S.)…)
    Killing demon: #{^WEB.7106: ^EXPECT …}
    Executing demon: #{^WEB.6906: ^FIND-P-ECON-PROTECTION …}
        #{^WEB.6861: ^P-ECON-PROTECTION…} =
            #{^P-ECON-PROTECTION.7130…}
    Killing demon: #{^WEB.6906: ^FIND-P-ECON-PROTECTION …}
    Executing demon: #{^WEB.6767: ^FIND-P-ECON-PROTECTION …}
        #{^WEB.6722: ^P-ECON-PROTECTION…} =
            #{^P-ECON-PROTECTION.7134…}
    Killing demon: #{^WEB.6767: ^FIND-P-ECON-PROTECTION …}
```

Concept Reference: Here, the word "nation" refers to the U.S. because: (1) a conceptualization of class COUNTRY has not been previously mentioned; and (2) the U.S. is the country where the editorial was written. Making this inference allows OpEd to understand that the U.S. is the character of the goal failure resulting from the import restrictions.

```
Executing demon: #{^WEB.6671: ^EXPECT-REALIZED-FAILURE …}
Inferring BELIEF:
   #{^WEB.7137: ^BELIEF …} = ((HEAD ^BELIEF)
                             (CONTENT ^WEB.7101)
                             (BELIEVER ^HUMAN.786)…)
Inferring SUPPORT RELATIONSHIP:
   #{^WEB.7151: ^SUPPORT …} = ((HEAD ^SUPPORT)
                              (SUPPORTER ^WEB.7137)
                              (SUPPORTED ^BELIEF.6664))
Spawning demon: #{^WEB.7148: ^FIND-BELIEF …}
   ((HEAD ^FIND-BELIEF)
   (ARGUMENTS ^WEB.7137))
Spawning demon: #{^WEB.7157: ^FIND-SUPPORT …}
   ((HEAD ^FIND-SUPPORT)
   (ARGUMENTS ^WEB.7151))
   If matching SUPPORT exists,
   Then return SUPPORT found.
   Otherwise, create a new instance of SUPPORT.
Killing demon: #{^WEB.6671: ^EXPECT-REALIZED-FAILURE …}
Executing demon: #{^WEB.7157: ^FIND-SUPPORT …}
   #{^WEB.7151: ^SUPPORT …} = #{^SUPPORT.7163}
Killing demon: #{^WEB.7157: ^FIND-SUPPORT …}
Executing demon: #{^WEB.7148: ^FIND-BELIEF …}
   #{^WEB.7137: ^BELIEF …} = #{^BELIEF.7174}
Killing demon: #{^WEB.7148: ^FIND-BELIEF …}
```

Belief Justification Based on Goal Failure: The goal failure involving the U.S. matches the expectation implemented in the active instance of the demon EXPECT-REALIZED-FAILURE. As a result, OpEd recognizes the given goal failure as one of the reasons for Friedman's belief that import restrictions are a bad idea. However, at this point it is not known whether the goal failure involves: (1) one of the goals associated with import restrictions; or (2) a goal more important than or equally important to the goals associated with import restrictions.

```
Executing demon: #{^WEB.7001: ^FIND-GROUP …}
   #{^WEB.6722: ^P-ECON-PROTECTION…} =
      #{^P-ECON-PROTECTION.6682…}
Killing demon: #{^WEB.7001: ^FIND-GROUP …}
Executing demon: #{^WEB.6900: ^INFER-PROTECTED-INDUSTRY …}
Inferring PROTECTED-INDUSTRY:
```

```
    PI.5019.6427 <-- ((HEAD ^INSTITUTION)
                      (NATION ^COUNTRY.587)
                      (NAME STEEL-INDUSTRY)
                      (TYPE INDUSTRY)...)
Killing demon: #{^WEB.6900: ^INFER-PROTECTED-INDUSTRY ...}
Killing demon: #{^WEB.6901: ^FILLER ...}
Executing demon: #{^WEB.6761: ^INFER-PROTECTED-INDUSTRY ...}
Inferring PROTECTED-INDUSTRY:
    PI.5019.6427 <-- ((HEAD ^INSTITUTION)
                      (NATION ^COUNTRY.587)
                      (NAME AUTOMOBILE-INDUSTRY)
                      (TYPE INDUSTRY)...)
Killing demon: #{^WEB.6761: ^INFER-PROTECTED-INDUSTRY ...}
Killing demon: #{^WEB.6762: ^FILLER ...}
```

Concept Unification and Domain-Specific Inferences: As a result
of executing the demon FIND-GROUP, the GROUP structure containing the
two instances of voluntary limits is unified with the existing
representation of P-ECON-PROTECTION in episodic memory.
Consequently OpEd realizes that "voluntary limits on Japanese
automobiles and voluntary limits on steel" refer to the policies
implemented by the Reagan administration to protect U.S. industries
against foreign competition. Once this unification takes place, it is
possible to infer that those industries are the U.S. auto industry and the
U.S. steel industry (see section 2.2.2). These inferences are
implemented by the active instances of the demon INFER-PROTECTED-
INDUSTRY.

```
Result of parse:
  ((HEAD ^LEAD-TO)
   (ANTE ((HEAD ^P-ECON-PROTECTION)
          (ACTOR ((HEAD ^AUTHORITY)
                  (TYPE EXECUTIVE-BRANCH)
                  (NAME REAGAN-ADMINISTRATION)
                  (NATION ^COUNTRY.587)...))
          (IMPORTING-COUNTRY ((HEAD ^COUNTRY)
                              (NAME U.S.)...))
          (GROUP-INSTANCES ((HEAD ^P-ECON-PROTECTION)
                            (ACTIONS ^RESOLVE.7219)
                            (IMPORT ^PHYS-OBJ.6855)
                            (EXPORTING-COUNTRY ^COUNTRY.604)
                            (PROTECTED-INDUSTRY ^INSTITUTION.912)
                            (IMPORTING-COUNTRY ^COUNTRY.587)
                            (ACTOR ^AUTHORITY.1136)...)
                           ((HEAD ^P-ECON-PROTECTION)
                            (ACTIONS ^RESOLVE.7185)
                            (IMPORT ^PHYS-OBJ.1401)
                            (PROTECTED-INDUSTRY ^INSTITUTION.984)
                            (EXPORTING-COUNTRY ^INSTITUTION.985)
```

```
                              (IMPORTING-COUNTRY ^COUNTRY.587)
                              (ACTOR ^AUTHORITY.1136)…))…)
      (CONSE ((HEAD ^GOAL-SITUATION)
             (GOAL ((HEAD ^GOAL)
                   (ACTOR ((HEAD ^COUNTRY) (NAME U.S.)…))…)
             (STATUS THWARTED)…)))
```

Inferred BELIEF:
```
     ((HEAD ^BELIEF)
      (CONTENT ((HEAD ^LEAD-TO)
               (ANTE ((HEAD ^P-ECON-PROTECTION)
                     (ACTOR ^AUTHORITY.1136)
                     (IMPORTING-COUNTRY ^COUNTRY.587)
                     (GROUP-INSTANCES ^P-ECON-PROTECTION.7134
                                      ^P-ECON-PROTECTION.7130)…))
               (CONSE ((HEAD ^GOAL-SITUATION)
                      (GOAL ((HEAD ^GOAL)
                            (ACTOR ^COUNTRY.587)…))
                      (STATUS THWARTED)…))))
      (BELIEVER ((HEAD ^HUMAN)
                (FIRST-NAME MILTON)
                (LAST-NAME FRIEDMAN)…))…)
```

Inferred SUPPORT:
```
     ((HEAD ^SUPPORT)
      (SUPPORTED ((HEAD ^BELIEF)
                 (CONTENT ((HEAD ^OUGHT-NOT-TO)
                          (OBJECT ^P-ECON-PROTECTION.6682)))
                 (BELIEVER ((HEAD ^HUMAN)
                           (FIRST-NAME MILTON)
                           (LAST-NAME FRIEDMAN)…))…))
      (SUPPORTER ((HEAD ^BELIEF)
                 (CONTENT ((HEAD ^LEAD-TO)
                          (ANTE ^P-ECON-PROTECTION.6682)
                          (CONSE ^GOAL-SITUATION.7104)…))
                 (BELIEVER ((HEAD ^HUMAN)
                           (FIRST-NAME MILTON)
                           (LAST-NAME FRIEDMAN)…))…)))
```

8.2.3. Third Sentence

Processing Sentence:
THEY DO NOT PROMOTE THE LONG-RUN HEALTH OF THE INDUSTRIES
AFFECTED *PERIOD*

```
THEY DO NOT PROMOTE ==>
   Adding to *working-memory*:
    #{^WEB.7351} = ((HEAD ^LEAD-TO)
                    (ANTE (*VAR* 'ANTE.5834))
                    (CONSE ((HEAD ^GOAL-SITUATION)
                            (GOAL ((HEAD ^GOAL)
                                   (TYPE ACHIEVEMENT)
                                   (OBJECT (*VAR* 'O.5837))…))
                            (STATUS ACHIEVED)…))…)
   Spawning demon: #{^WEB.7357: ^EXPECT …}
      ((HEAD ^EXPECT)
       (ARGUMENTS ^WEB.7351 ANTE.5834 (PLAN EVENT) BEFORE …))
   Spawning demon: #{^WEB.7360: ^EXPECT …}
      ((HEAD ^EXPECT)
       (ARGUMENTS ^WEB.7351 O.5837 STATE AFTER …))
   Executing demon: #{^WEB.7350: ^NEGATION …}
    #{^WEB.7351} = ((HEAD ^LEAD-TO)
                    (ANTE (*VAR* 'ANTE.5834))
                    (CONSE ((HEAD ^GOAL-SITUATION)
                            (GOAL ((HEAD ^GOAL)
                                   (TYPE ACHIEVEMENT)
                                   (OBJECT (*VAR* 'O.5837))…))
                            (STATUS NOT-ACHIEVED)…))…)
   Killing demon: #{^WEB.7350: ^NEGATION …}
   Executing demon: #{^WEB.7357: ^EXPECT …}
      ANTE.5834 <-- ((HEAD ^P-ECON-PROTECTION)
                     (ACTOR ((HEAD ^AUTHORITY)
                             (TYPE EXECUTIVE-BRANCH)
                             (NAME REAGAN-ADMINISTRATION)
                             (NATION ^COUNTRY.587)…))
                     (IMPORTING-COUNTRY ((HEAD ^COUNTRY)
                                         (NAME U.S.)…))
                     (GROUP-INSTANCES ^P-ECON-PROTECTION.7134
                                      ^P-ECON-PROTECTION.7130)…)
   Killing demon: #{^WEB.7357: ^EXPECT …}
```

Unrealized Success: Here, OpEd binds the word "they" to the content of the global variable MOST-RECENT-GROUP. This variable contains a pointer to the representation of the import restrictions on automobiles and steel, i.e., the variable contains a pointer to the most recently mentioned group. Then, that group is bound to the antecedent of the causal relationship underlying the word "promote." The consequent of that causal relationship is modified by a NEGATION demon associated with the word "not." As a result, OpEd understands the phrase "they do not promote" as a causal relationship in which the execution of P-ECON-PROTECTION fails to achieve a long-term goal or *achievement goal* (Schank and Abelson, 1977).

```
THE LONG-RUN ==>
    Adding to *working-memory*:
        #{^WEB.7381} = ()
    Spawning demon: #{^WEB.7383: ^MODIFY-CONCEPT …}
        ((HEAD ^MODIFY-CONCEPT)
         (ARGUMENTS ^WEB.7381
                        (GOAL PLAN EVENT STATE)
                        TIME
                        (LONG-TERM) …))

HEALTH ==>
    Adding to *working-memory*:
        #{^WEB.7384} = ((HEAD ^STATE)
                        (TYPE (*VAR* 'TYPE.5902))
                        (SCALE NORM)
                        (OBJECT (*VAR* 'OBJECT.5903))
                        (REFERENCE (*VAR* 'REFERENCE.5905)))
    Spawning demon: #{^WEB.7389: ^HEALTH-TYPE …}
        ((HEAD ^HEALTH-TYPE)
         (ARGUMENTS ^WEB.7384 …))
        If HUMAN found AFTER and modified by word OF,
        Then modify ^WEB.7384 with (TYPE = PHYSICAL),
        and (OBJECT = HUMAN found).
        If INSTITUTION found AFTER
        and modified by word OF,
        Then modify ^WEB.7384 with (TYPE = SIZE),
        and (OBJECT = EARNINGS of INSTITUTION found).
    Executing demon: #{^WEB.7381: ^MODIFY-CONCEPT …}
        #{^WEB.7384} <-- ((HEAD ^STATE)
                          (TYPE (*VAR* 'TYPE.5902))
                          (SCALE NORM)
                          (OBJECT (*VAR* 'OBJECT.5903))
                          (TIME LONG-TERM)
                          (REFERENCE (*VAR* 'REFERENCE.5905)))
    Killing demon: #{^WEB.7381: ^MODIFY-CONCEPT …}
    Executing demon: #{^WEB.7360: ^EXPECT …}
        0.5837 <-- ((HEAD ^STATE)
                    (TYPE (*VAR* 'TYPE.5902))
                    (OBJECT (*VAR* 'OBJECT.5903))
                    (SCALE NORM)
                    (TIME LONG-TERM)
                    (REFERENCE (*VAR* 'REFERENCE.5905)))
    Killing demon: #{^WEB.7360: ^EXPECT …}

OF THE INDUSTRIES ==>
    Recognized word: INDUSTRY
    Recognized suffix: ES
    Adding to *working-memory*:
        #{^WEB.7400} = ((HEAD ^INSTITUTION)
                        (TYPE INDUSTRY)
                        (NAME (*VAR* 'NAME.2522))
```

```
                    (NATION (*VAR* 'NATION.2524))…)
Spawning demon: #{^WEB.7405: ^PLURAL …}
    ((HEAD ^PLURAL)
     (ARGUMENTS ^WEB.7400))
Spawning demon: #{^WEB.7403: ^FIND-INSTITUTION …}
    ((HEAD ^FIND-INSTITUTION)
     (ARGUMENTS ^WEB.7400 …))
Executing demon: #{^WEB.7405: ^PLURAL …}
  #{^WEB.7400: ^INSTITUTION …} <-- ((HEAD ^INSTITUTION)
                                    (TYPE INDUSTRY)
                                    (NAME (*VAR* 'NAME.2522))
                                    (NATION (*VAR* 'NATION.2524))
                                    (GROUP-INSTANCES *MULTIPLE*))
Killing demon: #{^WEB.7405: ^PLURAL …}
Executing demon: #{^WEB.7389: ^HEALTH-TYPE …}
  #{^WEB.7386: ^STATE…} <-- ((HEAD ^STATE)
                            (TYPE SIZE)
                            (OBJECT ((HEAD ^EARNINGS)
                                    (ACTOR ^WEB.7400)…))
                            (SCALE NORM)
                            (TIME LONG-TERM)
                            (REFERENCE (*VAR* 'REFERENCE.5905)))
Killing demon: #{^WEB.7389: ^HEALTH-TYPE …}
```

Concept Refinement: The word "health" is represented in terms of a STATE. The lexical demon associated with "health" (i.e., HEALTH-TYPE) searches working memory for the actor associated with the given STATE. According to the actor found, the representation of "health" has to be refined. This concept refinement is necessary because "health" has at least two meanings: (a) the pattern <"health" "of" HUMAN> refers to the PHYSICAL-STATE of that HUMAN; and (b) the pattern <"health" "of" INSTITUTION> refers to that INSTITUTION's STATE of having a normal level of EARNINGS (i.e., being profitable).

```
AFFECTED *PERIOD* ==>
    Recognized word: AFFECT
    Recognized suffix: ED
    Adding to *working-memory*:
        #{^WEB.7426} = ()
Spawning demon: #{^WEB.7428: ^DISAMBIGUATE-USING-WORD …}
    ((HEAD ^DISAMBIGUATE-USING-WORD)
     (ARGUMENTS ^WEB.7426 BY (PLAN EVENT) AFTER (LEAD-TO …)) …)
Spawning demon: #{^WEB.7429: ^DISAMBIGUATE …}
    ((HEAD ^DISAMBIGUATE)
     (ARGUMENTS ^WEB.7426 (PLAN EVENT) AFTER (LEAD-TO …)) …)
Spawning demon: #{^WEB.7430: ^CONSEQUENT-RECIPIENT …}
    ((HEAD ^CONSEQUENT-RECIPIENT)
     (ARGUMENTS ^WEB.7426 …))
    If HUMAN or INSTITUTION precedes and a clause
```

```
boundary follows,
Then: (1) find a matching HUMAN or INSTITUTION
involved in a GOAL-SITUATION; and (2) return
the HUMAN or INSTITUTION found.
Executing demon: #{^WEB.7430: ^CONSEQUENT-RECIPIENT …}
  #{^WEB.7400: ^INSTITUTION …} <-- ((HEAD ^INSTITUTION)
                                   (TYPE INDUSTRY)
                                   (GROUP-INSTANCES
                                     ^INSTITUTION.912
                                     ^INSTITUTION.984)…)
Killing demon: #{^WEB.7430: ^CONSEQUENT-RECIPIENT …}
Killing demon: #{^WEB.7428: ^DISAMBIGUATE-USING-WORD …}
Killing demon: #{^WEB.7429: ^DISAMBIGUATE …}
Executing demon: #{^WEB.7403: ^FIND-INSTITUTION …}
  #{^WEB.7400: ^INSTITUTION …} = #{^INSTITUTION.7440 …}
Killing demon: #{^WEB.7403: ^FIND-INSTITUTION …}
```

Goal Situations: Recognizing the pattern <CHARACTER "affected"> at the end of the sentence causes OpEd to search episodic memory in order to find a CHARACTER involved in a goal-situation. In this case, the U.S. automobile and steel industries are found since they are being protected by the P-ECON-PROTECTIONs implemented by the Reagan administration. Thus, OpEd understands that P-ECON-PROTECTIONs do not achieve the goal of attaining a normal level of profits for the automobile and steel industries.

```
Executing demon: #{^WEB.6670: ^EXPECT-UNREALIZED-SUCCESS …}
Inferring BELIEF:
  #{^WEB.7433: ^BELIEF …} = ((HEAD ^BELIEF)
                             (CONTENT
                               ((HEAD ^LEAD-TO)
                                (ANTE ^P-ECON-PROTECTION.6682)
                                (CONSE ((HEAD ^GOAL-SITUATION)
                                        (GOAL ^GOAL.7359)
                                        (STATUS NOT-ACHIEVED)))))
                             (BELIEVER ^HUMAN.786)…)
Inferring SUPPORT RELATIONSHIP:
    #{^WEB.7447: ^SUPPORT …} = ((HEAD ^SUPPORT)
                                (TYPE UNREALIZED-SUCCESS)
                                (SUPPORTER ^WEB.7433)
                                (SUPPORTED ^BELIEF.6664))
Spawning demon: #{^WEB.7444: ^FIND-BELIEF …}
    ((HEAD ^FIND-BELIEF)
     (ARGUMENTS ^WEB.7433))
Spawning demon: #{^WEB.7453: ^FIND-SUPPORT …}
    ((HEAD ^FIND-SUPPORT)
     (ARGUMENTS ^WEB.7447))
Spawning demon: #{^WEB.7455: ^RECOGNIZE-AUS-FROM-PLAN-FAILURE …}
    If a matching GOAL SITUATION follows,
    Then recognize appropriate ARGUMENT UNIT.
```

```
Killing demon: #{^WEB.6670: ^EXPECT-UNREALIZED-SUCCESS …}
Executing demon: #{^WEB.7453: ^FIND-SUPPORT …}
   #{^WEB.7447: ^SUPPORT …} = #{^SUPPORT.7469 …}
Killing demon: #{^WEB.7453: ^FIND-SUPPORT …}
Executing demon: #{^WEB.7444: ^FIND-BELIEF …}
   #{^WEB.7433: ^BELIEF …} = #{^BELIEF.7481 …}
Killing demon: #{^WEB.7444: ^FIND-BELIEF …}
```

Belief Justification Based on Unrealized Success: The unrealized success relationship involving the automobile and steel industries matches the expectation implemented in the active instance of the demon EXPECT-UNREALIZED-SUCCESS. As a result, OpEd recognizes that goal relationship as another justification for Friedman's belief that import restrictions are a bad idea (see section 6.4).

Expectations for Recognizing Argument Units: The justification of Friedman's evaluative belief also amounts to an implicit attack on the Reagan administration's belief that P-ECON-PROTECTION achieves the goal of attaining a normal level of earnings. Consequently, OpEd generates expectations for recognizing AUs involving attacks on the reasoning associated with the execution of plan (see section 6.7). These expectations are implemented in the demon RECOGNIZE-AUS-FROM-PLAN-FAILURE.

```
Result of parse:
   ((HEAD ^LEAD-TO)
   (ANTE ((HEAD ^P-ECON-PROTECTION)
          (ACTOR ((HEAD ^AUTHORITY)
                  (TYPE EXECUTIVE-BRANCH)
                  (NAME REAGAN-ADMINISTRATION)
                  (NATION ^COUNTRY.587)…))
          (IMPORTING-COUNTRY ((HEAD ^COUNTRY)
                              (NAME U.S.)…))
          (GROUP-INSTANCES ^P-ECON-PROTECTION.7134
                           ^P-ECON-PROTECTION.7130)
          (PROTECTED-INDUSTRY ((HEAD ^INSTITUTION)
                               (TYPE INDUSTRY)
                               (GROUP-INSTANCES
                                 ^INSTITUTION.912
                                 ^INSTITUTION.984)…))))
   (CONSE ((HEAD ^GOAL-SITUATION)
          (GOAL ((HEAD ^GOAL)
                 (TYPE ACHIEVEMENT)
                 (ACTOR ((HEAD ^INSTITUTION)
                         (GROUP-INSTANCES ^INSTITUTION.912
                                          ^INSTITUTION.984)…))
                 (OBJECT ((HEAD ^STATE)
                          (TYPE SIZE)
```

```
                                    (OBJECT ^EARNINGS.7412)
                                    (SCALE NORM)
                                    (TIME LONG-TERM)))))
                   (STATUS NOT-ACHIEVED)…)))
```

Inferred BELIEF:
```
    ((HEAD ^BELIEF)
     (CONTENT ((HEAD ^LEAD-TO)
               (ANTE ^P-ECON-PROTECTION.6682)
               (CONSE ((HEAD ^GOAL-SITUATION)
                       (GOAL ^GOAL.7359)
                       (STATUS NOT-ACHIEVED)))))
     (BELIEVER ((HEAD ^HUMAN)
                (FIRST-NAME MILTON)
                (LAST-NAME FRIEDMAN)…)))
```

Inferred SUPPORT:
```
    ((HEAD ^SUPPORT)
     (TYPE UNREALIZED-SUCCESS)
     (SUPPORTED ((HEAD ^BELIEF)
                 (CONTENT ((HEAD ^OUGHT-NOT-TO)
                           (OBJECT ^P-ECON-PROTECTION.6682)))
                 (BELIEVER ((HEAD ^HUMAN)
                            (FIRST-NAME MILTON)
                            (LAST-NAME FRIEDMAN)…))))
     (SUPPORTER ((HEAD ^BELIEF)
                 (CONTENT ((HEAD ^LEAD-TO)
                           (ANTE ^P-ECON-PROTECTION.6682)
                           (CONSE ((HEAD ^GOAL-SITUATION)
                                   (GOAL ^GOAL.7359)
                                   (STATUS NOT-ACHIEVED)))))
                 (BELIEVER ((HEAD ^HUMAN)
                            (FIRST-NAME MILTON)
                            (LAST-NAME FRIEDMAN)…)))))
```

8.2.4. Fourth Sentence

Processing Sentence:
THE PROBLEM OF THE AUTOMOBILE AND STEEL INDUSTRIES
IS *COLON* IN BOTH INDUSTRIES AVERAGE WAGE RATES ARE
TWICE AS HIGH AS THE AVERAGE *PERIOD*

THE PROBLEM ==>
```
    Adding to *working-memory*:
        #{^WEB.7505} = ((HEAD ^LEAD-TO)
                        (ANTE (*VAR* 'ANTE.5979))
                        (CONSE ((HEAD ^GOAL-SITUATION)
                                (GOAL ((HEAD ^GOAL)
                                       (ACTOR 'C.5982)…))
```

```
                                    (STATUS THWARTED)…)))
    Spawning demon: #{^WEB.7506: ^*EXPECT-USING-WORD …}
        ((HEAD ^*EXPECT-USING-WORD)
         (ARGUMENTS ^WEB.7505
                    ANTE.5979 (IS WAS) (STATE EVENT PLAN) AFTER …))
        If an unbound STATE, EVENT, or PLAN found AFTER and modified
        by word IS or WAS,
        Then bind ANTE.5979 to STATE, EVENT, or PLAN found.
    Spawning demon: #{^WEB.7509: ^EXPECT-USING-WORD …}
        ((HEAD ^EXPECT-USING-WORD)
         (ARGUMENTS ^WEB.7505 C.5982
                    OF
                    (HUMAN COUNTRY INSTITUTION AUTHORITY)
                    AFTER …))
```

Goal-Failure Relationship: The word "problem" signals a cause-effect relationship in which a PLAN, EVENT, or STATE thwarts an active GOAL for a character C. The lexical demons associated to "problem" search episodic memory for this character and the cause of the goal failure.

OF THE AUTOMOBILE ==>
```
    Adding to *working-memory*:
        #{^WEB.7529} = ((HEAD ^PHYS-OBJ)
                        (TYPE TRANSPORTATION)
                        (NAME AUTOMOBILE)
                        (NATION (*VAR* 'NATION.2863)))
    Spawning demon: #{^WEB.7532: ^FIND-PHYS-OBJ …}
        ((HEAD ^FIND-PHYS-OBJ)
         (ARGUMENTS ^WEB.7529 …))
```

AND ==>
```
    Adding to *working-memory*:
        #{^WEB.7537} = ()
    Spawning demon: #{^WEB.7539: ^BUILD-GROUP …}
        ((HEAD ^BUILD-GROUP)
         (ARGUMENTS ^WEB.7537 …))
    Spawning demon: #{^WEB.7540: ^GROUP-MODIFIER …}
        ((HEAD ^GROUP-MODIFIER)
         (ARGUMENTS ^WEB.7537 …))
```

STEEL ==>
```
    Adding to *working-memory*:
        #{^WEB.7541} = ((HEAD ^PHYS-OBJ)
                        (TYPE MATERIAL)
                        (NAME STEEL)
                        (NATION (*VAR* 'NATION.2870)))
    Spawning demon: #{^WEB.7544: ^FIND-PHYS-OBJ …}
        ((HEAD ^FIND-PHYS-OBJ)
         (ARGUMENTS ^WEB.7541 …))
```

```
Executing demon: #{^WEB.7539: ^BUILD-GROUP …}
   #{^WEB.7537} = ((HEAD ^PHYS-OBJ)
                      (GROUP-INSTANCES ^WEB.7529 ^WEB.7541)…)
Spawning demon: #{^WEB.7559: ^FIND-GROUP …}
   ((HEAD ^FIND-GROUP)
    (ARGUMENTS ^WEB.7537))
Killing demon: #{^WEB.7539: ^BUILD-GROUP …}
```

INDUSTRIES ==>
```
   Recognized word: INDUSTRY
   Recognized suffix: ES
   Adding to *working-memory*:
      #{^WEB.7565} = ((HEAD ^INSTITUTION)
                       (TYPE INDUSTRY)
                       (NAME (*VAR* 'NAME.2522))
                       (NATION (*VAR* 'NATION.2524))
                       (GROUP-INSTANCES *MULTIPLE*)…))
Spawning demon: #{^WEB.7568: ^FIND-INSTITUTION …}
   ((HEAD ^FIND-INSTITUTION)
    (ARGUMENTS ^WEB.7565 …))
Executing demon: #{^WEB.7540: ^GROUP-MODIFIER …}
   #{^WEB.7565} <-- ((HEAD ^INSTITUTION)
                      (TYPE INDUSTRY)
                      (GROUP-INSTANCES
                         ((HEAD ^INSTITUTION)
                          (TYPE INDUSTRY)
                          (NAME AUTOMOBILE-INDUSTRY)…)
                         ((HEAD ^INSTITUTION)
                          (TYPE INDUSTRY)
                          (NAME STEEL-INDUSTRY)…))…)
Killing demon: #{^WEB.7540: ^GROUP-MODIFIER …}
Executing demon: #{^WEB.7509: ^EXPECT-USING-WORD …}
   C.5982 <-- ((HEAD ^INSTITUTION)
                (TYPE INDUSTRY)
                (GROUP-INSTANCES ^WEB.7577 ^WEB.7588)…)
Killing demon: #{^WEB.7509: ^EXPECT-USING-WORD …}
Executing demon: #{^WEB.7568: ^FIND-INSTITUTION …}
   #{^WEB.7567: ^INSTITUTION …} = #{^INSTITUTION.7440 …}
Killing demon: #{^WEB.7568: ^FIND-INSTITUTION …}
```

Noun Groups: The demons associated with the word "and" build the representation of the phrase "automobile and steel industries" in two steps. First, the demon BUILD-GROUP represents the phrase "automobile and steel" in terms of a GROUP structure composed of two PHYS-OBJ. That GROUP structure is then used by the demon GROUP-MODIFIER to modify the representation of the word "industries" and, consequently, create a GROUP structure containing representations of the "automobile industry" and the "steel industry."

```
IS *COLON* IN BOTH ==>
    Adding to *working-memory*:
        #{^WEB.7615} = ()
    Spawning demon: #{^WEB.7618: ^TWO-MEMBER-GROUP …}
        ((HEAD ^TWO-MEMBER-GROUP)
         (ARGUMENTS ^WEB.7615 …))
    If a GROUP follows,
    Then: (1) find a matching GROUP that contains
    two group instances and has been mentioned earlier;
    and (2) return GROUP found.
    Otherwise, find a GROUP that contains two group
    instances and has been mentioned earlier

INDUSTRIES ==>
    Recognized word: INDUSTRY
    Recognized suffix: ES
    Adding to *working-memory*:
        #{^WEB.7619} = ((HEAD ^INSTITUTION)
                        (TYPE INDUSTRY)
                        (NAME (*VAR* 'NAME.2522))
                        (NATION (*VAR* 'NATION.2524))
                        (GROUP-INSTANCES *MULTIPLE*)…))
    Spawning demon: #{^WEB.7622: ^FIND-INSTITUTION …}
        ((HEAD ^FIND-INSTITUTION)
         (ARGUMENTS ^WEB.7629 …)
    Executing demon: #{^WEB.7618: ^TWO-MEMBER-GROUP …}
        #{^WEB.7621: ^INSTITUTION …} <-- ((HEAD ^INSTITUTION)
                                          (TYPE INDUSTRY)
                                          (GROUP-INSTANCES
                                            ^INSTITUTION.912
                                            ^INSTITUTION.984)…)
    Killing demon: #{^WEB.7618: ^TWO-MEMBER-GROUP …}
    Killing demon: #{^WEB.7622: ^FIND-INSTITUTION …}
```

Group Reference: The word "both" acts as a place holder for a GROUP with two members. After reading that word, OpEd verifies whether the concept that follows "both" is a GROUP. Since that is the case in ED-JOBS, OpEd searches working memory in order to find a previously mentioned GROUP that matches the one that follows "both." The search is successful and the representation of the phrase "both industries" is unified with the representation of the phrase "automobile and the steel industries."

```
AVERAGE ==>
    Adding to *working-memory*:
        #{^WEB.7630} = ((HEAD ^STATE)
                        (SCALE NORM)
                        (OBJECT (*VAR* 'OBJECT.6199))…)
    Spawning demon: #{^WEB.7631: ^EXPECT …}
```

```
((HEAD ^EXPECT)
 (ARGUMENTS ^WEB.7630 OBJECT.6199
             (QUANTITY ECONOMIC-QUANTITY) AFTER …))
```

WAGE RATES ==>
```
Recognized phrase: WAGE RATES
Adding to *working-memory*:
  #{^WEB.7639} = ((HEAD ^SALARY)
                  (TYPE RATE)
                  (ACTOR (*VAR* 'C.6224))
                  (SETTING (*VAR* 'S.6235))
Spawning demon: #{^WEB.7640: ^EXPECT-USING-WORD …}
  ((HEAD ^EXPECT-USING-WORD)
   (ARGUMENTS ^WEB.7639 C.6224 OF HUMAN AFTER …))
Spawning demon: #{^WEB.7647: ^EXPECT-USING-WORD …}
  ((HEAD ^EXPECT-USING-WORD)
   (ARGUMENTS ^WEB.7639 S.6235 IN INSTITUTION BEFORE …))
Spawning demon: #{^WEB.7648: ^EXPECT-USING-WORD …}
  ((HEAD ^EXPECT-USING-WORD)
   (ARGUMENTS ^WEB.7639 S.6235 IN INSTITUTION AFTER …))
Executing demon: #{^WEB.7647: ^EXPECT-USING-WORD …}
   S.6235 <-- ((HEAD ^INSTITUTION)
               (TYPE INDUSTRY)
               (GROUP-INSTANCES ^INSTITUTION.912
                                ^INSTITUTION.984)…)
Killing demon: #{^WEB.7647: ^EXPECT-USING-WORD …}
Killing demon: #{^WEB.7648: ^EXPECT-USING-WORD …}
Executing demon: #{^WEB.7631: ^EXPECT …}
   OBJECT.6199 <-- ((HEAD ^SALARY)
                    (TYPE RATE)
                    (ACTOR (*VAR* 'C.6224))
                    (SETTING ((HEAD ^INSTITUTION)
                              (TYPE INDUSTRY)
                              (GROUP-INSTANCES
                                ^INSTITUTION.912
                                ^INSTITUTION.984)…)))
Killing demon: #{^WEB.7631: ^EXPECT …}
```

Economic Quantities: The phrase "wage rates" is represented in terms of the economic quantity SALARY. This economic quantity has three components: (1) the type of payment (i.e., RATE or FIXED-TERM); (2) the character receiving the payment; and (3) the setting associated with the payment (e.g., the industry that makes the payment). Once the representation of "wage rates" has been created in working memory, appropriate demons are activated to find the actor and setting components. In the case of ED-JOBS, the setting is identified as the automobile and steel industries.

States of Economic Quantities: Economic quantities can attain states, i.e., they can be equal, lower, or higher than their norms (see section 2.3). For example, the phrase "average wage rates" indicates that the state of the economic quantity SALARY is equal to its NORM.

```
ARE TWICE ==>
    Adding to *working-memory*:
        #{^WEB.7668} = ()
    Spawning demon: #{^WEB.7670: ^QUANTITATIVE-MODIFIER ...}
        ((HEAD ^QUANTITATIVE-MODIFIER)
         (ARGUMENTS ^WEB.7668 STATE SCALE DOUBLE ...))
        If a STATE follows,
        Then modify it with SCALE = DOUBLE.
AS ==>
    Adding to *working-memory*:
        #{^WEB.7671} = ()
    Spawning demon: #{^WEB.7673: ^COMPARISON-TRAP ...}
        ((HEAD ^COMPARISON-TRAP)
         (ARGUMENTS ^WEB.7671 ...))
        If the current word is the first instance of the word
        "as" in the comparison pattern:
        <OBJECT1 "as" STATE "as" OBJECT2>,
        Then modify STATE with (OBJECT = OBJECT1),
        (REFERENCE = OBJECT2), and (SCALE = EQUAL).
        If the current word is the second instance of the word
        "as" in the comparison pattern:
        <OBJECT1 "as" STATE "as" OBJECT2>,
        Then ignore it.


HIGH ==>
    Adding to *working-memory*:
        #{^WEB.7674} = ((HEAD ^STATE)
                        (TYPE SIZE)
                        (SCALE GREATER-THAN-NORM)
                        (OBJECT (*VAR* 'OBJECT.6295))...)
    Spawning demon: #{^WEB.7677: ^EXPECT ...}
        ((HEAD ^EXPECT)
         (ARGUMENTS ^WEB.7674
                    OBJECT.6295
                    (ECONOMIC-QUANTITY QUANTITY PHYS-OBJ)
                    AFTER ...))


AS THE AVERAGE *PERIOD* ==>
    Executing demon: #{^WEB.7673: ^COMPARISON-TRAP ...}
        #{^WEB.7671} <-- ((HEAD ^STATE)
                          (SCALE EQUAL)
                          (TYPE SIZE)
                          (OBJECT ((HEAD ^STATE)
                                   (SCALE NORM)
                                   (OBJECT
```

```
                            ((HEAD ^SALARY)              .
                             (TYPE RATE)
                             (SETTING
                                ^INSTITUTION.7440)…)))))
                   (REFERENCE ((HEAD ^STATE)
                              (SCALE NORM)…)))
Killing demon: #{^WEB.7673: ^COMPARISON-TRAP …}
Executing demon: #{^WEB.7670: ^QUANTITATIVE-MODIFIER …}
    #{^WEB.7674} <-- ((HEAD ^STATE)
                     (TYPE SIZE)
                     (SCALE DOUBLE)
                     (OBJECT ^STATE.7632)
                     (REFERENCE ^STATE.7692)…)
Killing demon: #{^WEB.7670: ^QUANTITATIVE-MODIFIER …}
Killing demon: #{^WEB.7640: ^EXPECT-USING-WORD …}
Executing demon: #{^WEB.7506: ^*EXPECT-USING-WORD …}
    ANTE.5979 <-- ((HEAD ^STATE)
                  (TYPE SIZE)
                  (SCALE DOUBLE)
                  (OBJECT ^STATE.7632)
                  (REFERENCE ^STATE.7692)…)
Killing demon: #{^WEB.7506: ^*EXPECT-USING-WORD …}
```

Comparisons, Modifiers, and Priority Demons: As shown by Dyer (1983a), demons may also be designed to have priority of execution over other demons. For example, the demons associated with the word "as" process the comparison pattern <OBJECT1 "as" STATE "as" OBJECT2> before demons associated with modifiers can access the given STATE. Due to this priority, the word "twice" in the phrase "average wage rates are twice as high as the average" modifies the representation of "high" only after that phrase has been processed using the COMPARISON-TRAP demon associated with the first occurrence of the word "as."

```
Executing demon: #{^WEB.7455: ^RECOGNIZE-AUS-FROM-PLAN-FAILURE…}
Recognizing AU-ACTUAL-CAUSE:
    #{^WEB.7715: ^AU-ACTUAL-CAUSE …} =
        ((HEAD ^AU-ACTUAL-CAUSE)
         (ARGUER ^HUMAN.786))
         (OPPONENT ^AUTHORITY.1136)
         (PLAN ^P-ECON-PROTECTION.6682)
         (GOAL ^GOAL.7359)
         (ACTUAL-STATE ^STATE.7676)
         (OPPOSITE-STATE ^STATE.7677))
   Spawning demon: #{^WEB.7735: ^FIND-AU-ACTUAL-CAUSE …}
     ((HEAD ^FIND-AU-ACTUAL-CAUSE)
      (ARGUMENTS ^WEB.7715))
     If matching AU-ACTUAL-CAUSE exists,
     Then return AU-ACTUAL-CAUSE found.
```

```
     Otherwise, create a new instance of AU-ACTUAL-CAUSE.
Killing demon: #{^WEB.7455: ^RECOGNIZE-AUS-FROM-PLAN-FAILURE …}
Executing demon: #{^WEB.7735: ^FIND-AU-ACTUAL-CAUSE …}
   #{^WEB.7715: ^AU-ACTUAL-CAUSE …} =
      #{^AU-ACTUAL-CAUSE.7886 …}
Killing demon: #{^WEB.7735: ^FIND-AU-ACTUAL-CAUSE …}
```

Recognizing Argument Units From Plan Failures: The failure of
a long-term goal involving the automobile and steel industries matches
the expectation implemented in the demon RECOGNIZE-AUS-FROM-
PLAN-FAILURE (see section 6.7). This demon creates an instance of AU-
ACTUAL-CAUSE that contains: (1) Friedman's attack on the Reagan
administration's position that import restrictions should be used to help
U.S. industries attain profitability; and (2) Friedman's position that
import restrictions are bad because they cannot reverse the decrease in
profits resulting from high salaries.

Result of parse:
```
((HEAD ^LEAD-TO)
 (ANTE ((HEAD ^STATE)
        (TYPE SIZE)
        (SCALE DOUBLE)
        (OBJECT ((HEAD ^STATE)
                 (SCALE NORM)
                 (OBJECT ^SALARY.7413)…))
        (REFERENCE ((HEAD ^STATE)
                    (SCALE NORM)…))))
 (CONSE ((HEAD ^GOAL-SITUATION)
         (GOAL ((HEAD ^GOAL)
                (TYPE ACHIEVEMENT)
                (ACTOR ((HEAD ^INSTITUTION)
                        (GROUP-INSTANCES ^INSTITUTION.912
                                         ^INSTITUTION.984)…))
                (OBJECT ((HEAD ^STATE)
                         (TYPE SIZE)
                         (OBJECT ^EARNINGS.7412)
                         (SCALE NORM)
                         (TIME LONG-TERM)…))))
         (STATUS THWARTED)…)))
```

Inferred AU-ACTUAL-CAUSE:
```
((HEAD ^AU-ACTUAL-CAUSE)
 (ARGUER ((HEAD ^HUMAN)
          (FIRST-NAME MILTON)
          (LAST-NAME FRIEDMAN)
          (GENDER MALE)…))
 (OPPONENT ((HEAD ^AUTHORITY)
            (TYPE EXECUTIVE-BRANCH)
            (NAME REAGAN-ADMINISTRATION))…))
```

```
(PLAN ((HEAD ^P-ECON-PROTECTION)
       (ACTOR ((HEAD ^AUTHORITY)
               (NAME REAGAN-ADMINISTRATION)
               (NATION ^COUNTRY.587)...))
       (GROUP-INSTANCES ^P-ECON-PROTECTION.7134
                        ^P-ECON-PROTECTION.7130)...))
 (GOAL ((HEAD ^GOAL)
        (TYPE ACHIEVEMENT)
        (ACTOR ((HEAD ^INSTITUTION)
                (GROUP-INSTANCES ^INSTITUTION.912
                                 ^INSTITUTION.984)...))
        (OBJECT ((HEAD ^STATE)
                 (TYPE SIZE)
                 (OBJECT ^EARNINGS.7412)
                 (SCALE NORM)
                 (TIME LONG-TERM)...))))
 (ACTUAL-STATE ((HEAD ^STATE)
                (TYPE SIZE)
                (SCALE DOUBLE)
                (OBJECT ((HEAD ^STATE)
                         (SCALE NORM)
                         (OBJECT ^SALARY.7413)...)))
                (REFERENCE ((HEAD ^STATE)
                            (SCALE NORM)...)))
 (OPPOSITE-STATE ((HEAD ^STATE)
                  (TYPE SIZE)
                  (SCALE LESS-THAN)
                  (OBJECT ((HEAD ^STATE)
                           (SCALE NORM)
                           (OBJECT ^SALARY.7413)...)))
                  (REFERENCE ((HEAD ^STATE)
                              (SCALE NORM)...))))
```

8.2.5. Fifth Sentence

Processing Sentence:
FAR FROM SAVING JOBS *COMMA* THE LIMITATIONS ON IMPORTS
WILL COST JOBS *PERIOD*

FAR FROM ==>
```
    Recognized phrase: FAR FROM
    Adding to *working-memory*:
       #(^WEB.7907) = ()
    Spawning demon: #(^WEB.7909: ^DISAMBIGUATE ...)
        ((HEAD ^DISAMBIGUATE)
         (ARGUMENTS ^WEB.7907
                    (PHYS-OBJ COUNTRY SETTING)
                    AFTER SPACE-RELATION ...))
    Spawning demon: #(^WEB.7910: ^EXPECT-OPPOSITE-EFFECTS ...)
```

```
((HEAD ^EXPECT-OPPOSITE-EFFECTS)
 (ARGUMENTS ^WEB.7907 …))
If current phrase is part of the
contradictory-effect construct:
<"Far from" PLAN--achieve-->GOAL, PLAN--thwart-->GOAL>,
Then bind ^WEB.7907 to RELATIONSHIP of OPPOSITION and infer
AU-OPPOSITE-EFFECT.
```

Ambiguous Argument Connective: "Far from" is an ambiguous phrase that can introduce: (1) a space relationship (e.g., "far from" LOCATION L); or (2) the contradictory-effect construct <"far from" P-achieve->G, P-thwart->G> (see section 6.6.1). If the second meaning is selected, a relationship of OPPOSITION and the argument unit AU-OPPOSITE-EFFECT are recognized.

SAVING ==>
```
    Recognized word: SAVE
    Recognized suffix: ING
    Adding to *working-memory*:
        #{^WEB.7911} = ((HEAD ^LEAD-TO)
                        (ANTE (*VAR* 'ANTE.5673))
                        (CONSE ((HEAD ^GOAL-SITUATION)
                                (GOAL ((HEAD ^GOAL)
                                       (TYPE PRESERVATION)
                                       (ACTOR (*VAR* 'A.5677))
                                       (OBJECT (*VAR* 'O.5679))…))
                                (STATUS ACHIEVED))))
    Spawning demon: #{^WEB.7912: ^EXPECT …}
        ((HEAD ^EXPECT)
         (ARGUMENTS ^WEB.7911 ANTE.5673 (PLAN EVENT) BEFORE …))
    Spawning demon: #{^WEB.7915: ^BIND-MEANING …}
        ((HEAD ^BIND-MEANING)
         (ARGUMENTS ^WEB.7911 ANTE.5673 HUMAN BEFORE DO …))
    Spawning demon: #{^WEB.7916: ^EXPECT ...}
        ((HEAD ^EXPECT)
         (ARGUMENTS ^WEB.7911
                    A.5677 (HUMAN INSTITUTION COUNTRY) AFTER …))
    Spawning demon: #{^WEB.7917: ^EXPECT …}
        ((HEAD ^EXPECT)
         (ARGUMENTS ^WEB.7911 O.5679 (OCCUPATION PHYS-OBJ) AFTER …))
```

JOBS *COMMA* ==>
```
    Recognized word: JOB
    Recognized suffix: S
    Adding to *working-memory*:
        #{^WEB.7931} = ((HEAD ^OCCUPATION)
                        (ACTOR (*VAR* 'ACTOR.2767))
                        (TYPE (*VAR* 'TYPE.2768))
                        (SETTING (*VAR* 'SETTING.2764))
                        (GROUP-INSTANCES *MULTIPLE*))
```

```
Spawning demon: #{^WEB.7932: ^EXPECT-USING-WORD ...}
   ((HEAD ^EXPECT-USING-WORD)
    (ARGUMENTS ^WEB.7931 ACTOR.2767 OF HUMAN AFTER ...))
Spawning demon: #{^WEB.7934: ^EXPECT ...}
   ((HEAD ^EXPECT)
    (ARGUMENTS ^WEB.7931 SETTING.2764 INSTITUTION AFTER ...))
Executing demon: #{^WEB.7917: ^EXPECT ...}
   0.5679 <-- ((HEAD ^OCCUPATION)
              (ACTOR (*VAR* 'ACTOR.2767)
              (TYPE (*VAR* 'TYPE.2768))
              (SETTING (*VAR* 'SETTING.2764))
              (GROUP-INSTANCES *MULTIPLE*))
Killing demon: #{^WEB.7917: ^EXPECT ...}
```

Achievement Relationship: The word "save" refers to an achievement relationship between a plan and a preservation goal. Demons associated with "save" search working memory for the plan and the object of the goal. In ED-JOBS, the plan is not mentioned explicitly, and the object of the goal corresponds to number of jobs.

```
THE LIMITATIONS ON IMPORTS ==>
   Recognized phrase: LIMITATIONS ON IMPORTS
   Adding to *working-memory*:
     #{^WEB.7949} = ((HEAD ^P-ECON-PROTECTION)
                     (IMPORTING-COUNTRY (*VAR* 'IC.5016.7982))
                     (EXPORTING-COUNTRY (*VAR* 'EC.5017.7983))
                     (IMPORT (*VAR* 'I.5018.7984))
                     (PROTECTED-INDUSTRY (*VAR* 'PI.5019.7985))
                     (STATE (*VAR* 'STATE.5096.8019))
                     (ACTIONS (*OR* #{^WEB.8011: ^AUTHORIZE ...}
                                    #{^WEB.7998: ^RESOLVE ...}))
                     (ACTOR (*VAR* 'ACTOR.7977)))
Spawning demon: #{^WEB.8054: ^FIND-P-ECON-PROTECTION ...}
   ((HEAD ^FIND-P-ECON-PROTECTION)
    (ARGUMENTS ^WEB.7949)...)
Spawning demon: #{^WEB.8051: ^FILLER ...}
   ((HEAD ^FILLER)
    (ARGUMENTS ^WEB.7949 (IMPORT NATION) (EXPORTING-COUNTRY)...))
Spawning demon: #{^WEB.8049: ^FILLER ...}
   ((HEAD ^FILLER)
    (ARGUMENTS ^WEB.7949 (ACTOR NATION) (IMPORTING-COUNTRY)...))
Spawning demon: #{^WEB.8048: ^INFER-PROTECTED-INDUSTRY ...}
   ((HEAD ^INFER-PROTECTED-INDUSTRY)
    (ARGUMENTS ^WEB.7949 ...))
Spawning demon: #{^WEB.7978: ^EXPECT-USING-WORD ...}
   ((HEAD ^EXPECT-USING-WORD)
    (ARGUMENTS ^WEB.7949
               ACTOR.7977 BY (AUTHORITY COUNTRY) AFTER ...))
```

```
WILL COST ==>
    Adding to *working-memory*:
        #{^WEB.8122} = ()
    Spawning demon: #{^WEB.8123: ^DISAMBIGUATE-USING-WORD …}
        ((HEAD ^DISAMBIGUATE-USING-WORD)
         (ARGUMENTS ^WEB.8122 OF (PHYS-OBJ FOOD) AFTER PRICE …))
    Spawning demon: #{^WEB.8124: ^DISAMBIGUATE …}
        ((HEAD ^DISAMBIGUATE)
         (ARGUMENTS ^WEB.8122 (PLAN EVENT) BEFORE LEAD-TO …))
    Executing demon: #{^WEB.8124: ^DISAMBIGUATE …}
        #{^WEB.8122} = ((HEAD ^LEAD-TO)
                        (ANTE (*VAR* 'ANTE.5705))
                        (CONSE ((HEAD ^GOAL-SITUATION)
                                (GOAL ((HEAD ^GOAL)
                                       (TYPE PRESERVATION)
                                       (ACTOR (*VAR* 'A.5709))
                                       (OBJECT (*VAR* 'O.5711))…))
                               (STATUS THWARTED)
                               (TIME FUTURE))))
    Spawning demon: #{^WEB.8125: ^EXPECT …}
        ((HEAD ^EXPECT)
         (ARGUMENTS ^WEB.8122 ANTE.5705 (PLAN ACT) BEFORE …))
    Spawning demon: #{^WEB.8128: ^BIND-MEANING …}
        ((HEAD ^BIND-MEANING)
         (ARGUMENTS ^WEB.8122 ANTE.5705 HUMAN BEFORE DO …))
    Spawning demon: #{^WEB.8129: ^EXPECT …}
        ((HEAD ^EXPECT)
         (ARGUMENTS ^WEB.8122
                    A.5709 (HUMAN INSTITUTION COUNTRY) AFTER …))
    Spawning demon: #{^WEB.8130: ^EXPECT …}
        ((HEAD ^EXPECT)
         (ARGUMENTS ^WEB.8122 O.5711 (OCCUPATION PHYS-OBJ) AFTER …))
    Killing demon: #{^WEB.8124: ^DISAMBIGUATE …}
    Executing demon: #{^WEB.8125: ^EXPECT …}
        ANTE.5705 <-- ((HEAD ^P-ECON-PROTECTION)
                       (IMPORTING-COUNTRY (*VAR* 'IC.5016.7982))
                       (EXPORTING-COUNTRY (*VAR* 'TC.5017.7983))
                       (IMPORT (*VAR* 'I.5018.7984))
                       (PROTECTED-INDUSTRY (*VAR* 'PI.5019.7985))
                       (ASSOCIATED-GOAL ^WEB.7986 ^WEB.7990)
                       (STATE (*VAR* 'STATE.5096.8019))
                       (ACTIONS (*OR* #{^WEB.8011: ^AUTHORIZE …}
                                      #{^WEB.7998: ^RESOLVE …}))
                       (ACTOR (*VAR* 'ACTOR.7977)))
    Killing demon: #{^WEB.8125: ^EXPECT …}
    Killing demon: #{^WEB.8128: ^BIND-MEANING …}
    Killing demon: #{^WEB.8123: ^DISAMBIGUATE-USING-WORD …}
```

Goal-Failure Relationship: The word "cost" is another ambiguous word. It may refer to: (1) the PRICE of an object; or (2) a goal-failure relationship between a plan and a preservation goal. When processing Friedman's argument, the second meaning is selected since "cost" is preceded by an instance of the plan P-ECON-PROTECTION.

```
JOBS *PERIOD* ==>
    Executing demon: #{^WEB.8130: ^EXPECT ...}
        0.5711 <-- ((HEAD ^OCCUPATION)
                    (ACTOR (*VAR* 'ACTOR.2767))
                    (TYPE (*VAR* 'TYPE.2768))
                    (SETTING (*VAR* 'SETTING.2764))
                    (GROUP-INSTANCES *MULTIPLE*)))
    Killing demon: #{^WEB.8130: ^EXPECT ...}
    Executing demon: #{^WEB.8054: ^FIND-P-ECON-PROTECTION ...}
        #{^WEB.7949: ^P-ECON-PROTECTION...} =
            #{^P-ECON-PROTECTION.6682...}
    Killing demon: #{^WEB.8054: ^FIND-P-ECON-PROTECTION ...}
    Executing demon: #{^WEB.7910: ^EXPECT-OPPOSITE-EFFECTS ...}
    Recognizing OPPOSITE RELATIONSHIP:
      #{^WEB.8208: ^OPPOSITE ...} = ((HEAD ^OPPOSITE)
                                     (FAILURE
                                       ((HEAD ^LEAD-TO)
                                        (ANTE ^P-ECON-PROTECTION.6682)
                                        (CONSE ((HEAD ^GOAL-SITUATION)
                                                (GOAL ^GOAL.7104)
                                                (STATUS THWARTED)))))
                                     (SUCCESS
                                       ((HEAD ^LEAD-TO)
                                        (ANTE ^P-ECON-PROTECTION.6682)
                                        (CONSE ((HEAD ^GOAL-SITUATION)
                                                (GOAL ^GOAL.7104)
                                                (STATUS ACHIEVED))))))
    Recognizing AU-OPPOSITE-EFFECT from Contradictory-Effect
    Construct:
        #{^WEB.8227: ^AU-OPPOSITE-EFFECT ...} =
            ((HEAD ^AU-OPPOSITE-EFFECT)
             (ARGUER ^HUMAN.786))
             (OPPONENT ^AUTHORITY.1136)
             (PLAN ^P-ECON-PROTECTION.6682)
             (GOAL ^GOAL.7104))
    Spawning demon: #{^WEB.8213: ^FIND-OPPOSITE ...}
        ((HEAD ^FIND-OPPOSITE)
         (ARGUMENTS ^WEB.8208))
        If matching OPPOSITE exists,
        Then return OPPOSITE found.
        Otherwise, create a new instance of OPPOSITE.
    Spawning demon:#{^WEB.8244: ^FIND-AU-OPPOSITE-EFFECT ...}
        ((HEAD ^FIND-AU-OPPOSITE-EFFECT)
         (ARGUMENTS ^WEB.8227))
        If matching AU-OPPOSITE-EFFECT exists,
        Then return AU-OPPOSITE-EFFECT found.
        Otherwise, create a new instance of AU-OPPOSITE-EFFECT.
```

Recognizing Argument Units From Linguistic Constructs: The goal-achievement and goal-failure relationships involve the same goal of preserving jobs. These relationships match the expectation implemented in the demon EXPECT-OPPOSITE-EFFECTS. As a result, the relationship OPPOSITE and the argument unit AU-OPPOSITE-EFFECT are instantiated in episodic memory. This AU contains: (1) Friedman's attack on the Reagan administration's position that import restrictions should be used to preserve jobs; and (2) Friedman's position that import restrictions are bad because they will not save jobs but, instead, cost jobs. As a side effect of instantiating AU-OPPOSITE-EFFECT, Friedman's belief that import restrictions cost jobs is unified with his belief that import restrictions cause a goal failure for the U.S.

```
Spawning demon: #{^WEB.8245: ^EXPECT-CAUSE-EFFECT-CHAIN …}
    ((HEAD ^EXPECT-CAUSE-EFFECT-CHAIN)
    (ARGUMENTS ^BELIEF.7174
                $R-ECON-PROTECTION-->FEWER-EXPORT-JOBS))
    If a CAUSE-EFFECT CHAIN follows and conforms to
    the reasoning script $R-ECON-PROTECTION-->FEWER-EXPORT-JOBS,
    Then reinterpret it as the SUPPORT of ^BELIEF.7174.
Killing demon: #{^WEB.7910: ^EXPECT-OPPOSITE-EFFECTS …}
Executing demon: #{^WEB.8244: ^FIND-AU-OPPOSITE-EFFECT …}
    #{^WEB.8227: AU-OPPOSITE-EFFECT…} =
        #{^AU-OPPOSITE-EFFECT.8369…}
Killing demon: #{^WEB.8244: ^FIND-AU-OPPOSITE-EFFECT …}
```

Expectations for Recognizing Reasoning Scripts: From abstract argument knowledge, OpEd can determine that: (1) the editorial writer may use an AU in combination with a support structure to further elaborate on the goal failures caused by a plan (see section 4.3); and (2) beliefs containing goal-failure relationships signal the occurrence of reasoning scripts (see section 6.5). Consequently, the reasoning script $R-ECON-PROTECTION-->FEWER-EXPORT-JOBS is expected as a justification for Friedman's belief that import restrictions cost jobs. This expectation is implemented in an instance of the demon EXPECT-CAUSE-EFFECT-CHAIN.

Result of parse:
```
    ((HEAD ^OPPOSITE)
    (FAILURE ((HEAD ^LEAD-TO)
                (ANTE ((HEAD ^P-ECON-PROTECTION)
                        (ACTOR ^AUTHORITY.1136)
                        (IMPORTING-COUNTRY ^COUNTRY.587)
                        (GROUP-INSTANCES ^P-ECON-PROTECTION.7134
                                         ^P-ECON-PROTECTION.7130)…))
                (CONSE ((HEAD ^GOAL-SITUATION)
                        (GOAL ((HEAD ^GOAL)
```

```
                                    (TYPE PRESERVATION)
                                    (ACTOR ^COUNTRY.587)
                                    (OBJECT ^OCCUPATION.8197)))
                          (STATUS THWARTED)…))))
        (SUCCESS ((HEAD ^LEAD-TO)
                 (ANTE ((HEAD ^P-ECON-PROTECTION)
                        (ACTOR ^AUTHORITY.1136)
                        (IMPORTING-COUNTRY ^COUNTRY.587)
                        (GROUP-INSTANCES ^P-ECON-PROTECTION.7134
                                         ^P-ECON-PROTECTION.7130)…))
                     (CONSE ((HEAD ^GOAL-SITUATION)
                            (GOAL ((HEAD ^GOAL)
                                   (TYPE PRESERVATION)
                                   (ACTOR ^COUNTRY.587)
                                   (OBJECT ^OCCUPATION.8197)))
                            (STATUS ACHIEVED)…)))))
```

Inferred AU-OPPOSITE-EFFECT:
```
    ((HEAD ^AU-OPPOSITE-EFFECT)
     (ARGUER ((HEAD ^HUMAN)
              (FIRST-NAME MILTON)
              (LAST-NAME FRIEDMAN)
              (GENDER MALE)…))
     (OPPONENT ((HEAD ^AUTHORITY)
                (TYPE EXECUTIVE-BRANCH)
                (NAME REAGAN-ADMINISTRATION))…))
     (PLAN ((HEAD ^P-ECON-PROTECTION)
            (ACTOR ((HEAD ^AUTHORITY)
                    (NAME REAGAN-ADMINISTRATION)
                    (NATION ^COUNTRY.587)…))
            (GROUP-INSTANCES ^P-ECON-PROTECTION.7134
                             ^P-ECON-PROTECTION.7130)…))
     (GOAL ((HEAD ^GOAL)
            (TYPE PRESERVATION)
            (ACTOR ^COUNTRY.587)
            (OBJECT ^OCCUPATION.8197))))
```

8.2.6. Sixth Sentence

Processing Sentence:
IF WE IMPORT LESS *COMMA* FOREIGN COUNTRIES WILL EARN
FEWER DOLLARS *PERIOD*

IF ==>
```
    Adding to *working-memory*:
        #{^WEB.8447} = ((HEAD ^LEAD-TO)
                        (ANTE (*VAR* 'ANTE.5737))
                        (CONSE (*VAR* 'CONSE.5739)))
    Spawning demon: #{^WEB.8448: ^EXPECT-ANTECEDENT …}
```

```
((HEAD ^EXPECT-ANTECEDENT)
 (ARGUMENTS ^WEB.8447
              ANTE.5737
              (PLAN EVENT STATE STATE-CHANGE)…)
If an unbound PLAN, EVENT, STATE, OR STATE-CHANGE
found BEFORE next clause boundary,
Then bind it to ANTE.5737.
Spawning demon: #{^WEB.8450: ^EXPECT-CONSEQUENT …}
 ((HEAD ^EXPECT-CONSEQUENT)
  (ARGUMENTS ^WEB.8447
               CONSE.5739
               (STATE STATE-CHANGE GOAL-SITUATION)…)
If an unbound STATE, STATE-CHANGE, or GOAL-SITUATION
found AFTER next clause boundary,
Then bind it to CONSE.5739.
```

Causal Constructs: The pattern <"if" X, Y> is handled by the demons EXPECT-ANTECEDENT and EXPECT-CONSEQUENT. These demons use the syntactic information provided by the clause boundary "comma" in order to locate the appropriate filler of the ANTE and CONSE slots in LEAD-TO structures.

WE ⟹
```
Adding to *working-memory*:
    #{^WEB.8458} = ()
Spawning demon: #{^WEB.8460: ^ACTOR-REFERENCE-1 …}
 ((HEAD ^ACTOR-REFERENCE-1)
  (ARGUMENTS ^WEB.8458 …))
  1) If a GROUP containing the WRITER was
     previously mentioned,
     Then bind ^WEB.8458 to the GROUP found.
  2) If a GROUP containing the WRITER was not
     previously mentioned and a BELIEF follows,
     Then bind ^WEB.8458 to the WRITER.
  3) If a GROUP containing the WRITER was not
     previously mentioned and a PLAN, EVENT, or
     ECONOMIC QUANTITY follows,
     Then bind ^WEB.8458 to the COUNTRY where the
     editorial was written.
```

IMPORT ⟹
```
Adding to *working-memory*:
    #{^WEB.8462} = ()
Spawning demon: #{^WEB.8464: ^DISAMBIGUATE …}
 ((HEAD ^DISAMBIGUATE)
  (ARGUMENTS ^WEB.8462 (COUNTRY INSTITUTION) BEFORE
               (SPENDING ACTIVITY (M-TRADE)…) …))
Spawning demon: #{^WEB.8465: ^DISAMBIGUATE-USING-WORD …}
 ((HEAD ^DISAMBIGUATE-USING-WORD)
  (ARGUMENTS ^WEB.8462 FROM COUNTRY AFTER
```

```
                    (PHYS-OBJ TYPE (IMPORT)) …))
Spawning demon: #{^WEB.8466: ^IMPORT-MODIFIER …}
    ((HEAD ^IMPORT-MODIFIER)
    (ARGUMENTS ^WEB.8462 …)
    1) If (INSTITUTION TYPE (INDUSTRY)) follows,
       Then modify it with TYPE = IMPORT.
    2) If PHYS-OBJ or FOOD found AFTER and modified by the
       word OF,
       Then modify it with TYPE = IMPORT.
Executing demon: #{^WEB.8460: ^ACTOR-REFERENCE-1 …}
    #{^WEB.8458} = ((HEAD ^COUNTRY) (NAME U.S.)…)
    #{^WEB.8462} = ((HEAD ^SPENDING)
                    (ACTOR (*VAR* 'B.2779))
                    (OBJECT (*VAR* 'P.2787))
                    (ACTIVITY ((HEAD ^M-TRADE)
                               (BUYER (*VAR* 'B.2779))
                               (SELLER (*VAR* 'S.2781))
                               (GOODS (*VAR* 'G.2786))
                               (PAYMENT ((HEAD ^PHYS-OBJ)
                                         (TYPE MONEY))))))
Spawning demon: #{^WEB.8471: ^EXPECT …}
    ((HEAD ^EXPECT)
    (ARGUMENTS ^WEB.8462 OBJECT.2783 (FOOD PHYS-OBJ) AFTER …))
Spawning demon:#{^WEB.8470: ^EXPECT-USING-WORD …}
    ((HEAD ^EXPECT-USING-WORD)
    (ARGUMENTS ^WEB.8462 S.2781 FROM COUNTRY AFTER …))
Spawning demon: #{^WEB.8468: ^EXPECT …}
    ((HEAD ^EXPECT)
    (ARGUMENTS ^WEB.8462 B.2779 COUNTRY BEFORE …))
Killing demon: #{^WEB.8460: ^ACTOR-REFERENCE-1 …}
Executing demon: #{^WEB.8468: ^EXPECT …}
    B.2779 <-- ((HEAD ^COUNTRY) (NAME U.S.)…)
Killing demon: #{^WEB.8468: ^EXPECT …}
Killing demon: #{^WEB.8466: ^IMPORT-MODIFIER …}
Killing demon: #{^WEB.8465: ^DISAMBIGUATE-USING-WORD …}
Killing demon: #{^WEB.8464: ^DISAMBIGUATE …}
```

Modeling Trade Relationships: In OpEd, the activity of trade and lexical items associated with it are modeled in terms of economic quantities and their relationships (see section 2.3.2). For example, the pattern:

```
<COUNTRY1 "import" PRODUCT "from" COUNTRY2>
```

is represented in terms of the economic quantity SPENDING:

```
((HEAD ^SPENDING)
 (ACTOR COUNTRY1)
 (OBJECT PRODUCT)
 (ACTIVITY ((HEAD ^M-TRADE)
            (BUYER COUNTRY1)
            (SELLER COUNTRY2)
```

```
(GOODS PRODUCT))))
(PAYMENT ((HEAD ^PHYS-OBJ)
         (TYPE MONEY))))))
```

Here, the structure M-TRADE is a *memory organization packet (MOP)* (Schank, 1982) that organizes two events: (1) COUNTRY2 transfers possession of PRODUCT to COUNTRY1; and (2) COUNTRY1 transfers possession of MONEY to COUNTRY2. Each transfer of possession is represented in terms of an ATRANS, one of eleven primitives of Schank's (1973, 1975) Conceptual Dependency theory. In contrast, the pattern:

```
<COUNTRY1 "export" PRODUCT "to" COUNTRY2>
```

is represented in terms of the economic quantity EARNINGS:

```
((HEAD ^EARNINGS)
 (ACTOR COUNTRY1)
 (OBJECT ((HEAD ^PHYS-OBJ)
          (TYPE MONEY)))
 (ACTIVITY ((HEAD ^M-TRADE)
            (BUYER COUNTRY2)
            (SELLER COUNTRY1)
            (GOODS PRODUCT))))
 (PAYMENT ((HEAD ^PHYS-OBJ)
           (TYPE MONEY))))))
```

Here, the events organized by the structure M-TRADE are: (1) COUNTRY1 transfers possession of PRODUCT to COUNTRY2; and (2) COUNTRY2 transfers possession of MONEY to COUNTRY1.

LESS *COMMA*==>
```
Adding to *working-memory*:
    #{^WEB.8478} = ((HEAD ^STATE-CHANGE)
                    (TYPE DECREASE)
                    (OBJECT (*VAR* '0.2655))...)
Spawning demon: #{^WEB.8479: ^EXPECT ...}
    ((HEAD ^EXPECT)
     (ARGUMENTS ^WEB.8478
                OBJECT.2655
                (ECONOMIC-QUANTITY)
                BEFORE ...))
Spawning demon: #{^WEB.8481: ^EXPECT ...}
    ((HEAD ^EXPECT)
     (ARGUMENTS ^WEB.8478
                OBJECT.2655
                (ECONOMIC-QUANTITY PHYS-OBJ FOOD)
                AFTER ...))
Executing demon: #{^WEB.8479: ^EXPECT ...}
    0.2655 <-- ((HEAD ^SPENDING)
                (ACTOR ^COUNTRY.587)
```

```
                    (OBJECT (*VAR* 'P.2787))
                    (ACTIVITY ((HEAD ^M-TRADE)
                               (BUYER ^COUNTRY.587)
                               (SELLER (*VAR* 'S.2781))
                               (GOODS (*VAR* 'G.2786))
                               (PAYMENT ((HEAD ^PHYS-OBJ)
                                         (TYPE MONEY))))))
Killing demon: #{^WEB.8479: ^EXPECT …}
Killing demon: #{^WEB.8481: ^EXPECT …}
Executing demon: #{^WEB.8448: ^EXPECT-ANTECEDENT …}
    ANTE.5737 <-- ((HEAD ^STATE-CHANGE)
                   (TYPE DECREASE)
                   (OBJECT ^SPENDING.8469)…)
Killing demon: #{^WEB.8448: ^EXPECT-ANTECEDENT …}
```

Lexical Items for State Changes: Words such as "less" and "fewer" indicate state changes. Associated with those words are demons that search working memory in order to locate the object that changes state. Those demons implement the following expectation:

- If an unbound economic quantity precedes a state-change lexical item I1, then that economic quantity is the object of the state change. Otherwise, the object of the state change follows I1.

FOREIGN ==>
```
    Adding to *working-memory*:
        #{^WEB.8491} = ()
    Spawning demon: #{^WEB.8493: ^FOREIGN-MODIFIER …}
        ((HEAD ^FOREIGN-MODIFIER)
         (ARGUMENTS ^WEB.8491…))
        1) If PHYS-OBJ, FOOD, HUMAN, or AUTHORITY follows,
           Then modify it with
           (NATION ≠ COUNTRY where editorial was written).
        2) If GROUP of class COUNTRY follows,
           Then modify it with
           (EXCLUDED-INSTANCE = COUNTRY where editorial was written).
        3) If single instance of COUNTRY follows,
           Then modify it with
           (NAME ≠ COUNTRY where editorial was written).
```

COUNTRIES ==>
```
    Recognized word: COUNTRY
    Recognized suffix: ES
    Adding to *working-memory*:
        #{^WEB.8494} = ((HEAD ^COUNTRY)
                        (GROUP-INSTANCES *MULTIPLE*)…)
    Executing demon: #{^WEB.8493: ^FOREIGN-MODIFIER …}
        #{^WEB.8494} = ((HEAD ^COUNTRY)
                        (GROUP-INSTANCES *MULTIPLE*)
```

```
                          (EXCLUDED-INSTANCE ((HEAD ^COUNTRY)
                                             (NAME U.S.)…))…)
        Killing demon: #{^WEB.8493: ^FOREIGN-MODIFIER …}
```

WILL EARN FEWER DOLLARS *PERIOD* ==>
```
        #{^WEB.8537} = ((HEAD ^STATE-CHANGE)
                        (TYPE DECREASE)
                        (OBJECT
                          ((HEAD ^EARNINGS)
                           (ACTOR ((HEAD ^COUNTRY)
                                   (GROUP-INSTANCES *MULTIPLE*)
                                   (EXCLUDED-INSTANCE
                                     ((HEAD ^COUNTRY)
                                      (NAME U.S.)…)))))
                           (OBJECT ((HEAD ^PHYS-OBJ)
                                    (TYPE MONEY)
                                    (NAME DOLLAR)
                                    (NATION ((HEAD ^COUNTRY)
                                             (NAME U.S.)…))))…)))
        Executing demon: #{^WEB.8450: ^EXPECT-CONSEQUENT …}
           CONSE.5739 <-- ((HEAD ^STATE-CHANGE)
                           (TYPE DECREASE)
                           (OBJECT ^EARNINGS.8529)…)
        Killing demon: #{^WEB.8450: ^EXPECT-CONSEQUENT …}
        Executing demon: #{^WEB.8245: ^EXPECT-CAUSE-EFFECT-CHAIN …}
        Recognized CAUSAL RELATIONSHIPS in reasoning script
        #{^$R-ECON-PROTECTION-->FEWER-EXPORT-JOBS.8703}:
           ((HEAD ^LEAD-TO)
            (ANTE ^P-ECON-PROTECTION.6682)
            (CONSE ((HEAD ^STATE-CHANGE)
                    (TYPE DECREASE)
                    (OBJECT ^SPENDING.8469))))
           ((HEAD ^LEAD-TO)
            (ANTE ((HEAD ^STATE-CHANGE)
                   (TYPE DECREASE)
                   (OBJECT ^SPENDING.8469)))
            (CONSE ((HEAD ^STATE-CHANGE)
                    (TYPE DECREASE)
                    (OBJECT ^SALES.8644))))
           ((HEAD ^LEAD-TO)
            (ANTE ((HEAD ^STATE-CHANGE)
                   (TYPE DECREASE)
                   (OBJECT ^SALES.8644)))
            (CONSE ((HEAD ^STATE-CHANGE)
                    (TYPE DECREASE)
                    (OBJECT ^EARNINGS.8529))))
        Spawning demon:  #{^WEB.8858: ^FOLLOW-CAUSE-EFFECT-CHAIN …}
           ((HEAD ^FOLLOW-CAUSE-EFFECT-CHAIN)
            (ARGUMENTS ^$R-ECON-PROTECTION-->FEWER-EXPORT-JOBS.8703
                       ^BELIEF.7174))
        If representation R of next input
```

```
      sentence matches the components of
      ^$R-ECON-PROTECTION-->FEWER-EXPORT-JOBS.8703,
      Then instantiate
      ^$R-ECON-PROTECTION-->FEWER-EXPORT-JOBS.8703
      up to the point referred to by R.
Killing demon: #{^WEB.8375: ^EXPECT-CAUSE-EFFECT-CHAIN …}
```

Beginning Script Application: The representation of the current input sentence is matched against the causal chain in the script $R-ECON-PROTECTION-->FEWER-EXPORT-JOBS. Since the match succeeds, $R-ECON-PROTECTION-->FEWER-EXPORT-JOBS is instantiated up to the point referred to by the input. This instantiation allows OpEd to infer that the relationship between the decrease in SPENDING by the U.S. and the decrease in EARNINGS of foreign countries is mediated by a decrease in the volume of SALES by foreign countries. In addition, an instance of the demon FOLLOW-CAUSE-EFFECT-CHAIN is spawned to attempt to understand successive input sentences from the context of $R-ECON-PROTECTION-->FEWER-EXPORT-JOBS.

8.2.7. Seventh Sentence

```
Processing Sentence:
THEY WILL HAVE LESS TO SPEND ON AMERICAN EXPORTS *PERIOD*

THEY WILL HAVE LESS TO SPEND ==>
      #{^WEB.8905} = ((HEAD ^STATE-CHANGE)
                      (TYPE DECREASE)
                      (OBJECT
                       ((HEAD ^SPENDING)
                       (ACTOR (*VAR* 'A.6345))
                       (OBJECT (*VAR* 'P.6347)
                       (ACTIVITY ((HEAD ^M-TRADE)
                                  (BUYER (*VAR* 'A.6345))
                                  (SELLER (*VAR* 'S.6350))
                                  (GOODS (*VAR* 'G.6351))
                                  (PAYMENT (*VAR* 'P.6347)))))))))
Spawning demon: #{^WEB.8918: ^EXPECT …}
      ((HEAD ^EXPECT)
       (ARGUMENTS ^WEB.8917
                  A.6345 (HUMAN COUNTRY INSTITUTION) BEFORE …))
Spawning demon: #{^WEB.8918: ^EXPECT-USING-WORD …}
      ((HEAD ^EXPECT-USING-WORD)
       (ARGUMENTS ^SPENDING.8917 S.6350 FROM COUNTRY AFTER …))
Spawning demon: #{^WEB.8920: ^EXPECT-USING-WORD …}
      ((HEAD ^EXPECT-USING-WORD)
       (ARGUMENTS ^SPENDING.8917
                  G.6351 ON (PHYS-OBJ FOOD) AFTER …))
```

```
Spawning demon: #{^WEB.8921: ^EXPECT …}
    ((HEAD ^EXPECT)
    (ARGUMENTS ^SPENDING.8917
                P.6347
                (PHYS-OBJ TYPE (MONEY))
                AFTER …))
Executing demon: #{^WEB.8918: ^EXPECT ...}
    A.6345 <-- ((HEAD ^COUNTRY)
                (GROUP-INSTANCES *MULTIPLE*)
                (EXCLUDED-INSTANCE ^COUNTRY.587))
Killing demon: #{^WEB.8918: ^EXPECT …}
```

Another State Change: OpEd recognizes that the object of the decrease indicated by the phrase "have less" corresponds to the economic quantity SPENDING underlying the word "spend." The actor of that economic quantity is bound to the group referent of the pronoun "they," i.e., countries on which the U.S. has imposed trade restrictions. In addition, the demons spawned by the word "spend" search working memory for conceptualizations that correspond to the money spent and the object received in exchange.

```
ON AMERICAN ==>
    Adding to *working-memory*:
        #{^WEB.8930} = ()
    Spawning demon: #{^WEB.8931: ^MODIFY-CONCEPT …}
        ((HEAD ^MODIFY-CONCEPT)
        (ARGUMENTS ^WEB.8930
                    (HUMAN PHYS-OBJ INSTITUTION AUTHORITY FOOD)
                    NATION
                    (COUNTRY NAME (U.S.))…))
    Spawning demon: #{^WEB.8932: ^DISAMBIGUATE …}
        ((HEAD ^DISAMBIGUATE)
        (ARGUMENTS ^WEB.6819 (EVENT PLAN) AFTER HUMAN …))

EXPORTS *PERIOD* ==>
    Recognized word: EXPORT
    Recognized suffix: S
    Adding to *working-memory*:
        #{^WEB.8933} = ()
    Spawning demon: #{^WEB.8939: ^PLURAL …}
        ((HEAD ^PLURAL)
        (ARGUMENTS ^WEB.8933))
    Spawning demon: #{^WEB.8935: ^DISAMBIGUATE-USING-WORD …}
        ((HEAD ^DISAMBIGUATE-USING-WORD)
        (ARGUMENTS ^WEB.8933 FROM COUNTRY AFTER
                    (PHYS-OBJ TYPE (EXPORT)) …))
    Spawning demon: #{^WEB.8936: ^EXPORT-MODIFIER …}
        ((HEAD ^EXPORT-MODIFIER)
        (ARGUMENTS ^WEB.8933 …)
```

```
    1) If (INSTITUTION TYPE (INDUSTRY)) follows,
       Then modify it with TYPE = EXPORT.
    2) If PHYS-OBJ or FOOD found AFTER and modified by
       the word OF,
       Then modify it with TYPE = EXPORT.
Spawning demon: #{^WEB.8937: ^DISAMBIGUATE …}
  ((HEAD ^DISAMBIGUATE)
   (ARGUMENTS ^WEB.8933 (COUNTRY INSTITUTION) BEFORE
                        (SPENDING ACTIVITY (M-TRADE)…) …))
Executing demon: #{^WEB.8931: ^MODIFY-CONCEPT …}
  #{^WEB.8933} = ((HEAD ^PHYS-OBJ)
                 (TYPE EXPORT)
                 (NAME (*VAR* 'NAME.2823))
                 (NATION ((HEAD ^COUNTRY)
                          (NAME U.S.))))
Killing demon: #{^WEB.8932: ^MODIFY-CONCEPT …}
Killing demon: #{^WEB.8937: ^DISAMBIGUATE …}
Killing demon: #{^WEB.8936: ^EXPORT-MODIFIER …}
Killing demon: #{^WEB.8935: ^DISAMBIGUATE-USING-WORD …}
Executing demon: #{^WEB.8939: ^PLURAL …}
   #{^WEB.8933} <-- ((HEAD ^PHYS-OBJ)
                    (TYPE EXPORT)
                    (NAME (*VAR* 'NAME.2823))
                    (NATION ^COUNTRY.587)
                    (GROUP-INSTANCES *MULTIPLE*))
Killing demon: #{^WEB.8939: ^PLURAL …}
Executing demon: #{^WEB.8920: ^EXPECT-USING-WORD …}
   G.6351 <-- ((HEAD ^PHYS-OBJ)
              (TYPE EXPORT)
              (NAME (*VAR* 'NAME.2823))
              (NATION ^COUNTRY.587)
              (GROUP-INSTANCES *MULTIPLE*))
Killing demon: #{^WEB.8920: ^EXPECT-USING-WORD …}
```

Bottom-Up Disambiguation and Top-Down Disambiguation:
The instance of the demon MODIFY-CONCEPT associated with the word
"American" expects a PHYS-OBJ. This expectation matches one of the
meanings of the word "exports." As a result, the word "American" is
disambiguated in a bottom-up manner, the word "exports" is
disambiguated in a top-down manner, and the phrase "American
exports" is understood as "products sold by the U.S. to foreign
countries."

```
Executing demon: #{^WEB.8858: ^FOLLOW-CAUSE-EFFECT-CHAIN …}
Recognized CAUSAL RELATIONSHIPS from active reasoning script
#{^$R-ECON-PROTECTION-->FEWER-EXPORT-JOBS.8703}:
    ((HEAD ^LEAD-TO)
     (ANTE ((HEAD ^STATE-CHANGE)
            (TYPE DECREASE)
            (OBJECT ^EARNINGS.8529)))
```

```
            (CONSE ((HEAD ^STATE-CHANGE)
                   (TYPE DECREASE)
                   (OBJECT ^SPENDING.8917))))
    Spawning demon: #{^WEB.9004: ^FOLLOW-CAUSE-EFFECT-CHAIN ...}
       ((HEAD ^FOLLOW-CAUSE-EFFECT-CHAIN)
        (ARGUMENTS ^$R-ECON-PROTECTION-->FEWER-EXPORT-JOBS.8703
                   ^BELIEF.7174))
    Killing demon: #{^WEB.8858: ^FOLLOW-CAUSE-EFFECT-CHAIN ...}
```

Continuing Script Application: OpEd uses $R-ECON-PROTECTION-->FEWER-EXPORT-JOBS to understand that the decrease in SPENDING by foreign countries is caused by the decrease in their level of EARNINGS. Once this causal relationship has been instantiated in episodic memory, OpEd spawns another instance of the demon FOLLOW-CAUSE-EFFECT-CHAIN to continue the script application.

8.2.8. Eighth Sentence

Processing Sentence:
THE RESULT WILL BE FEWER JOBS IN EXPORT
INDUSTRIES *PERIOD*

THE RESULT ==>
```
    Adding to *working-memory*:
       #{^WEB.9097} = ((HEAD ^LEAD-TO)
                       (ANTE (*VAR* 'ANTE.5763))
                       (CONSE (*VAR* 'CONSE.5765)))
    Spawning demon: #{^WEB.9098: ^EXPECT-USING-WORD ...}
       ((HEAD ^EXPECT-USING-WORD)
        (ARGUMENTS ^WEB.9097 ANTE.5763 OF
                   (PLAN EVENT STATE STATE-CHANGE) AFTER ...))
    Spawning demon: #{^WEB.9101: ^EXPECT-USING-WORD ...}
       ((HEAD ^EXPECT-USING-WORD)
        (ARGUMENTS ^WEB.9097 CONSE.5765 (BE IS WAS)
                   (STATE STATE-CHANGE GOAL-SITUATION) AFTER ...))
```

WILL BE FEWER JOBS IN EXPORT INDUSTRIES *PERIOD* ==>
```
    Executing demon: #{^WEB.9101: ^EXPECT-USING-WORD ...}
       CONSE.5765 <-- ((HEAD ^STATE-CHANGE)
                       (TYPE DECREASE)
                       (OBJECT
                        ((HEAD ^OCCUPATION)
                         (SETTING ((HEAD ^INSTITUTION)
                                   (TYPE EXPORT INDUSTRY)
                                   (GROUP-INSTANCES *MULTIPLE*)...))
                         (GROUP-INSTANCES *MULTIPLE*))))
    Killing demon: #{^WEB.9129: ^EXPECT ...}
    Executing demon: #{^WEB.9004: ^FOLLOW-CAUSE-EFFECT-CHAIN ...}
```

```
Recognized CAUSAL RELATIONSHIPS from active reasoning script
#{^R-ECON-PROTECTION-->FEWER-EXPORT-JOBS.8703}:
    ((HEAD ^LEAD-TO)
     (ANTE ((HEAD ^STATE-CHANGE)
            (TYPE DECREASE)
            (OBJECT ^SPENDING.8917)))
     (CONSE ((HEAD ^STATE-CHANGE)
             (TYPE DECREASE)
             (OBJECT ^SALES.9198))))
    ((HEAD ^LEAD-TO)
     (ANTE ((HEAD ^STATE-CHANGE)
            (TYPE DECREASE)
            (OBJECT ^SALES.9198)))
     (CONSE ((HEAD ^STATE-CHANGE)
             (TYPE DECREASE)
             (OBJECT ^EARNINGS.9209))))
    ((HEAD ^LEAD-TO)
     (ANTE ((HEAD ^STATE-CHANGE)
            (TYPE DECREASE)
            (OBJECT ^EARNINGS.9209)))
     (CONSE ((HEAD ^STATE-CHANGE)
             (TYPE DECREASE)
             (OBJECT ^OCCUPATION.8197))))
    ((HEAD ^LEAD-TO)
     (ANTE ((HEAD ^STATE-CHANGE)
            (TYPE DECREASE)
            (OBJECT ^OCCUPATION.8197)))
     (CONSE ((HEAD ^GOAL-SITUATION)
             (GOAL ^GOAL.7104)
             (STATUS THWARTED)))))
Inferred BELIEF:
    #{^WEB.9231: ^BELIEF ...} =
        ((HEAD ^BELIEF)
         (CONTENT ^$R-ECON-PROTECTION-->FEWER-EXPORT-JOBS.8703)
         (BELIEVER ((HEAD ^HUMAN)
                    (FIRST-NAME MILTON)
                    (LAST-NAME FRIEDMAN)...))...)
Inferred SUPPORT RELATIONSHIP:
    #{^WEB.9247: ^SUPPORT ...} = ((HEAD ^SUPPORT)
                                  (TYPE POSSIBLE-FAILURE)
                                  (SUPPORTED ^BELIEF.7174)
                                  (SUPPORTER ^WEB.9231))
Spawning demon: #{^WEB.9252: ^FIND-BELIEF ...}
    ((HEAD ^MARK-INSTANCE)
     (ARGUMENTS ^WEB.9231))
Spawning demon: #{^WEB.9253: ^FIND-SUPPORT ...}
    ((HEAD ^FIND-SUPPORT)
     (ARGUMENTS ^WEB.9247))
Killing demon: #{^WEB.9004: ^FOLLOW-CAUSE-EFFECT-CHAIN ...}
Executing demon: #{^WEB.9253: ^FIND-SUPPORT ...}
    #{^WEB.9247: ^SUPPORT ...} = #{^SUPPORT.9262: ^SUPPORT ...}
Killing demon: #{^WEB.9253: ^FIND-SUPPORT ...}
```

```
Executing demon: #{^WEB.9252: ^FIND-BELIEF …}
   #{^WEB.9231: ^BELIEF …} = #{^BELIEF.9277: ^BELIEF …}
Killing demon: #{^WEB.9252: ^FIND-BELIEF …}
```

Ending Script Application: The use of $R-ECON-PROTECTION-
->FEWER-EXPORT-JOBS allows OpEd to make the following inferences:
(1) the decrease in SPENDING by foreign countries causes a decrease in
SALES of U.S. exports; (2) this decrease in SALES causes a decrease in
EARNINGS of U.S. export industries; (3) the decrease in EARNINGS
results in a decrease in OCCUPATIONs in U.S. export industries; and (4)
the decrease in OCCUPATIONs thwarts the goal of preserving
OCCUPATIONs in the U.S. In addition, OpEd instantiates a support
structure in which Friedman's belief that import restrictions cost jobs is
supported by the instance of $R-ECON-PROTECTION-->FEWER-EXPORT-
JOBS.

8.3.   Question-Answering Traces

After reading ED-JOBS, OpEd is ready for a question-
answering session. Each input question is parsed by OpEd's
expectation-based parser and the question's conceptual representation is
built in working memory. The context for understanding the question is
provided by the argument graph that contains the beliefs, belief
relationships, and argument units instantiated during editorial
comprehension. Question answering demons attached to question words
(e.g., who, what, why, etc.) are activated whenever such words are
found at the beginning of the question. These demons determine the
question's conceptual category and activate appropriate search and
retrieval demons that access the argument graph and return conceptual
answers. Once an answer is found, it is generated in English by a
recursive-descent generator. These processes of question
understanding, memory search, and answer generation are illustrated in
the following sections using traces of how OpEd answers five types of
questions characterized in chapter 7, namely: belief-holder, causal-
belief, belief-justification, affect/belief, and top-belief/AU. Since
questions are parsed by the same parser used for editorial
comprehension, only highlights of the parsing process are shown.

8.3.1. Belief-Holder Question

Processing Question:
WHO BELIEVES THAT THE LIMITATIONS ON IMPORTS WILL SAVE
JOBS *QMARK*

WHO ==>
```
    Adding to *working-memory*:
       #{^WEB.11289} = ()
    Spawning demon: #{^WEB.11291: ^WHO-BELIEF? …}
       ((HEAD ^WHO-BELIEF?)
        (ARGUMENTS ^WEB.11289 …))
       If a BELIEF follows,
       Then spawn appropriate demons that retrieve
       answers to BELIEF-HOLDER questions.
    Spawning demon: #{^WEB.11292: ^WHO-CONCEPT? …}
       ((HEAD ^WHO-PLAN?)
        (ARGUMENTS ^WEB.11289…))
       If a PLAN or EVENT follows,
       Then spawn appropriate demons that retrieve
       answers to CONCEPT-COMPLETION questions.
```

BELIEVES ==>
```
    Adding to *working-memory*:
       #{^WEB.11293} = ((HEAD ^BELIEF)
                        (BELIEVER (*VAR* 'BELIEVER.2630))
                        (CONTENT (*VAR* 'CONTENT.2634)))
    Spawning demon: #{^WEB.11294: ^EXPECT …}
       ((HEAD ^EXPECT)
        (ARGUMENTS ^WEB.11293 BELIEVER.2630
                   (HUMAN INSTITUTION AUTHORITY) BEFORE …))
    Spawning demon: #{^WEB.11297: ^EXPECT-USING-WORD …}
       ((HEAD ^EXPECT-USING-WORD)
        (ARGUMENTS ^WEB.11293 CONTENT.2634 THAT
                   (OUGHT-TO OUGHT-NOT-TO LEAD-TO) AFTER …))
    Spawning demon: #{^WEB.11304: ^FIND-BELIEF …}
       ((HEAD ^FIND-BELIEF)
        (ARGUMENTS ^WEB.11293 …))
    Executing demon: #{^WEB.11291: ^WHO-BELIEF? …}
    Spawning demon: #{^WEB.11310: ^EVALUATIVE-BELIEF-->BELIEVER …}
       ((HEAD ^EVALUATIVE-BELIEF-->BELIEVER)
        (ARGUMENTS ^WEB.11293))
       If the given BELIEF contains a PLAN EVALUATION,
       Then retrieve BELIEVER of matching EVALUATIVE BELIEF
       indexed by given PLAN.
    Spawning demon: #{^WEB.11311: ^CAUSAL-BELIEF-->BELIEVER …}
       ((HEAD ^CAUSAL-BELIEF-->BELIEVER)
        (ARGUMENTS ^WEB.11293))
       1) If the given BELIEF contains a CAUSAL RELATIONSHIP of the
```

```
        form: (PLAN -lead-to-> GOAL-SITUATION),
        Then retrieve BELIEVER of matching CAUSAL BELIEF
        indexed by the given PLAN.
     2) If the given BELIEF contains a CAUSAL RELATIONSHIP
        of the form: (*?* -lead-to-> GOAL-SITUATION),
        Then retrieve BELIEVER of matching CAUSAL BELIEF
        indexed by the given GOAL.
Killing demon: #{^WEB.11291: ^WHO-BELIEF? …}
Killing demon: #{^WEB.11292: ^WHO-CONCEPT? …}
```

The word "who" spawns demons that determine whether a question is: (1) a belief-holder question, such as "who believes that import restrictions are bad?"; or (2) a concept-completion question, such as "who gave Mary a book?" (see Lehnert (1978) for a detailed explanation of concept-completion questions). Strategies for answering belief-holder questions depend upon the content of the given belief (see section 7.3.1). If the belief contains a plan evaluation or a plan-goal relationship, then OpEd searches for a matching belief indexed by the given plan. In contrast, if the belief only contains a goal-situation, OpEd searches for a matching belief indexed by the given goal. Once a matching belief has been found, OpEd retrieves the holder of that belief.

```
THAT THE LIMITATIONS ON IMPORTS
WILL SAVE JOBS *QMARK* ==>
Executing demon: #{^WEB.11297: ^EXPECT-USING-WORD …}
     C.2634 <-- ((HEAD ^LEAD-TO)
                 (ANTE ((HEAD ^P-ECON-PROTECTION)…))
                 (CONSE ((HEAD ^GOAL-SITUATION)
                         (GOAL ((HEAD ^GOAL)
                                (TYPE PRESERVATION)
                                (OBJECT ((HEAD ^OCCUPATION)…)))))
                        (STATUS ACHIEVED)
                        (TIME FUTURE))))
Killing demon: #{^WEB.11297: ^EXPECT-USING-WORD …}
Executing demon: #{^WEB.11311: ^CAUSAL-BELIEF-->BELIEVER …}
BELIEF found:
     #{^BELIEF.8319 …} =
        ((HEAD ^BELIEF)
         (CONTENT ((HEAD ^LEAD-TO)
                   (ANTE ^P-ECON-PROTECTION.6682)
                   (CONSE ((HEAD ^GOAL-SITUATION)
                           (GOAL ^GOAL.7104)
                           (STATUS ACHIEVED)))))
         (BELIEVER ^AUTHORITY.1136))
Answer found:
     #{^AUTHORITY.1136 …}
Killing demon: #{^WEB.11311: ^CAUSAL-BELIEF-->BELIEVER …}
Killing demon: #{^WEB.11310: ^EVALUATIVE-BELIEF-->BELIEVER …}
```

Calling English Generator:
```
#{^AUTHORITY.1136 …}:
    THE REAGAN ADMINISTRATION *PERIOD*
```

Here, OpEd finds the answer to the belief-holder question by:
(1) accessing the causal beliefs indexed by P-ECON-PROTECTION; and
(2) retrieving the holder of the belief that matches the relationship
P-ECON-PROTECTION--achieve-->G-PRESERVE-JOB.

8.3.2. Causal-Belief Question

Processing Question:
```
WHAT IS THE RESULT OF THE LIMITATIONS ON IMPORTS *QMARK*
```

WHAT ==>
```
    Adding to *working-memory*:
        #{^WEB.10109} = ()
    Spawning demon: #{^WEB.10111: ^WHAT-BELIEF? …}
        ((HEAD ^WHAT-BELIEF?)
         ARGUMENTS ^WEB.10109 …))
        If a BELIEF follows,
        Then spawn appropriate demons that retrieve
        answers to TOP-BELIEF/AU questions.
    Spawning demon: #{^WEB.10112: ^WHAT-LEAD-TO? …}
        ((HEAD ^WHAT-LEAD-TO?)
         (ARGUMENTS ^WEB.10109 …))
        If a CAUSAL RELATIONSHIP or a BELIEF containing
        a CAUSAL RELATIONSHIP follows,
        Then spawn appropriate demons that retrieve
        answers to CAUSAL-BELIEF questions.
    Spawning demon: #{^WEB.10113: ^WHAT-AFFECT? …}
        ((HEAD ^WHAT-AFFECT?)
         (ARGUMENTS ^WEB.10109 …))
        If an AFFECT follows,
        Then spawn appropriate demons that retrieve
        answers to AFFECT/BELIEF questions.
```

IS THE RESULT ==>
```
    Adding to *working-memory*:
        #{^WEB.10119} = ((HEAD ^LEAD-TO)
                         (ANTE (*VAR* 'ANTE.5763))
                         (CONSE (*VAR* 'CONSE.5765)))
    Spawning demon: #{^WEB.10120: ^EXPECT-USING-WORD …}
        ((HEAD ^EXPECT-USING-WORD)
         (ARGUMENTS ^WEB.10119 ANTE.5763 OF
                    (PLAN EVENT STATE STATE-CHANGE) AFTER …))
    Spawning demon: #{^WEB.10122: ^EXPECT-USING-WORD …}
        ((HEAD ^EXPECT-USING-WORD)
```

```
(ARGUMENTS ^WEB.10119 CONSE.5765 (BE IS WAS)
          (STATE STATE-CHANGE GOAL-SITUATION) AFTER …))
Executing demon: #{^WEB.10112: ^WHAT-LEAD-TO? …}
Spawning demon: #{^WEB.10131: ^ANTECEDENT-->BELIEF …}
   ((HEAD ^ANTECEDENT-->BELIEF)
   (ARGUMENTS ^WEB.10119))
   If the given CAUSAL RELATIONSHIP is of the form:
   (PLAN -lead-to-> *?*),
   Then retrieve BELIEF about PLAN-GOAL RELATIONSHIPS
   indexed by the given PLAN.
Spawning demon: #{^WEB.10132: ^CONSEQUENT-->BELIEF …}
   ((HEAD ^CONSEQUENT-->BELIEF)
   (ARGUMENTS ^WEB.10119))
   If the given CAUSAL RELATIONSHIP is of the form:
   (*?* -lead-to-> GOAL-SITUATION),
   Then retrieve BELIEF about GOAL SITUATIONS
   indexed by the given GOAL.
Killing demon: #{^WEB.10112: ^WHAT-LEAD-TO? …}
Killing demon: #{^WEB.10113: ^WHAT-AFFECT? …}
Killing demon: #{^WEB.10111: ^WHAT-BELIEF? …}
```

The word "what" indicates at least three types of conceptual question categories: causal-belief, affect/belief, and top-belief/AU. For example:

- <u>Causal-Belief Question</u>: What does the Reagan administration think the result of the limitations on imports will be?

- <u>Affect/Belief Question:</u> What has disappointed Milton Friedman?

- <u>Top-Belief/AU Question:</u> What does the Reagan administration believe about the limitations on imports?

In order to answer causal-belief questions, OpEd must examine the conceptualization that follows the word "what" (see section 7.3.2). For example, if "what" is followed by a causal relationship of the form:

```
PLAN -lead-to-> *?*
```

then OpEd retrieves the causal beliefs that are indexed by P and contain goal situations caused by P. Similarly, if "what" is followed by a causal relationship of the form:

```
*?* -lead-to-> GOAL-SITUATION
```

then OpEd retrieves the causal beliefs that are indexed by the given goal and contain the given goal situation.

```
OF THE LIMITATIONS ON IMPORTS *QMARK* ==>
    Executing demon: #{^WEB.10120: ^EXPECT-USING-WORD …}
        ANTE.5763 <-- ((HEAD ^P-ECON-PROTECTION)…))
    Killing demon: #{^WEB.10120: ^EXPECT-USING-WORD …}
    Executing demon: #{^WEB.10131: ^ANTECEDENT-->BELIEF …}
    Answer found:
        #{^BELIEF.7174 …}
        #{^BELIEF.7481 …}
        #{^BELIEF.7813 …}
        #{^BELIEF.8319 …}
    Killing demon: #{^WEB.10131: ^ANTECEDENT-->BELIEF …}
    Killing demon: #{^WEB.10132: ^CONSEQUENT-->BELIEF …}
```

Calling English Generator:
```
#{^BELIEF.7174 …}:
    MILTON FRIEDMAN BELIEVES THAT PROTECTIONIST POLICIES BY THE
    REAGAN ADMINISTRATION WILL THWART THE PRESERVATION OF JOBS FOR
    U.S.
#{^BELIEF.7481 …}:
    MILTON FRIEDMAN BELIEVES THAT PROTECTIONIST POLICIES BY THE
    REAGAN ADMINISTRATION DO NOT LEAD TO THE ACHIEVEMENT OF NORMAL
    PROFITS OF THE STEEL INDUSTRY AND THE AUTOMOBILE INDUSTRY.
#{^BELIEF.7813 …}:
    THE REAGAN ADMINISTRATION BELIEVES THAT PROTECTIONIST POLICIES
    BY THE REAGAN ADMINISTRATION LEAD TO THE ACHIEVEMENT OF NORMAL
    PROFITS OF THE STEEL INDUSTRY AND THE AUTOMOBILE INDUSTRY.
#{^BELIEF.8319 …}:
    THE REAGAN ADMINISTRATION BELIEVES THAT PROTECTIONIST POLICIES
    BY THE REAGAN ADMINISTRATION ACHIEVE THE PRESERVATION OF JOBS
    FOR U.S.
```

Answer generation in OpEd is by recursive descent through instantiated concepts. OpEd produces English sentences in a left-to-right manner by using generation patterns associated with each class of knowledge structure. For example, a BELIEF is generated using the pattern:

<BELIEVER "believe" "that" CONTENT>

This pattern indicates that: (1) the generation procedure must be invoked recursively on the fillers of the BELIEVER and CONTENT slots of the BELIEF; and (2) the verb "to believe" must be conjugated according to the fillers of those slots. For instance, BELIEF.8319 is generated as follows:

Calling English Generator:
```
#{^BELIEF.8319 …}:
    generating #{^BELIEF.8319 …}: #{^AUTHORITY.1136 …} "BELIEVES"
                                   "THAT" #{^LEAD-TO.8290 …}
    generating #{^AUTHORITY.1136 …}: "THE" "REAGAN" "ADMINISTRATION"
```

```
generating #{^LEAD-TO.8290 …}: #{^P-ECON-PROTECTION.6682 …}
                               #{^GOAL-SITUATION.8126 …}
generating #{^P-ECON-PROTECTION.6682 …}: "PROTECTIONIST"
                                         "POLICIES" "BY"
                                         #{^AUTHORITY.1136 …}
generating #{^AUTHORITY.1136 …}: "THE" "REAGAN" "ADMINISTRATION"
generating #{^GOAL-SITUATION.8126 …}: "ACHIEVE" #{^GOAL.7104 …}
generating #{^GOAL.7104 …}: "THE" "PRESERVATION" "OF"
                           #{^OCCUPATION.8197 …} "FOR"
                           #{^COUNTRY.587 …}
generating #{^OCCUPATIONS.8197 …}: "JOBS"
generating #{^COUNTRY.587 …}: "U.S."
```

THE REAGAN ADMINISTRATION BELIEVES THAT PROTECTIONIST POLICIES
BY THE REAGAN ADMINISTRATION ACHIEVE THE PRESERVATION OF JOBS
FOR U.S.

8.3.3. Belief-Justification Question

Processing Question:
WHY DOES MILTON FRIEDMAN BELIEVE THAT THE LIMITATIONS ON
IMPORTS WILL COST JOBS *QMARK*

WHY ==>
```
    Adding to *working-memory*:
        #{^WEB.10309} = ()
    Spawning demon: #{^WEB.10311: ^WHY-AFFECT? …}
        ((HEAD ^WHY-AFFECT?)
         (ARGUMENTS ^WEB.10309 …))
        If an AFFECT follows,
        Then spawn appropriate demons that retrieve
        answers to AFFECT/BELIEF questions.
    Spawning demon: #{^WEB.10312: ^WHY-BELIEF? …}
        ((HEAD ^WHY-BELIEF?)
         (ARGUMENTS ^WEB.10309 …))
        If a BELIEF, PLAN EVALUATION, or
        PLAN-GOAL RELATIONSHIP follows,
        Then spawn appropriate demons that retrieve
        answers to BELIEF-JUSTIFICATION questions.
```

DOES MILTON FRIEDMAN BELIEVE ==>
```
    Adding to *working-memory*:
        #{^WEB.10342} = ((HEAD ^BELIEF)
                        (BELIEVER (*VAR* 'BELIEVER.2630))
                        (CONTENT (*VAR* 'CONTENT.2634)))
    Spawning demon: #{^WEB.10343: ^EXPECT …}
        ((HEAD ^EXPECT)
         (ARGUMENTS ^WEB.10342 BELIEVER.2630
                    (HUMAN INSTITUTION AUTHORITY) BEFORE …))
```

```
Spawning demon: #{^WEB.10345: ^EXPECT-USING-WORD …}
    ((HEAD ^EXPECT-USING-WORD)
     (ARGUMENTS ^WEB.10342 CONTENT.2634 THAT
                     (OUGHT-TO OUGHT-NOT-TO LEAD-TO) AFTER …))
Spawning demon: #{^WEB.10353: ^FIND-BELIEF …}
    ((HEAD ^FIND-BELIEF)
     (ARGUMENTS ^WEB.10342 …))
Executing demon: #{^WEB.10343: ^EXPECT …}
    BELIEVER.2630 <-- ((HEAD ^HUMAN)
                       (FIRST-NAME MILTON)
                       (LAST-NAME FRIEDMAN)…)
Killing demon: #{^WEB.10343: ^EXPECT …}
Executing demon: #{^WEB.10312: ^WHY-BELIEF? …}
Spawning demon: #{^WEB.10358: ^BELIEF-->BELIEF-JUSTIFICATION …}
    ((HEAD ^BELIEF-->BELIEF-JUSTIFICATION)
     (ARGUMENTS ^WEB.10342))
    1) If the given BELIEF contains a PLAN EVALUATION,
       Then retrieve the JUSTIFICATION of matching
       EVALUATIVE BELIEF indexed by the given PLAN.
    2) If the given BELIEF contains a CAUSAL RELATIONSHIP of the
       form: (PLAN -lead-to-> GOAL-SITUATION),
       Then retrieve the JUSTIFICATION of matching
       CAUSAL BELIEF indexed by given PLAN.
    3) If the given BELIEF contains a CAUSAL RELATIONSHIP
       of the form: (*?* -lead-to-> GOAL-SITUATION),
       Then retrieve JUSTIFICATION of matching
       CAUSAL BELIEF indexed by given GOAL.
Killing demon: #{^WEB.10312: ^WHY-BELIEF? …}
Killing demon: #{^WEB.10311: ^WHY-AFFECT? …}
```

The word "why" spawns demons for recognizing belief-justification questions and affect/belief questions. A belief-justification question is answered by accessing the editorial's argument graph through two levels of indexing (see section 7.3.3). First, OpEd must access the belief that matches the information provided in the question. Then, OpEd must retrieve the justifications indexed by that belief.

```
THAT THE LIMITATIONS ON IMPORTS
WILL COST JOBS *QMARK* ==>
    Executing demon: #{^WEB.10345: ^EXPECT-USING-WORD …}
        C.2634 <-- ((HEAD ^LEAD-TO)
                    (ANTE ((HEAD ^P-ECON-PROTECTION)…))
                         (CONSE ((HEAD ^GOAL-SITUATION)
                             (GOAL ((HEAD ^GOAL)
                                    (TYPE PRESERVATION)
                                    (OBJECT
                                        ((HEAD ^OCCUPATION)…))))
                             (STATUS THWARTED)
                             (TIME FUTURE))))
    Killing demon: #{^WEB.10345: ^EXPECT-USING-WORD …}
```

```
Executing demon: #{^WEB.10358: ^BELIEF-->BELIEF-JUSTIFICATION …}
Answer found:
    #{^SUPPORT.9262 …} =
        ((HEAD ^SUPPORT)
         (SUPPORTER ^BELIEF.9277)
         (SUPPORTED ^BELIEF.7174))
Killing demon: #{^WEB.10358: ^BELIEF-->BELIEF-JUSTIFICATION …}
```

Calling English Generator:
```
#{^SUPPORT.9262 …}:
```
MILTON FRIEDMAN BELIEVES THAT PROTECTIONIST POLICIES BY THE
REAGAN ADMINISTRATION WILL THWART THE PRESERVATION OF JOBS FOR
U.S. BECAUSE MILTON FRIEDMAN BELIEVES THAT AS A CONSEQUENCE OF
PROTECTIONIST POLICIES BY THE REAGAN ADMINISTRATION, U.S.
IMPORTS FEWER PRODUCTS; AND IF U.S. IMPORTS FEWER PRODUCTS,
THEN THERE IS A DECREASE IN PROFITS OF FOREIGN COUNTRIES; AND
IF THERE IS A DECREASE IN PROFITS OF FOREIGN COUNTRIES, THEN
FOREIGN COUNTRIES BUY FEWER AMERICAN EXPORTS; AND IF FOREIGN
COUNTRIES BUY FEWER AMERICAN EXPORTS, THEN THERE IS A DECREASE
IN PROFITS OF EXPORT INDUSTRIES; AND IF THERE IS A DECREASE IN
PROFITS OF EXPORT INDUSTRIES, THEN THERE IS A DECREASE IN JOBS
IN EXPORT INDUSTRIES; AND A DECREASE IN JOBS IN EXPORT
INDUSTRIES THWARTS THE PRESERVATION OF JOBS FOR U.S

Here, OpEd finds the answer by: (1) using the planning
structure P-ECON-PROTECTION to access Friedman's belief that import
restrictions cost jobs; and (2) retrieving the justification indexed by that
belief. That justification corresponds to Friedman's causal chain of
reasoning on how import restrictions cause a decrease in U.S. exports
and, consequently, a decrease in U.S. jobs.

8.3.4. Affect/Belief Question

Processing Question:
WHY HAVE THE LIMITATIONS ON IMPORTS DISAPPOINTED MILTON
FRIEDMAN *QMARK*

WHY ==>
```
    Adding to *working-memory*:
        #{^WEB.9835} = ()
    Spawning demon: #{^WEB.9837: ^WHY-AFFECT? …}
        ((HEAD ^WHY-AFFECT?)
         (ARGUMENTS ^WEB.9835 …))
    Spawning demon: #{^WEB.9838: ^WHY-BELIEF? …}
        ((HEAD ^WHY-BELIEF?)
         (ARGUMENTS ^WEB.9835 …))
```

```
HAVE THE LIMITATIONS ON IMPORTS DISAPPOINTED ==>
    Adding to *working-memory*:
        #{^WEB.10016} = ((HEAD ^AFFECT)
                         (TYPE NEGATIVE)
                         (CHARACTER (*VAR* 'A.2617))
                         (CAUSE (*VAR* 'C.2619))...)
    Spawning demon: #{^WEB.10019: ^EXPECT ...}
        ((HEAD ^EXPECT)
         (ARGUMENTS ^WEB.10016 C.2619 (PLAN EVENT) BEFORE ...))
    Spawning demon: #{^WEB.10017: ^EXPECT ...}
        ((HEAD ^EXPECT)
         (ARGUMENTS ^WEB.10016 A.2617 HUMAN AFTER ...))
    Spawning demon: #{^WEB.10021: ^INFER-BELIEF-FROM-AFFECT ...}
        ((HEAD ^INFER-BELIEF-FROM-AFFECT)
         (ARGUMENTS ^WEB.10016 ...))
    Executing demon: #{^WEB.10019: ^EXPECT ...}
        C.2619 <-- ((HEAD ^P-ECON-PROTECTION) ...)
    Killing demon: #{^WEB.10019: ^EXPECT ...}
    Executing demon: #{^WEB.9837: ^WHY-AFFECT? ...}
    Spawning demon: #{^WEB.10029: ^AFFECT-->BELIEF-JUSTIFICATION ...}
        ((HEAD ^AFFECT-->BELIEF-JUSTIFICATION)
         (ARGUMENTS ^WEB.10016))
        If the BELIEF associated with the given AFFECT matches an
        existing EVALUATIVE BELIEF indexed by the ACTOR of
        the AFFECT,
        Then: (1) access the JUSTIFICATIONS of the matching
        EVALUATIVE BELIEF; and (2) retrieve those JUSTIFICATIONS
        that contain the most specific plan-goal situations.
    Killing demon: #{^WEB.9837: ^WHY-AFFECT? ...}
    Killing demon: #{^WEB.9838: ^WHY-BELIEF? ...}
```

Although affect descriptions do not serve as indices for the editorial memory, they organize inferences for evaluative beliefs about plans (see section 6.3). As a result, answering an affect/belief question of the form:

Why has plan P produced emotional reaction R on argument participant A?

requires: (1) accessing an evaluative belief B that is indexed by A and corresponds to the the emotional reaction R; and (2) accessing recursively the justifications of that belief in order to find the most specific plan-goal situations underlying the emotional reaction R (see section 7.3.4).

```
MILTON FRIEDMAN *QMARK* ==>
    Executing demon: #{^WEB.10017: ^EXPECT ...}
        A.2617 <-- ((HEAD ^HUMAN)
                    (FIRST-NAME MILTON)
                    (LAST-NAME FRIEDMAN)...)
```

```
Killing demon: #{^WEB.10017: ^EXPECT …}
Executing demon: #{^WEB.10021: ^INFER-BELIEF-FROM-AFFECT …}
Inferring BELIEF:
    #{^WEB.10064: ^BELIEF …} =
        ((HEAD ^BELIEF)
         (CONTENT ((HEAD ^OUGHT-NOT-TO)
                   (OBJECT ((HEAD ^P-ECON-PROTECTION)…))))
         (BELIEVER ((HEAD ^HUMAN)
                    (FIRST-NAME MILTON)
                    (LAST-NAME FRIEDMAN)…)))
Spawning demon: #{^WEB.11075: ^FIND-BELIEF …}
    ((HEAD ^FIND-BELIEF)
     (ARGUMENTS ^WEB.10064))
Killing demon: #{^WEB.10021: ^INFER-BELIEF-FROM-AFFECT …}
Executing demon: #{^WEB.11075: ^FIND-BELIEF …}
    #{^WEB.10064: ^BELIEF …} = #{^BELIEF.6664 …}
Killing demon: #{^WEB.11075: ^FIND-BELIEF …}
Executing demon: #{^WEB.10029: ^AFFECT-->BELIEF-JUSTIFICATION …}
Answer found:
    #{^BELIEF.7174 …}
    #{^BELIEF.7481 …}
Killing demon: #{^WEB.10029: ^AFFECT-->BELIEF-JUSTIFICATION …}
```

Calling English Generator:

```
#{^BELIEF.7174 …}:
```
    MILTON FRIEDMAN BELIEVES THAT PROTECTIONIST POLICIES BY THE
    REAGAN ADMINISTRATION WILL THWART THE PRESERVATION OF JOBS FOR
    U.S.
```
#{^BELIEF.7481 …}:
```
    MILTON FRIEDMAN BELIEVES THAT PROTECTIONIST POLICIES BY THE
    REAGAN ADMINISTRATION DO NOT LEAD TO THE ACHIEVEMENT OF NORMAL
    PROFITS OF THE STEEL INDUSTRY AND THE AUTOMOBILE INDUSTRY.

Once OpEd has understood the question in terms of Friedman's belief that import restrictions are bad, the retrieval of the answer involves accessing Friedman's beliefs about the specific goal failures and unrealized successes associated with those policies. Thus, OpEd's answer includes Friedman's beliefs that import restrictions cost jobs and can not help U.S. industries.

8.3.5. Top-Belief/AU Question

Processing Question:
```
WHAT DOES MILTON FRIEDMAN BELIEVE *QMARK*
```

WHAT ==>
```
    Adding to *working-memory*:
        #{^WEB.9458} = ()
```

```
Spawning demon: #{^WEB.9460: ^WHAT-BELIEF? …}
    ((HEAD ^WHAT-BELIEF?)
     ARGUMENTS ^WEB.9458 …))
Spawning demon: #{^WEB.9461: ^WHAT-LEAD-TO? …}
    ((HEAD ^WHAT-LEAD-TO?)
     (ARGUMENTS ^WEB.9458 …))
Spawning demon: #{^WEB.9462: ^WHAT-AFFECT? …}
    ((HEAD ^WHAT-AFFECT?)
     (ARGUMENTS ^WEB.9458 …))
```

DOES MILTON FRIEDMAN BELIEVE ==>
```
    Adding to *working-memory*:
      #{^WEB.9491} = ((HEAD ^BELIEF)
                      (BELIEVER (*VAR* 'BELIEVER.2630))
                      (CONTENT (*VAR* 'CONTENT.2634)))
    Spawning demon: #{^WEB.9493: ^EXPECT …}
      ((HEAD ^EXPECT)
       (ARGUMENTS ^WEB.9491 BELIEVER.2630
                  (HUMAN INSTITUTION AUTHORITY) BEFORE …))
    Spawning demon: #{^WEB.9494: ^EXPECT-USING-WORD …}
      ((HEAD ^EXPECT-USING-WORD)
       (ARGUMENTS ^WEB.9491 CONTENT.2634 THAT
                  (OUGHT-TO OUGHT-NOT-TO LEAD-TO) AFTER …))
    Spawning demon: #{^WEB.9502: ^FIND-BELIEF …}
      ((HEAD ^FIND-BELIEF)
       (ARGUMENTS ^WEB.9491 …))
    Executing demon: #{^WEB.9493: ^EXPECT …}
      BELIEVER.2630 <-- ((HEAD ^HUMAN)
                         (FIRST-NAME MILTON)
                         (LAST-NAME FRIEDMAN)…)
    Killing demon: #{^WEB.9493: ^EXPECT …}
    Executing demon: #{^WEB.9460: ^WHAT-BELIEF? …}
    Spawning demon: #{^WEB.9507: ^BELIEVER-->TOP-BELIEF/AU …}
      ((HEAD ^BELIEVER-->TOP-BELIEF/AU)
       (ARGUMENTS ^WEB.9491 …))
      If a question boundary follows,
      Then: (1) If the TOP BELIEFS indexed by the given
                BELIEF HOLDER are contained in AUs used
                by the BELIEF HOLDER,
                Then retrieve those AUs.
            (2) If the TOP BELIEFS indexed by the given
                BELIEF HOLDER are not contained in AUs,
                Then retrieve the TOP BELIEFS and their
                immediate JUSTIFICATIONS.
    Spawning demon: #{^WEB.9508: ^BELIEF-OBJECT-->TOP-BELIEF …}
      ((HEAD ^BELIEF-OBJECT-->TOP-BELIEF)
       (ARGUMENTS ^WEB.9493 …))
      If a PLAN follows,
      Then retrieve the TOP BELIEFS of the giver BELIEF HOLDER
      about the given PLAN, and the immediate JUSTIFICATIONS
      of those BELIEFS.
```

```
Killing demon: #{^WEB.9460: ^WHAT-BELIEF? …}
Killing demon: #{^WEB.9462: ^WHAT-AFFECT? …}
Killing demon: #{^WEB.9461: ^WHAT-LEAD-TO? …}
```

To answer a top-belief/AU question, OpEd must determine whether the question provides: (1) an argument participant A and a plan P; or (2) only an argument participant A. In the first case, OpEd retrieves A's top belief about P and its immediate justifications. In the second case, OpEd retrieves the argument units that have been used by A and contain A's top belief (see section 7.3.5).

QMARK ==>
```
Executing demon: #{^WEB.9507: ^BELIEVER-->TOP-BELIEF/AU …}
Answer found:
    #{^AU-ACTUAL-CAUSE.7886 …}
    #{^AU-OPPOSITE-EFFECT.8369 …}
Killing demon: #{^WEB.9507: ^BELIEVER-->TOP-BELIEF/AU …}
Killing demon: #{^WEB.9508: ^BELIEF-OBJECT-->TOP-BELIEF …}
```

Calling English Generator:
```
#{^AU-ACTUAL-CAUSE.7886 …}:
```
   MILTON FRIEDMAN BELIEVES THAT PROTECTIONIST POLICIES BY THE REAGAN ADMINISTRATION ARE BAD BECAUSE MILTON FRIEDMAN BELIEVES THAT PROTECTIONIST POLICIES BY THE REAGAN ADMINISTRATION DO NOT LEAD TO THE ACHIEVEMENT OF NORMAL PROFITS OF THE STEEL INDUSTRY AND THE AUTOMOBILE INDUSTRY. MILTON FRIEDMAN BELIEVES THAT PROTECTIONIST POLICIES BY THE REAGAN ADMINISTRATION DO NOT LEAD TO THE ACHIEVEMENT OF NORMAL PROFITS OF THE STEEL INDUSTRY AND THE AUTOMOBILE INDUSTRY BECAUSE MILTON FRIEDMAN BELIEVES THAT NORMAL SALARY IN THE STEEL INDUSTRY AND THE AUTOMOBILE INDUSTRY HIGHER THAN THE NORM THWARTS THE ACHIEVEMENT OF NORMAL PROFITS OF THE STEEL INDUSTRY AND THE AUTOMOBILE INDUSTRY. MILTON FRIEDMAN BELIEVES THAT THE REAGAN ADMINISTRATION IS WRONG BECAUSE THE REAGAN ADMINISTRATION BELIEVES THAT PROTECTIONIST POLICIES BY THE REAGAN ADMINISTRATION LEAD TO THE ACHIEVEMENT OF NORMAL PROFITS OF THE STEEL INDUSTRY AND THE AUTOMOBILE INDUSTRY.

```
#{^AU-OPPOSITE-EFFECT.8369 …}:
```
   MILTON FRIEDMAN BELIEVES THAT PROTECTIONIST POLICIES BY THE REAGAN ADMINISTRATION ARE BAD BECAUSE MILTON FRIEDMAN BELIEVES THAT PROTECTIONIST POLICIES BY THE REAGAN ADMINISTRATION WILL THWART THE PRESERVATION OF JOBS FOR U.S. MILTON FRIEDMAN BELIEVES THAT THE REAGAN ADMINISTRATION IS WRONG BECAUSE THE REAGAN ADMINISTRATION BELIEVES THAT PROTECTIONIST POLICIES BY THE REAGAN ADMINISTRATION ACHIEVE THE PRESERVATION OF JOBS FOR U.S.

The above answers contain a detailed account of what OpEd knows about Friedman's opinion in ED-JOBS. These answers are produced using the following patterns:

- AU-ACTUAL-CAUSE:
  ```
  <B1-SELF "because" B2-SELF>.
  <B2-SELF "because" B3-SELF>.
  <SELF "believe that"
       OPPONENT "be wrong because" B1-OPPONENT>.
  ```

- AU-OPPOSITE-EFFECT:
  ```
  <B1-SELF "because" B4-SELF>.
  <SELF "believe that"
       OPPONENT "be wrong because" B1-OPPONENT>.
  ```

where: (1) SELF is the arguer using the argument unit; (2) OPPONENT is the arguer's opponent; (3) B1-SELF is the belief "plan P should not be executed"; (4) B2-SELF is the belief "P does not achieve goal G"; (5) B3-SELF is the belief "state S thwarts G"; (6) B4-SELF is the belief that "P thwarts G"; and (7) B1-OPPONENT is the belief "P achieves G." Although these generation patterns produce answers that are very detailed, such answers are also verbose and contain redundant information. However, linguistic style in answer generation is not a major issue addressed in OpEd. As a result, OpEd's natural language generation strategies are not as well developed as its strategies for argument comprehension, representation, and retrieval.

8.4. Current Status of OpEd

OpEd is written in T (Rees et al., 1984; Slade, 1987), a lexically-scoped Scheme-based dialect of Lisp running on Apollo Domain workstations. OpEd uses the knowledge representation system provided by GATE (Mueller and Zernik, 1984; Mueller, 1987b), an integrated set of Artificial Intelligence development tools. Currently OpEd can: (1) read two conceptually different editorial segments, namely ED-JOBS and ED-RESTRICTIONS (see section 1.3); and (2) answer belief-related questions about the contents of those editorials. In addition, OpEd can answer belief-related questions concerning the conceptual content of a number of other argument graphs, which have been handcoded in memory to test OpEd's retrieval strategies.

OpEd has more than 100 demons and requires approximately 3.3 megabytes of memory (interpreted) in order to maintain the lexicon, knowledge structures, and demons used when reading ED-JOBS and

ED-RESTRICTIONS. OpEd takes about 15 minutes to process each editorial and spawns an average of 30 demons per editorial sentence.

The initial version of OpEd (Alvarado et al., 1985a) contained enough knowledge to handle ED-JOBS. The scope of OpEd was later extended (Alvarado et al., 1986) to read ED-RESTRICTIONS. This expansion did not require modifying OpEd's process model of argument comprehension, but rather: (a) augmenting its lexicon and politico-economic knowledge; (b) augmenting its knowledge of argument units to include two more AUs, namely AU-EQUIVALENCE and AU-SPIRAL-EFFECT; and (c) specifying the demons needed to manipulate the conceptual structures added. In addition, OpEd's search and retrieval processes did not need any modifications to retrieve answers to questions about ED-RESTRICTIONS. This follows from the fact that those search and retrieval processes do not depend on the specific contents of the editorial memory, but rather on the knowledge dependencies that exist among plans, goals, beliefs, support relationships, attack relationships, and AUs. OpEd's ability to handle both ED-JOBS and ED-RESTRICTIONS indicates that its process model is not tailored to any specific editorial and, consequently, can be viewed as a prototype of computer comprehension of editorial text.

Chapter 9

Future Work and Conclusions

9.1. Introduction

This dissertation has presented a theory of argument comprehension, representation, and retrieval. The theory has been implemented in the OpEd system to read editorials about the effects of economic-protection policies and answer questions about the contents of those editorials. The theory characterizes eight major sources of knowledge:

1) Domain-Specific Knowledge: OpEd has a politico-economic model that represents: (a) conflicts in international trade; (b) economic quantities associated with trade and their causal relationships; and (c) cause-effect chains between protectionist plans and economic goals.

2) Taxonomy of Beliefs: Beliefs are predications about goals, plans, events, and states. Three type of predications are distinguished: (a) evaluations about plans; (b) causal relationships; and (c) beliefs about beliefs.

3) Taxonomy of Attack Structures: Attacks are relationships between two beliefs whose contents involve mutually-exclusive planning situations or opposite effects of a plan on interrelated goals.

4) Taxonomy of Support Structures: Supports are relationships between beliefs and belief justifications based on refinements

of plan evaluations, refinements of plan-goal relationships, analogies, and examples.

5) <u>Taxonomy of Argument Units:</u> AUs are abstract configurations of support and attack relationships that represent the possible ways to refute an opponent's argument for endorsing or rejecting the use of a plan.

6) <u>Taxonomy of Meta-Argument Units:</u> Meta-AUs organize abstract knowledge about the use of support strategies and can be used to argue against the underlying logic of an opponent' argument.

7) <u>Strategies for Recognizing Argument Structures:</u> These strategies allow OpEd to: (a) extract the beliefs, belief relationships, and AUs underlying an editorial; and (b) integrate those structures into an argument graph.

8) <u>Strategies for Memory Search and Retrieval:</u> These strategies allow OpEd to: (a) gain initial entry to an editorial's argument graph; and (b) locate appropriate beliefs, belief relationships, or AUs in that graph in order to answer questions.

The approach taken to develop this theory has been to consider argument comprehension as an integral part of natural language understanding. As a result, OpEd builds upon theories developed for comprehension of narrative text. Specifically, OpEd's process model is based on: (1) the conceptual parser developed by Dyer (1983a); (2) the question-answering theory developed by Dyer and Lehnert (1982) as an extension to previous work by Lehnert (1978); and (3) the argument-graph technique developed by Flowers et al. (1982). Clearly, OpEd can be characterized as a conceptual model of argument comprehension.

This chapter compares OpEd's model of argument comprehension with other models of belief and argument analysis. The chapter also includes a discussion of the limitations of OpEd and the corresponding directions for future related research. Finally, the chapter presents a summary of the claims made in this dissertation along with some closing comments.

9.2.   Comparison With Other Work

The problem of modeling beliefs and argument knowledge has been addressed by other researchers in the fields of rhetoric, logic, artificial intelligence, and psychology. Those research efforts differ from OpEd in terms of objectives, scope, and methodology. This section presents a brief overview of the approaches taken in those fields and compares them with OpEd.

9.2.1. Argument Analysis in Rhetoric

Toulmin (1958) has proposed a model for analyzing the structure of arguments. According to Toulmin, an argument is composed of six major elements: (1) a claim, or conclusion of the argument; (2) the grounds for believing the claim; (3) a warrant that justifies using the grounds as the basis for the claim; (4) the backing (e.g., statistics) that supports the grounds and/or the warrant; (5) a modal qualifier (e.g., "certainly") that indicates the degree of reliance on the claim; and (6) a rebuttal that indicates the circumstances on which the claim can be questioned. The central element of Toulmin's model is the warrant. Warrants may involve: a general principle (e.g., "all men are mortal"), a cause-effect relationship, a generalization, an analogy, a statement that associates the occurrence of two states or events, or a statement about the credibility of the source of a belief.

As pointed out by Toulmin et al. (1979) and Rieke and Sillars (1984), Toulmin's model can be used to test the structure of arguments in disparate domains, including science, law, religion, politics, economics, and the arts. In addition, Windes and Hastings (1966) have shown that decomposing an argument into its grounds, warrant, and claim provides a method for deciding how to attack an argument. That is, an argument can be attacked from three perspectives: (1) attacking the claim directly; (2) attacking the grounds; and (3) attacking the warrant.

Although Toulmin's model provides the basis for the analysis of argument structure, it does not provide a method for: (a) mapping the argument text into its grounds-warrant-claim representation; or (b) inferring missing components of an argument from the argument text. In contrast, argument comprehension in OpEd involves mapping input editorial text into an argument graph where configurations of support and attack relationships among beliefs are organized by argument units. This comprehension process involves applying OpEd's strategies for recognizing: (1) evaluative beliefs from descriptions of emotional reactions and standpoints; (2) causal beliefs from evaluative beliefs; (3) reasoning scripts from causal beliefs; and (4) AUs from various linguistic constructs and from beliefs involving plan failures.

9.2.2. Formal/Logical Approaches to Belief Systems

Logicians have a long history in examining the notions of knowledge and belief (Hintikka 1962; Chellas 1980), but their approach has been to establish axiomatic systems for deducing consistent beliefs, without regard as to how humans understand the beliefs of others and relate them to their own beliefs. Belief research in artificial intelligence has concentrated on truth maintenance (Doyle 1979; de Kleer 1986) and evidential reasoning (Pearl 1986; Dechter and Dechter 1988). The goal of these systems is to maintain and/or propagate evidence for/against beliefs, once these beliefs and their relationships are already resident in a knowledge base. A major task of such systems is to maintain logical consistency among a set of beliefs by dynamically altering the truth value of tentative beliefs (i.e., assumptions). None of these groups of researchers have addressed the natural language comprehension task, which involves dynamically constructing a knowledge base of the beliefs and belief justifications of an arguer "on the fly," from textual input. In OpEd, the vast majority of the processing and knowledge structures are not involved in logical operations *per se*. Major tasks involve common sense inference, memory search, planning, application of world knowledge, and recognition of argument structures.

9.2.3. Artificial Intelligence Approaches to Argument Comprehension

Cohen (1983) has postulated a purely *structural* model for argument understanding, in contrast to the *conceptual* model presented in OpEd. In Cohen's model, understanding an argument requires building a tree where argument propositions are connected by a single evidence link. The root of the tree contains the major claim made in an argument. Relations between propositions are determined by using: (a) a proposition analyzer that produces a proposition from the input and integrates it into the tree built so far; (b) a clue interpreter that analyzes the role of special linguistic connectives (e.g., "as a result" and "similarly"); and (c) an evidence oracle that accesses a knowledge base and model of the speaker in order to determine whether any evidence relation exists between two propositions. Unfortunately, Cohen's model has not been fully implemented (Cohen, 1987), so it is difficult to assess its potential. One limitation of the model stems from the fact that arguments do not conform to a simple tree structure, but rather consist of a complex directed graph. In addition, since Cohen's trees lack conceptual content, they cannot indicate how either explicit or implicit conceptualizations (contained in a given proposition) relate to, and/or provide evidence for, conceptualizations contained in other propositions. Moreover, by using an "oracle," the model avoids having to deal with the critical problems of: (1) how lexical items are mapped from natural language to conceptual structures; (2) how world knowledge is represented and applied during the comprehension process; and (3) how argument strategies are represented and applied within a given domain.

In contrast to Cohen's strictly structural approach, OpEd analyzes editorial arguments by building a conceptual graph which captures interactions between goals, plans, events, emotional states, beliefs, and argument units. This conceptual graph results from recognizing and instantiating those knowledge structures along with causal relationships and belief relationships. In addition, OpEd's comprehension process also results in building indices that are subsequently used during question answering. All these knowledge structures and processes are missing in Cohen's model.

Another model for computer comprehension of arguments is the one developed by Roesner (1985). That model has been designed to understand newspaper text dealing with job market developments. Roesner's model assumes that it is possible to: (a) determine the propositions that compose a given text; and (b) recognize the logical and causal dependencies that exist among those propositions. Those relationships are cued by surface structures (e.g., "in spite of" proposition1, proposition2) in which two propositions are linked by a surface connective that may signal a cause-effect dependency, a refinement dependency, or a contradiction. Surface structures are mapped into argumentation schemata (or frames) whose slots take propositions as arguments. Roesner's model characterizes three types of argumentation schemata: (1) explanation schemata that deal with reasons for a given fact; (2) interpretation schemata that deal with the consequences of a given fact; and (3) rhetorical schemata that contrast contradictory interpretations of factual statements in order to favor one over the others.

In Roesner's model, understanding argumentation text in terms of schemata is viewed as the process of establishing constraint relationships between given propositions. This process is handled by an inference mechanism that has access to a network of domain-specific causal dependencies. Unfortunately, no theory of the content of argument schemata is provided in Roesner's model. That is, Roesner's model characterizes argument schemata as frames with slots, but it does not state what goal, plan, or belief relationships may be used to fill in those slots. In contrast to Roesner's argument schemata, OpEd represents abstract knowledge of argumentation in terms of argument units that organize goals, plans, beliefs, support relationships, and attack relationships. In OpEd, each AU can be cued by specific constructs that involve: (a) argument connectives (e.g., "far from", "but", and "yet") that signal opposition and expectation failures; and (b) goal, plan, and belief relationships. In order to follow an argument, OpEd must recognize these linguistic constructs, access the specific conceptualizations they refer to, and map from these conceptualizations into their appropriate AUs. This process of recognizing AUs relies on expectations generated after an argument connective is found. These expectations involve specific information about the type of conceptualization that may follow and/or precede the argument connective.

A third computer model designed to address the problem of argument comprehension and generation is the ABDUL/ILANA system (Birnbaum et al., 1980; Flowers et al., 1982; McGuire et al., 1981). ABDUL/ILANA embodies a partial theory of the reasoning processes that an arguer may use when engaged in an *adversary argument*, i.e., an argument in which the participants intend to remain adversaries and present their views for the judgement of an audience. The program models either side of an argument between an Arab (ABDUL) and an Israeli (ILANA) over who was responsible for the 1967 Arab-Israeli war. During the argument dialogue, ABDUL/ILANA constructs an argument graph that represents the entire history of the argument between the program and its opponent. That argument graph aids understanding because the role of every input utterance is determined by finding how that utterance can be integrated into the graph using support and attack links. Furthermore, the program uses the argument graph to determine how to respond to an opponent's statement according to three *argument tactics*: (a) attacking the given statement directly; (b) attacking the statement's supporting evidences; or (c) attacking the warrants connecting the given statement to its supporting evidences.

ABDUL/ILANA has also provided a model to investigate functional properties of commonly occurring substructures in the argument graph (Birnbaum, 1982; Flowers et al., 1982). Those substructures, known as *argument molecules*, organize knowledge about the logical structure of arguments and provide expectations about: (a) which propositions are likely to be attacked or supported by the program's opponent; and (b) which propositions should be attacked or supported by the program. Two argument molecules have been identified within the context of ABDUL/ILANA: contrastive-positions and stand-off. The contrastive-positions molecule characterizes arguments centered on two mutually-exclusive propositions that summarize the main positions of two arguers. In arguments that conform to this molecule, each arguer may try to offer additional support for his/her own position, or attack the position of his/her opponent by using an appropriate argument tactic. In contrast, the stand-off molecule characterizes arguments in which an arguer attacks his/her opponent's use of a warrant by showing that such a warrant can also be used to support a position that is unacceptable to the opponent. In arguments that conform to this molecule, each arguer may try to support his/her own position or attack directly the evidence supporting his/her opponent's position.

Argument molecules differ from OpEd's argument units in terms of the type of abstract argument knowledge they organize. That is, argument molecules contain functional knowledge on how to determine which beliefs should be attacked in an argument, while AUs contain declarative knowledge on how to represent those attacks in terms of goals, plans, beliefs, and belief relationships. However, functional and declarative knowledge are two sides of the same coin. That is, the contrastive-positions molecule provides the functional knowledge associated with the AUs that are used to refute an opponent's argument about a plan on the basis of goal achievements and goal failures. Similarly, the stand-off molecule organizes the functional knowledge associated with the meta-AUs that are used to attack the underlying logic of an opponent's argument on the basis of that opponent's hypocritical behavior. Clearly, argument molecules and argument units provide two complementary methods for modeling argument comprehension and generation.

9.2.4. Psycholinguistic Analysis of Editorial Text

While there has been an extensive examination of expository, narrative, and discourse text in the psychological literature (Britton and Black, 1985; Spiro et al., 1980; van Dijk, 1985), there appears to be little direct analysis of argument-based editorial text. van Dijk and Kintsch (1983) have performed an analysis of an editorial that discusses the effect of Reagan's election on Guatemala, military aid to Guatemala from Israel, mass murders committed by the Guatemalan "regime," and so on. van Dijk and Kintsch apply a very general theory of discourse and schema coherency to the text, which includes coherency structures at the local (sentence), macrostructure, and schematic levels. Much of the discussion is concerned with the discourse structure of what is actually expository text. Unfortunately, van Dijk and Kintsch do not have any computer implementation of their model, so the discussion is at a very general descriptive level. However, the work is useful, to the extent that it gives one an idea of a number of discourse issues (e.g. topic shifts) involved in complex, expository text—issues that fall outside the scope of OpEd.

9.3.   Future Work

The theory of argument comprehension, representation, and retrieval presented in this dissertation provides the basis for understanding how computers may someday be able to engage in discussions about politics, economics, law, or religion. Although OpEd has provided an initial testbed for this theory, much remains to be done since OpEd is currently a prototype of computer comprehension of editorial text. Designing programs capable of arguing will require addressing the following issues: (1) long-term memory organization of arguments; (2) subjective comprehension of arguments; (3) belief inferences based on past arguments; (4) modeling persuasion; (5) meta-argument comprehension; and (6) knowledge engineering bottlenecks.

9.3.1. Long-Term Memory Organization of Arguments

OpEd is capable of reading only one editorial at a time. After the argument graph has been formed and OpEd has answered questions based on it, in the current model the argument graph is "thrown away" before OpEd is given the next editorial to read. In contrast, an adult human is able to read many editorials in a given domain, over a period of months, and begin to form a coherent picture of ideological positions in that domain. A human expert is able to interpret a given editorial in the light of all previous editorials stored in his/her long-term memory.

Integrating multiple editorials in long-term memory does not just require maintaining prior argument graphs. As many more beliefs, plans, goals, etc. are added to memory, they have to be organized in a more sophisticated manner. One direction of research is to augment OpEd's indexing structures, creating hierarchical memories of the type used in the CYRUS system (Kolodner 1984) and OCCAM system (Pazzani 1988). CYRUS modeled the organization and retrieval of former Secretary of State Cyrus Vance's numerous memories of travel and diplomatic meetings, while OCCAM acquired, indexed, and generalized events involving international economic sanctions.

9.3.2. Subjective Comprehension of Arguments

OpEd is an objective model of argumentation. That is, OpEd attempts to understand the beliefs of others, but does not have any beliefs of its own. In contrast, humans do not read in a totally objective manner. They come to a text (or argument) with their own points of view and their own justifications for these positions. When people read an editorial that disagrees with their own beliefs and/or presents arguments that they feel are flawed, they will often become angry while reading and find themselves generating counter arguments as they read. Examples of subjective systems are PARRY (Colby 1981), DAYDREAMER (Mueller 1987b), and POLITICS (Carbonell 1981). PARRY models paranoid behavior while DAYDREAMER models the generation of a continual stream of thought, including daydreams of wish fulfillment and retaliation. The behaviors of both these systems are influenced by representations concerning the subjective beliefs and emotional states of the comprehension system itself.

POLITICS maintains both conservative and liberal political ideologies. Each ideology is modeled as a goal hierarchy, termed *goal tree,* where goals relate to one another via goal-subgoal links and relative-importance links. For example, in the U.S. conservative tree, Communist containment is the most important goal and has three associated subgoals: high military strength, establishment of anti-Communist allies, and prevention of internal subversion. In addition, the conservative has a different goal hierarchy than the liberal for modeling the Soviet's ideology. In the POLITICS system, the conservative ideology ranks world domination as the most important Soviet goal, while the liberal ranks the Soviet goal of avoiding military conflicts higher than the Soviet goal of increasing world domination. Thus, when POLITICS is in conservative mode, it interprets a Soviet troop build-up on the Afghanistan border as part of a Soviet invasion plan. While in liberal mode, POLITICS predicts that the Soviet Union will not invade Afghanistan.

Goal hierarchies can also be used to model aspects of personality (Carbonell 1980). For example, a "greedy" personality model has object-possession goals that are higher up in the goal hierarchy than a "brave" personality model, which has self-preservation goals relatively lower in the hierarchy.

A direction of future research is to make OpEd a more subjective model. Such a model would: (1) have its own beliefs, ideology, and personality; and (2) experience emotional responses (Dyer 1987; 1983b) according to arguments that it encounters.

9.3.3. Belief Inferences Based on Past Arguments

Currently, OpEd answers belief-related questions by accessing indices into the argument graph and then traversing causal links and attack/support links. There are questions, however, that require beliefs to be inferred from beliefs already instantiated in the argument graph. Consider hypothetical questions of the sort: "Would A agree/disagree with B over issue U?" Here, the system must generate plausibly held beliefs of an arguer A, given knowledge of A's beliefs and arguments (in possibly unrelated domains). Getting OpEd to handle hypothetical questions will require modeling the process of belief inference in relation to models of ideology and long-term memory organization of arguments.

9.3.4. Modeling Persuasion

Since OpEd lacks any beliefs of its own, it cannot be persuaded by the arguments that it reads. Persuasion involves not simply understanding an argument, but having one's beliefs modified by the arguments encountered. The problem of persuasion is a difficult one. For instance, one can be totally beaten in an argument and still not be persuaded. A possible response of the loser can be "I lost the argument because I don't know as much about the domain as you do, but I am still not convinced because I know that there exist experts who hold my opinion, and who could generate rebuttals to your arguments." Persuasion appears to be intimately bound up with personal goals. For instance, a factory worker may tend to be more persuaded by arguments for the need for unions than would the capitalist who owns the factory.

Giving OpEd the ability to be persuaded would require that OpEd possess methods for assessing the relative strengths and weaknesses of arguments—a difficult task, given that relatively little is known about why one argument is more forceful or persuasive than another.

9.3.5. Meta-Argument Comprehension

A subset of the task of persuasion involves recognizing logical flaws in arguments, since arguments with logical flaws should lack persuasive power (although that is not always the case; people are often persuaded by logically unsound arguments). A first step in this direction has been taken with the representation of meta-AUs in OpEd. Currently, however, OpEd is not able to dynamically instantiate meta-AUs from input text. All meta-AU instantiations in OpEd are encoded by hand.

As one can see by examining the text of the religious meta-arguments presented in Chapter 5, meta-arguments are highly abstract and in general appear to be more difficult to comprehend than standard arguments. A realistic test of human-level intelligence for future AI programs will be to manipulate meta-AUs, to abstract and/or learn previously unknown meta-AUs from input text, and to use this knowledge during subsequent argument comprehension.

9.3.6. Knowledge Engineering Bottlenecks

The language understanding technology used in OpEd is based on the demon architecture used in the BORIS (Dyer 1983a; Lehnert et al. 1983) narrative comprehension system. In recent years, spreading activation models have gained popularity, based on their ability to perform soft constraint satisfaction in parallel. A direction for future research is to replace both the demon-based parser and pattern-based generator in OpEd with a spreading activation mechanism, such as those developed by Gasser (1988), Waltz and Pollack (1985), and Sumida et al. (1988).

Finally, the design of OpEd is a labor intensive process, involving the handcoding of many knowledge constructs, along with processing rules that integrate these constructs during comprehension. OpEd's ability to handle a given fragment of editorial text is directly dependent on the knowledge constructs (of a given domain, of forms of argumentation, and of a given natural language) encoded in the system. This knowledge engineering bottleneck could be overcome if OpEd could dynamically acquire and augment its knowledge and processing structures. However, learning in symbolic systems, particularly the learning of fundamentally new symbols and symbolic relationships, has proved to be highly problematic in Artificial Intelligence. In addition, OpEd suffers from the same problems that plague all rule-based systems: (a) a lack of robustness in handling exceptions to rules; (b) unanticipated rule interactions; and (c) an inability to recover from the incorrect application of rules. A direction for future research is to explore a variety of "subsymbolic" processing, generalization, and knowledge representation methods, such as those used in connectionist and parallel distributed processing (PDP) systems (Dolan, 1989; Dyer, 1989; Feldman and Ballard, 1982; Rumelhart et al., 1986). Those methods may prove helpful in addressing fragility of rules and engineering bottlenecks.

9.4.   Summary and Conclusions

This dissertation has presented a theory of argument comprehension, representation, and retrieval implemented in OpEd to read politico-economic editorials and answer questions about their contents. Editorial comprehension in OpEd is achieved through the use of a wide variety of representational and processing constructs. At the level of domain-specific knowledge, OpEd has a politico-economic model that includes four major elements: (1) *authority triangles and social acts* represent explicitly all the information associated with conflicts in international trade, including beliefs, goals, and conflict-resolution methods; (2) *goals and plans* represent political and economic actions in terms of desired economic states; (3) a *trade graph* represents causal relationships among the economic quantities associated with producers and consumers; and (4) *reasoning scripts* represent common chains of cause-effect relationships in editorials.

During editorial comprehension, OpEd represents explicitly the *beliefs* of both the editorial writer and his/her implicit opponents. Each belief consists of a belief holder, the content of the belief, and links representing relationships of support and attack. The content of a belief corresponds to an evaluative component, a causal relationship, or a reasoning script. Evaluative components categorize plans in terms of the possible goal achievements and goal failures resulting from those plans.

Beliefs in an editorial may relate to one another in two systematic ways: *support* relationships and *attack* relationships. An attack is a relationship between two beliefs whose contents involve mutually-exclusive planning situations or opposite effects of a plan on interrelated goals. A support is a relationship that consists of a belief, the justification for the belief, and a warrant (itself a belief) that connects a belief to its justification. Belief justifications are based on refinements of plan evaluations, refinements of plan-goal relationships, analogies, and examples.

Beliefs, attack relationships, and support relationships are the basic building blocks organized by *argument units (AUs),* which encode language-free and domain-free knowledge about argument structure and content. With the aid of domain-specific knowledge, AUs can be instantiated to model arguments in which an arguer refutes his/her opponent's position that a given plan should/shouldn't be used. Those refutations are based on goal achievements and/or goal failures associated with the given plan.

Arguments about proper argument structure are represented as *meta-AUs*. Two types of meta-AUs have been characterized: (1) Meta-AUs based on hypocritical behavior, which specify argument errors that result from inconsistencies between actions and professed beliefs or from inconsistencies between actions and criticisms; and (2) Meta-AUs based on unsound reasoning, which specify argument errors that result from shifting the burden of proof or from using support strategies based on plausibilities, circularities, or self-contradictions. Meta-AUs are represented in OpEd as attacks on warrants and are used to model discussions about the nature of valid reasoning.

Associated with each knowledge construct in OpEd are one or more processing strategies. These strategies are invoked to recognize knowledge constructs that are not explicitly stated in the text, but which must be inferred to understand the argument, planning, and causal structure of the text. Processing strategies include: (a) inferring beliefs from positions concerning the beliefs of others, and from descriptions of emotional reactions; (b) constructing belief justifications by applying knowledge of plan-based reasoning, knowledge of domain-specific plans and goals, and reasoning scripts; (c) recognizing reasoning scripts through script headers; (d) following an argument by tracking specific linguistic constructs and plan-failures; and (e) instantiating AUs to help recognize implicitly stated beliefs, support relationships, and attack relationships.

The result of processing strategies is the construction of an *argument graph*, organized in terms of beliefs, belief relationships, and argument units (AUs). Initial entry to the editorial's argument graph is provided by indexing structures associated with argument participants, plans, and goals.

During question-answering, the argument graph represents and maintains the context from which questions about an editorial are understood. To answer belief-related questions, it is necessary to analyze the contents of the question into one of five conceptual question categories: belief holder, causal belief, belief justification, affect/belief, and top-belief/AU. Each conceptual question category leads to the selection of specific search and retrieval processes which use indexing structures to gain access to the argument graph. Once an index is selected, these processes traverse access and memory links in order to locate appropriate beliefs, belief relationships, or AUs in the argument graph.

The experience of designing and implementing a prototype of computer comprehension of editorial text has shed light on some of the basic problems any intelligent computer system must address: knowledge representation, organization, and application. The model demonstrates both the knowledge intensive nature of the task of argument comprehension and the complexity of the representational constructs and processing strategies needed to perform that task. The major benefit derived from building OpEd has been to characterize a framework for making explicit the knowledge required for understanding complex editorial text. As such, OpEd can be viewed as one small step toward understanding the nature of argument comprehension and modeling the basic components of intelligence.

References

Abelson, R. P. (1973). The Structure of Belief Systems. In R. C. Schank and K. M. Colby (Eds.), *Computer Models of Thought and Language*. San Francisco: Freeman.

Abelson, R. P. (1979). Differences between Beliefs and Knowledge Systems. *Cognitive Science, 3,* 355-366.

Alvarado, S. J., Dyer, M. G., and Flowers, M. (1985a). Memory Representation and Retrieval for Editorial Comprehension. *Proceedings of the Seventh Annual Conference of the Cognitive Science Society.* University of California, Irvine, pp. 228-235.

Alvarado, S. J., Dyer, M. G., and Flowers, M. (1985b). *Understanding Editorials: The Process of Reasoning Comprehension* (Technical Report UCLA-AI-85-3). Artificial Intelligence Laboratory. Computer Science Department. University of California, Los Angeles.

Alvarado, S. J., Dyer, M. G., and Flowers, M. (1985c). *Recognizing Argument Units* (Technical Note UCLA-AI-85-2). Artificial Intelligence Laboratory. Computer Science Department. University of California, Los Angeles.

Alvarado, S. J., Dyer, M. G., and Flowers, M. (1986). Editorial Comprehension in OpEd Through Argument Units. *Proceedings of the Fifth National Conference on Artificial Intelligence.* University of Pennsylvania, Philadelphia, pp. 250-256.

Alvarado, S. J., Dyer, M. G., and Flowers, M. (in press). Natural Language Processing: Computer Comprehension of Editorial Text. In H. Adeli (Ed.), *Knowledge Engineering*. New York: McGraw-Hill.

Alvarado, S. J., Dyer, M. G., and Flowers, M. (in press). Argument Representation for Editorial Text. *Knowledge-Based Systems*.

Alvarado, S. J., Dyer, M. G., and Flowers, M. (in press). Argument Comprehension and Retrieval for Editorial Text. *Knowledge-Based Systems*.

August, S. E., and Dyer, M. G. (1985a). Analogy Recognition and Comprehension in Editorials. *Proceedings of the Seventh Annual Conference of the Cognitive Science Society*. University of California, Irvine, pp. 228-235.

August, S. E. and Dyer, M. G. (1985b). Understanding Analogies in Editorials. *Proceedings of the Ninth International Joint Conference on Artificial Intelligence*. University of California, Los Angeles, pp. 845-847.

Birnbaum, L. (1982). Argument Molecules: A Functional Representation of Argument Structure. *Proceedings of the Second National Conference on Artificial Intelligence*. Pittsburgh, Pennsylvania, pp. 63-65.

Birnbaum, L., Flowers, M., and McGuire, R. (1980). Towards an AI Model of Argumentation. *Proceedings of the First National Conference on Artificial Intelligence*. Standford, California, pp. 313-315.

Birnbaum, L. and Selfridge, M. (1981). Conceptual Analysis of Natural Language. In R. C. Schank and C. K. Reisbeck (Eds.), *Inside Computer Understanding*. Hillsdale, NJ: Lawrence Earlbaum.

Britton, B. K. and Black, J. B. (Eds.) (1985). *Understanding Expository Text*. Hillsdale, NJ: Lawrence Earlbaum.

Bresnaham, T. F. (1984, May 11). Quotas, Not Bonuses, Hurt Auto Industry (Editorial). *Los Angeles Times*, part II, p. 7.

Bush, C. R. (1932). *Editorial Thinking and Writing*. New York: D. Appleton.

Carbonell, J. G. (1980). Toward a Process Model of Human Personality Traits. *Artificial Intelligence, 15*, 49-74.

Carbonell, J. G. (1981). *Subjective Understanding: Computer Models of Belief Systems*. Ann Arbor, MI: UMI Research Press.

Charniak, E. (1977). A framed PAINTING: The Representation of a Commonsense Knowledge Fragment. *Cognitive Science, 1*, 355-394.

Charniak, E. (1978). On the Use of Framed Knowledge in Language Comprehension. *Artificial Intelligence, 11*, 225-265.

Charniak, E., Riesbeck, C. K., and McDermott, D. V. (1980). *Artificial Intelligence Programming*. Hillsdale, NJ: Lawrence Earlbaum.

Cheit, E. F. (1984, October 7). Protectionism Is Alive and Well Under a Variety of Names and Methods (Editorial). *Los Angeles Times*, part VI, p. 3.

Chellas, B. F. (1980). *Modal Logic*. Cambridge, MA: Cambridge University Press.

Cohen, R. (1983). *A Computational Model for the Analysis of Arguments* (Ph.D. Thesis, Research Report CSRG-151). Department of Computer Science. University of Toronto.

Cohen, R. (1987). Analyzing the Structure of Argumentative Discourse. *Computational Linguistics, 13*, 11-30.

Colby, K. M. (1981). Modeling a Paranoid Mind. *The Behavioral and Brain Sciences, 4*, pp. 515-534.

Cuddington, J. T. and McKinnon, R. I. (1979). Free Trade Versus Protectionism: A Perspective. In Institute of Contemporary Studies (Ed.), *Tariffs, Quotas, and Trade: The Politics of Protectionism*. San Francisco: Institute of Contemporary Studies.

Cullingford, R. E. (1978). *Script Application: Computer Understanding of Newspaper Stories* (Ph.D. Thesis, Research Report #116). Department of Computer Science. Yale University, New Haven, CT.

Cullingford, R. E. (1981). SAM. In R. C. Schank and C. K. Reisbeck (Eds.), *Inside Computer Understanding*. Hillsdale, NJ: Lawrence Earlbaum.

Dechter, R. and Dechter, A. (1988). Belief Maintenance in Dynamic Constraint Networks. *Proceedings of the Seventh National Conference on Artificial Intelligence*. St. Paul, MN.

DeJong II, G. F. (1979). *Skimming Stories in Real TIme: An Experiment in Integrated Understanding* (Ph.D. Thesis, Research Report #158). Department of Computer Science. Yale University, New Haven, CT.

de Kleer, J. (1986). An Assumption-Based TMS. *Artificial Intelligence,* **28**, 127-162.

Doyle, J. (1979). A Truth Maintenance System. *Artificial Intelligence,* **12**, 231-272.

Dolan, C. P. (1989). *Tensor Manipulation Networks: Connectionist and Symbolic Approaches to Comprehension, Learning, and Planning* (Ph.D. Dissertation). Computer Science Department. University of California, Los Angeles.

Dyer, M. G. (1983a). *In-Depth Understanding: A Computer Model of Integrated Processing for Narrative Comprehension.* Cambridge, MA: MIT Press.

Dyer, M. G. (1983b). The Role of Affect in Narratives. *Cognitive Science,* **7**, 211-242.

Dyer, M. G. (1987). Emotions and Their Computations: Three Computer Models. *Cognition and Emotion,* **1**, 323-347.

Dyer, M. G. (1989). Symbolic NeuroEngineering for Natural Language Processing: A Multilevel Research Approach. In J. Barnden and J. Pollack (Eds.), *Advances in Connectionist and Neural Computation Theory*. Norwood, NJ: Ablex.

Dyer, M. G., Cullingford, R. E., and Alvarado, S. J. (1987). SCRIPTS. In S. C. Shapiro (Ed.), *Encyclopedia of Artificial Intelligence*. New York: Wiley.

Dyer, M. G. and Lehnert, W. G. (1982). Question Answering for Narrative Memory. In J. F. Le Ny and W. Kintsch (Eds.), *Language and Comprehension*. Amsterdam. North-Holland.

Feldman, J. A. and Ballard, D. H. (1982). Connectionist Models and Their Properties. *Cognitive Science, 6*, 205-254.

Feldstein, M. and Feldstein, K. (1985, April 10). Judicious Steps at Home Can Lessen Trade Deficit (Editorial). *Los Angeles Times,* part IV, p. 5.

Flowers, M. (1982). On Being Contradictory. *Proceedings of the Second National Conference on Artificial Intelligence*. Pittsburgh, Pennsylvania, pp. 63-65.

Flowers, M. and Dyer, M. G. (1984). Really Arguing with your Computer in Natural Language. *Proceedings of the National Computer Conference*. Las Vegas, Nevada, pp. 651-659.

Flowers, M., McGuire, R., and Birnbaum, L. (1982). Adversary Arguments and the Logic of Personal Attacks. In W. G. Lehnert and M. G. Ringle (Eds.), *Strategies for Natural Language Processing*. Hillsdale, NJ: Lawrence Earlbaum.

Friedman, M. (1982, November 15). Protection that Hurts (Editorial). *Newsweek,* p. 90.

Gasser, M. (1988). *A Connectionist Model of Sentence Generation in a First and Second Language* (Ph.D. Dissertation). Applied Linguistics Program. University of California, Los Angeles.

Goldman, S. R., Dyer, M. G., and Flowers, M. (1987). Precedent-based Legal Reasoning and Knowledge Acquisition in Contract Law: A Process Model. *Proceedings of the First International Conference on Artificial Intelligence and Law*. Boston, MA, pp. 210-221.

Green, C. J. (1985, April 14). But if We Hurt Japan We Hurt Ourselves (Editorial). *Los Angeles Times,* part II, p. 5.

Greenaway, D. (1983). *Trade Policy and the New Protectionism.* New York: St. Martin Press.

Greenaway, D. and Milner, C. (1979). *Protectionism Again ...? Causes and Consequences of a Retreat from Freer Trade to Economic Nationalism.* Hobart Paper 84. London: The Institute of Economic Affairs.

Harman, G. (1986). *Change in View: Principles of Reasoning.* Cambridge, MA: MIT Press.

Hintikka, J. (1962). *Knowledge and Belief.* Ithaca, New York: Cornell University Press.

Iacocca, L. A. (1986, October 26). How Many Jobs Do We Save as Doormat of World Trade? (Editorial). *Los Angeles Times,* part IV, p. 5.

Institute of Contemporary Studies (Ed.) (1979). *Tariffs, Quotas, and Trade: The Politics of Protectionism.* San Francisco: Institute of Contemporary Studies.

Johnson, B. C. (1981). *The Atheist Debater's Handbook.* Buffalo, NY: Prometheus Books.

Kolodner, J. L. (1984). *Retrieval and Organizational Strategies in Conceptual Memory: A Computer Model.* Hillsdale, NJ: Lawrence Erlbaum.

Lebowitz, M. (1980). *Generalization and Memory in an Integrated Understanding System* (Ph.D. Thesis, Research Report #186). Department of Computer Science. Yale University, New Haven, CT.

Lehnert, W. G. (1978). *The Process of Question Answering: A Computer Simulation of Cognition.* Hillsdale, NJ: Lawrence Earlbaum.

Lehnert, W. G., Dyer, M. G., Johnson, P. N., Yang, P. J., and Harley, S. (1983). BORIS—An Experiment in In-Depth Understanding of Narratives. *Artificial Intelligence,* 20, 15-62.

Los Angeles Times. (1984, February 16). Car Quotas: Costly Folly (Editorial). *Los Angeles Times,* part II, p. 6.

Los Angeles Times. (1984, March 19). The Great Consumer Rip-Off (Editorial). *Los Angeles Times,* part II, p. 4.

Los Angeles Times. (1984, March 23). Overkill, Overmisery (Editorial). *Los Angeles Times,* part II, p. 6.

Los Angeles Times. (1984, April 11). Japan's Hopeful Signal (Editorial). *Los Angeles Times,* part II, p. 5.

Los Angeles Times. (1984, May 3). Right On, Bill Brock (Editorial). *Los Angeles Times,* part II, p. 6.

Los Angeles Times. (1984, June 14). Protection for Dinosaurs (Editorial). *Los Angeles Times,* part II, p. 6.

Los Angeles Times. (1984, December 9). No Walls or New Walls (Editorial). *Los Angeles Times,* part V, p. 4.

Los Angeles Times. (1984a, December 26). High Price for Profit (Editorial). *Los Angeles Times,* part II, p. 4.

Los Angeles Times. (1984b, December 26). Weapons in Space (Editorial). *Los Angeles Times,* part II, p. 4.

Los Angeles Times. (1985, October 4). The Wrong Solution (Editorial). *Los Angeles Times,* part II, p. 4.

Los Angeles Times. (1986, November 7). Facing the Consequences (Editorial). *Los Angeles Times,* part II, p. 4.

McGuire, R., Birnbaum, L., and Flowers, M. (1981). Opportunistic Processing in Arguments. *Proceedings of the Seventh International Joint Conference on Artificial Intelligence.* Vancouver, Canada, pp. 58-60.

Minsky, M. A. (1975). Framework for Representing Knowledge. In P. Winston (Ed.), *Psychology of Computer Vision.* New York: McGraw-Hill.

Minsky, M. A. (1977). Frame-System Theory. In P. Johnson and O. Wason (Eds.), *Thinking: Readings in Cognitive Science*. Cambridge, MA: MIT Press.

Morrow, L. (1983, January 10). The Protectionist Temptation (Editorial). *Time*, p. 68.

Mueller, E. T. (1987a). *Daydreaming and Computation: A Computer Model of Everyday Creativity, Learning, and Emotions in the Human Stream of Thought* (Ph.D. Dissertation). Computer Science Department. University of California, Los Angeles.

Mueller, E. T. (1987b). *Gate Reference Manual* (Second Edition, Technical Report UCLA-AI-87-6). Artificial Intelligence Laboratory. Computer Science Department. University of California, Los Angeles.

Mueller, E. T. and Zernik, U. (1984). *Gate Reference Manual* (Technical Report UCLA-AI-84-5). Artificial Intelligence Laboratory. Computer Science Department. University of California, Los Angeles.

Musto, D. F. (1986, September 16). Drug Use and Abstinence: Two Routes to the Most You Can Be (Editorial). *Los Angeles Times*, part II, p. 5.

Pazzani, M. J. (1988). *Learning Causal Relationships: An Integration of Empirical and Explanation-Based Learning Methods* (Ph.D. Dissertation). Computer Science Department. University of California, Los Angeles.

Pearl, J. (1986). Fusion, Propagation,and Structuring in Belief Networks. *Artificial Intelligence, 29*, 241-288.

Rees, J. A., Adams, N. I., and Meehan, J. R. (1984). *The T Manual*. Department of Computer Science. Yale University, New Haven, CT.

Rieke, R. D. and Sillars, M. O. (1984). *Argumentation and the Decision Making Process*. Glenview, IL: Scott, Foresman and Company.

Riesbeck, C. K. (1984). Knowledge Reorganization and Reasoning Style. *International Journal of Man-Machine Studies,* **20,** 45-61.

Roesner, D. (1985). Schemata for Understanding of Argumentation in Newspaper Texts. In L. Steels and J. A. Campbell (Eds.), *Progress in Artificial Intelligence.* Chichester, England: Ellis Horwood.

Rumelhart, D. E., McClelland, J. L., and the PDP Research Group (Eds.) (1986). *Parallel Distributed Processing: Explorations in the Microstructure of Cognition* (Vols. 1 and 2). Cambridge, MA: MIT Press.

Samuelson, R. J. (1984, March 7). Backward Policies Restrict Our Exports (Editorial). *Los Angeles Times,* part II, p. 5.

Samuelson, R. J. (1984, September 12). Politics of Trade Protection: Opponents Shifting Balance (Editorial). *Los Angeles Times,* part II, p. 5.

Schank, R. C. (1973). Identification of Conceptualizations Underlying Natural Language. In R. C. Schank and K. M. Colby (Eds.), *Computer Models of Thought and Language.* San Francisco: Freeman.

Schank, R. C. (Ed.) (1975). *Conceptual Information Processing.* Amsterdam: North-Holland.

Schank, R. C. (1978). What Makes Something "Ad Hoc." *Proceedings of Theoretical Issues in Natural Language Processing-2.* University of Illinois, Urbana-Champaign, pp. 8-13.

Schank, R. C. (1982). *Dynamic Memory: A Theory of Reminding and Learning in Computers and People.* Cambridge: Cambridge University Press.

Schank, R. C. and Abelson, R. P. (1977). *Scripts, Plans, Goals, and Understanding.* Hillsdale, NJ: Lawrence Earlbaum.

Schank, R. C. and Carbonell, J. G. (1979). Re: The Gettysburg Address, Representing Social and Political Acts. In N. Findler (Ed.), *Associative Networks.* New York: Academic Press.

Schneider, W. (1985, September 22). Free Trade: Fury Grows in Congress—President vs. Protectionism (Editorial). *Los Angeles Times,* part IV, pp. 1, 3.

Slade, S. (1987). *The T Programming Language: A Dialect of Lisp.* Englewood Cliffs, NJ: Prentice-Hall.

Spich, R. and McKelvey, B. (1985, April 10). Using Trade Strength Against Japan—U.S. Should Bargain Hard, Consider Tokyo an Economic Rival (Editorial). *Los Angeles Times,* part II, p. 5.

Spiro, R. J., Bruce, B. C., and Brewer, W. F. (Eds.) (1980). *Theoretical Issues in Language Comprehension.* Hillsdale, NJ: Lawrence Earlbaum.

Staebler, N. and Ross, D. (1965). *How to Argue with a Conservative.* New York: Grossman Publishers.

Stonecipher, H. W. (1979). *Editorial and Persuasive Writing.* New York: Hastings House.

Sumida, R. A., Dyer, M., G. and Flowers, M. (1988). Integrating Marker Passing and Connectionism for Handling Conceptual and Structural Ambiguities. *Proceedings of the Tenth Annual Conference of the Cognitive Science Society.* Montreal, Canada.

Thurow, L. C. (1983, April 25). The Road to Lemon Socialism (Editorial). *Newsweek,* p. 63.

Toulmin, S. (1958). *The Uses of Argument.* Cambridge, MA: Cambridge University Press.

Toulmin, S., Rieke, R. D., and Janik, A. (1979). *An Introduction to Reasoning.* New York: Macmillan.

Tulving, E. (1972). Episodic and Semantic Memory. In E. Tulving and W. Donaldson (Eds.), *Organization of Memory.* New York: Academic Press.

van Dijk, T. A. (Ed.) (1985). *Handbook of Discourse Analysis* (Vols. 1-4). New York: Academic Press.

van Dijk, T. A. and Kintsch, W. (1983). *Strategies of Discourse Comprehension*. New York: Academic Press.

Waltz, D. L. and Pollack, J. B. (1985). Massive Parallel Parsing: A Strongly Interactive Model of Natural Language Interpretation. *Cognitive Science, 9*, 75-112.

Wilensky, R. (1983). *Planning and Understanding*. Reading, MA: Addison-Wesley.

Wilks, Y. and Bien, J. (1983). Beliefs, Points of View, and Multiple Environments. *Cognitive Science, 7*, 95-119.

Windes, R. R. and Hastings, A. (1966). *Argumentation and Advocacy*. New York: Random House.

Yoffie, D. B. (1983). *Power and Protectionism*. New York: Columbia University Press.

Zycher, B. (1984, April 3). Society Would Lose to a Trade Department (Editorial). *Los Angeles Times,* part II, p. 7.

Index